Reducing juvenile violence in American culture is a challenge which requires serious commitments from all fronts. . . . Gordon McLean has a long history and a deep understanding of the important role of faith in turning a life around. *[Too Young to Die]* demonstrates the value of an approach which integrates programs, services and moral principles.

Jim Ryan
Attorney General of Illinois

Young people *do* respond in a positive way to caring, committed individuals who take the time to invest in them. *Too Young to Die* powerfully reinforces that reality.

William J. Hibbler, Presiding Judge
Juvenile Justice Division
Circuit Court of Cook County, Illinois

This book ambushed me—not with despair, but with hope that the God Who once walked the streets of this world seeking the lost is still on the move in our cities today.

Daniel Dominick Meyer, Senior Pastor
Christ Church of Oak Brook, Illinois

Too Young to Die is must reading for anyone who cares about children and the future. Its message . . . support(s) the notion that young or old, rich or poor, of color or not, church-going or non-believer, we really do need one another to survive. *Too Young to Die* is a book of life.

Richard S. Kling, Clinical Professor of Law
Chicago Kent College of Law

LINCOLN CHRISTIAN COLLEGE AND SEMINARY

TOO YOUNG TO DIE

Other Books by Gordon McLean:
Coming in on the Beam
We're Holding Your Son
Let God Manage Your Money
Where the Love Is
High on the Campus
Man, I Need Help
Christians and Crime
How to Raise Your Parents
The Care and Feeding of Parents
Hell Bent Kid
What's a Parent to Do?
Devil at the Wheel
Terror in the Streets
Danger at Your Door
Cities of Lonesome Fear—with Dave & Neta Jackson

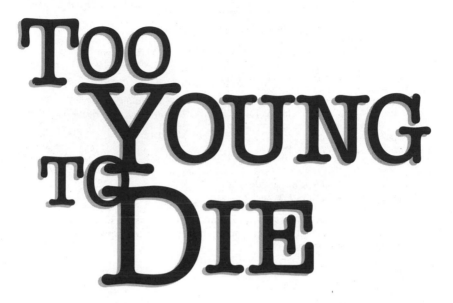

TOO YOUNG TO DIE

Gordon McLean

with
Dave and Neta Jackson

Tyndale House Publishers, Wheaton, Illinois

TOO YOUNG TO DIE
Copyright ©1998 by Gordon McLean. All rights reserved. International copyright secured.

Library of Congress Cataloging-in-Publication Data
McLean, Gordon R.
    Too young to die/by Gordon McLean with Dave and Neta Jackson.
       p. cm.
    Includes bibliographical references (p.).
    ISBN 1-56179-629-8
    1. Christian biography—Illinois—Chicago Region. 2. Gang members—Illinois—Chicago
Region—Biography. 3. Chicago Youth for Christ. Juvenile Justice Ministry—Biography.
4. McLean, Gordon R. I. Jackson, Dave. II. Jackson, Neta. III. Title.
BR1702.M35 1998
261.8'33106'0977311—dc21   98-21950
                                                          CIP

A Focus on the Family book published by
Tyndale House Publishers, Wheaton, Illinois.

All Scripture quotations are from the HOLY BIBLE, NEW INTERNATIONAL VERSION®
(NIV). Copyright ©1973, 1978, 1984 by International Bible Society. Used by permission of
Zondervan Publishing House.

The quotations of Max Lucado are from his book *In The Grip of Grace* (Dallas: Word, 1996).
Used by permission.

The quotation from George MacLeod appeared in Carl F. Burke, *God Is for Real, Man* (New
York: Association Press, 1966). Used by permission.

People's names and certain details of the stories in this book have been changed to protect
the privacy of the individuals involved. However, the facts of what happened and the under-
lying principles have been conveyed as accurately as possible.

No part of this publication may be reproduced, stored in a retrieval system, or transmitted
in any form or by any means—electronic, mechanical, photocopy, recording, or otherwise—without prior permission of the publisher.

Editor: Larry K. Weeden
Front cover design: Candi Park D'Agnese
Front cover photo: Barbara Leslie/FPG International

Printed in the United States of America

98 99 00 01 02/10 9 8 7 6 5 4 3 2 1

Contents

6. 59 *

99562

C 33.
133.
1

to
Dr. Robert H. and Dr. Robert A. Schuller,
in appreciation of your presenting the message of
positive faith in a negative world

"You will be called Repairer of Broken Walls."
Isaiah 58:12

Publisher's Note

Because this book tells the stories of juveniles involved in street gangs, readers should be aware that some violent scenes are included. Also, because these stories are based on the kids' accounts of what happened, the police aren't always presented in the best light. Nonetheless, Focus on the Family and the author believe that the vast majority of officers do their vital job with honesty and integrity, and we fully support them in their God-given mission. Further, while the author's views on the juvenile justice system make an important contribution to the ongoing national debate over such issues, they do not necessarily reflect the official views of Focus on the Family.

Finally, we would emphasize that what these stories portray most of all is the redemptive power of Jesus Christ. He is still at work in our world today, bringing spiritually dead people to new, eternal life through the gospel—many times even those society considers the most unlikely candidates for His grace.

Acknowledgments

To write a book such as this would be impossible without some unique and talented assistance. I was more than fortunate in finding generous quantities of both, a strong indication that these pages carry an important message people need to hear.

The excellent cooperation of the professional staff and chaplains at the Cook County Temporary Juvenile Detention Center and the Cook County Department of Corrections is an ongoing, essential part of our team's ministry.

The various police agencies, the office of the state's attorney, and the county sheriff were consistently helpful, and I thank them, not only for their assistance here, but also for the fine work they carry on every day to protect us all. I am a volunteer chaplain with the Cook County Sheriff's Department under the able leadership of Lorenzo Clemons, who coordinates community volunteer activity.

I also drew on the expertise of some respected private attorneys, among them: Clarence Burch, John DeLeon, George Howard, and Richard Kling—it's always a pleasure to meet and address Richard's students at Kent College of Law. Kendall Hill, a public defender, took time to carefully review our material for legal accuracy.

My colleagues and staff members in Youth for Christ are invaluable behind-the-scenes builders of the ministry described on these pages, especially Dick and Mary Norton. Dick provides the administrative leadership as executive director of the ministry, and Mary has built a team that daily and specifically prays for the work. Brian Kiel in our office and Esther Patterson in our community public relations work add valued support. Our front-line ministry team includes Mario and Maria Tamayo, Cheryl Larsen, Juan Chavez, Volney

McGhee, Eric Matthews, Jorge Roque, Pat Williams, and two young men you will meet in these pages, Boyce Allen and John Johnson. I also appreciate the help of Glen and Jane Fitzjerrell of Mission USA.

The editorial team from Focus on the Family is one of the most-talented, eager, and dedicated groups of people it has ever been my privilege to work with on any project. Al Janssen, who early on had insight into what this book could be, was ably assisted by managing editor Larry Weeden, along with Betsy Holt, Kathi Allen, Melanie Dobson, Bruce Peppin, Robert Turnbull, Robin Wilson, and Heidi Isaac in bringing it all together.

No choice was more vital to the success of the project than the coming aboard of Dave and Neta Jackson, two of the finest writers and friends any author could hope to enlist. They make me look like an accomplished writer, a feat that I'm sure tested the limits of their considerable ability. Most importantly, they cared deeply about the young people and the families presented on these pages, and that interest and prayer support will continue long after this book has gone to press.

Some personal friends have been close to encourage and strengthen me in all my ministry, and now with this book. Among them are Mark Beedle, Mike and Cathy Brickley, Howard Eklind, Gil and Dresden Erickson, Stan and Anita Johnson, Peter and Heidi Huizenge, Nancy Stolz, Roger Cross, Barbara Edgar, Bob and Joyce Venemon, Charles Alexander, Leonard Ramirez, Franklin Robbie, Bruce Love, and Bufford Karraker.

Pastor Daniel and Amy Meyer and Dr. and Mrs. Arthur DeKruyter and my many friends at Christ Church of Oak Brook have been a constant source of encouragement, for which I am most grateful. The youth group at Saratoga Federated Church, Saratoga, California, with sponsors Kirt and Lonnie Priest, were real friends to the Hardaway brothers and helped share the brothers' special testimony with teens across the country, as well as being gracious hosts to me and our Chicago young people who visited them.

Finally, this book would never have been possible without the total cooperation of the many young people and their families whose stories are told here. Nearly all of them have been through deep heartbreak and crisis, and like all of us, they want to put such events behind them. Still, they opened their hearts to help others by generously joining me to tell their experiences on these pages as I perceived them, certainly not always in the most flattering light, but I hope presenting truth with compassion. Several, especially Cragg Hardaway and Xavier McElrath-Bey, may well decide now to be authors themselves, and I wish them well.

Perhaps most encouraging, even amazing, are the numbers of young people who, on learning of the book, invited me to include their story if it could help someone else. They weren't seeking money, and recognition was not even a factor—many said their story could be told anonymously to avoid any thought of them seeking personal publicity.

As a result, I had far more material than I could hope to use unless I planned to fill a library, not just a book. It was necessary to protect the identity of some youths because of the confidentiality afforded juvenile offenders, and also that of a few law-enforcement agents. I shielded as well several victims' families from too much detailed discussion so as not to add to their hurt. Except for those qualifications, the material is factual and real. Obviously, various sources and readers will evaluate the serious cases, the offenders, and the recommendations I make on these pages and reach conclusions different from mine. That's to be expected in reporting highly controversial cases and proposed changes in the system.

Here are young people I know and how I view them. Many in the justice system and the media who have strong negative opinions of these youths have never talked with them. All they've done is read reports from others of like mind. In contrast, I *do* know them—certainly not totally, but with far greater and longer-term knowledge than many others wanting to condemn them and assign their fate.

More than anything, I want to view troubled kids as God sees them, candidates for His love and forgiveness. Some people will reject that view, but the fact is that many youths start a new and better life, turning away from a failed past. Isn't that what's needed to some degree in every life? That's the message of hope I have acknowledged on these pages.

Introduction

The emergency room at Cook County Hospital resembles a field hospital just behind the front lines in a war zone. And it is. But this institution gets the casualties of street wars between rival youth gangs in Chicago.

It's an ongoing and deadly battle for power, control, and profits from drug sales. The kids involved—part of 140 street "organizations"—are as young as eight years old. The figures for shootings and killings on the streets go up and down, and even the slightest drop is greeted as a hopeful sign. But sadly, the trend is up among the 15- to 19-year-olds. This age group is now the most violent in the nation, and their numbers will grow by 31 percent by the year 2010.

This is not a story told in cold statistics and popular television dramas, however. It's all too real. The kids this hospital and others across the city and suburbs treat are part of my parish as a minister of the gospel.

My name is Gordon McLean, and I direct the Juvenile Justice Ministry of Metro Chicago Youth for Christ. Since 1950, when I founded this type of program on the west coast of Canada and then took it to Tacoma, Washington, and San Jose, California, before arriving in Chicago in 1982, my life has been spent with hurting, broken kids and their families. Early in my career, most gangs were limited to the urban ghettos. But increasingly, they have moved to the suburbs—ironically because concerned families have sought to escape the problems of the inner city, only to find they've brought the problem with them. And, as drug use has spread among all socioeconomic groups, some entrepreneurial gangs have staked out new territories in the suburbs and even small towns for lucrative drug dealing—bringing the ensuing violence that results over disputed territory.

Say "gang" and many people automatically think of African-American or Hispanic youths. But gangs cross all racial lines—including the Tap Boys and Arab Posse (Arab Muslims), plus Cambodian and other recent Asian immigrants. (I know of no Japanese youth gangs, however.) White kids remain largely at the fringe of gang involvement, though there are several significant white gangs, including the Popes, Simon City Royals, and Gaylords. Many white gangs consist of wanna-bes trying to copy their minority counterparts. But one significant difference is that the members of minority gangs are often the "cream of the crop," unusually intelligent and sharp, the kids whom other young people admire. This is rarely true of white gang members, who are more apt to be considered "losers" among their peers—the dropouts, druggies, and racists. They're loners, more likely to be suicidal, interested in the occult and committing random violent acts. They're often slovenly, reckless, and have little motivation. But what they lack in respect, they try to make up for in ferocity, and a bullet fired by a wanna-be is just as deadly as one from a sophisticated gangbanger's gun.

Our staff and volunteers minister to kids in trouble from urban ghettos and tree-lined suburbs, from dysfunctional families and bewildered "good parents" who still can't believe their kids are involved. Often we meet these kids for the first time at the Cook County Temporary Juvenile Detention Center (for kids younger than 17), the youth wings of the notorious Cook County Jail (for youths 17 to 19), and the Illinois Youth Centers at St. Charles and Valley View. We work with the chaplains of the Good News Jail and Prison Ministry—Marcus Baird, Len Maselli, Steve Thompson, and Harry Roundtree—as well as the state chaplain, Marvin Manar.

We see kids on the bricks (i.e., on the street) or at their homes when they get released; we meet with some of them at our "United Nations" meetings of former gang rivals. We know many young men and women once in trouble who are now doing well—and we also see the ones caught in the battle zones who are rushed to the hospitals . . . and the morgues.

Jim Leslie, our staff minister in the Pilsen area of Chicago, recently called me to come to Cook County Hospital. I met him at the emergency room. Carlos, a 21-year-old nicknamed Bandit, was on life support. Jim and I knew Carlos well. He had grown up with all the problems of the streets, but he was "chilling out," getting away from the gang, working two jobs, and determined to make good. Jim and Carlos had held some serious talks about changes in his life that only the Lord Jesus could make.

Some of the boys from his old gang didn't understand his efforts to withdraw from gangbanging (a catchall term to describe the gang lifestyle of using fists and weapons to control a neighborhood by keeping out rivals, usually a gang of the same race). They thought Carlos had joined a rival gang. They had caught him in the alley behind his house as he was emptying the garbage into the Dumpster and shot him six times.

Carlos's mother, stepfather, and the rest of his family all gathered at the hospital, fearing the worst. We embraced, shook hands, and prayed and cried together. From outside Carlos's room, I could see him lying unconscious on the bed, his powerful, young body penetrated by numerous tubes sustaining his life as he struggled for every breath.

In spite of the heroic efforts of the emergency-room team and the aid of technology, Carlos soon died. His murderers have never been caught. To the media, Carlos's death was just another passing story. Human life seems so cheap on urban streets. But to his family and friends, it was a tragedy of immense proportions. Carlos's mother was devastated; she remains in a deep depression. Because the killers of her son remain at large, she feels no justice or closure for her family. The passing of time has not healed the hurt, and she continues to grieve the loss of her son.

I have been in this situation more times than I care to count, every one of them heartbreaking. And no, I don't get used to it after all these years.

Some victims of violence take solace in faith, but many want to strike out in understandable rage at the offender, seeking closure in places it can't be found—a courtroom or an execution chamber. Temporary satisfaction? Sometimes. Permanent release? Not likely.

Theirs surely is a heart-rending cry we all must hear and reach out to answer. But there's another sorrow I also share with many hurting families I have come to know well.

It happens in our courtrooms when kids' lives are thrown aside and even destroyed because it's politically popular to give heavy sentences to young offenders and lock them up in adult prisons. The tears of their brothers and sisters, grandparents, and moms and dads express a deep grief and regret that are multiplied daily in cities all over this nation.

The regret goes beyond a family loss, too, as great as that is. Aside from the enormous bill we pay to warehouse young people in expensive misery, we're wasting so much good potential.

Understand that in this book I'm writing about young people—mostly teenagers—not older adults. The repercussions for older, sophisticated criminals or sexual molesters may be much different from what we should consider for kids. And I'm certainly not denying that some young people need to be locked away to protect the rest of us. But that's a small number out of the total now confined in our penal system.

To our shame, we no longer ask, "What can we do to help this kid in trouble rehabilitate himself and become a good citizen?" Instead, we simply look at the offense and figure out how long he can be confined. Our lawmakers have taken discretion away from the judges and simply said, "Nothing can change these kids. Just let the crime dictate the sentence." No attitude could be more callous, shortsighted, and in error. We must allow judges to make a decision in each case based on the circumstances, background, potential for rehabilitation, and attitude of the young accused. At the end of the book, I will discuss alternatives that hold kids responsible for their behavior but do so in a redemptive way.

All over our land, we hear pleas for an end to the violence, for sensible solutions, for a release for suffering families. Often I would like to scream in the middle of the street wars or in a courtroom where another tragedy of destruction is being played out, "Stop! This is madness!" But on the street, the noise of weapons firing drowns out any shout, and courtroom decorum forbids it.

The calamity of kids destroyed—some by gunfire and others by the bang of a judge's gavel—is all too real. I know it well. I live with it every day.

But . . . there's another side to the story. Without it, there would be little to offset the parade of heartbreak and shattered dreams. I've been a front-row spectator at numerous miracles, seeing young people change in ways that can't be explained outside of divine intervention at a critical time in their lives.

Some change because of caring help in the justice system. A police officer, counselor, teacher, chapel volunteer, or coach reaches out, giving of himself or herself to be an instrument of God's mercy to kids in trouble. I get to reap the spiritual harvest in our chapel services at the jail and Bible studies at the Juvenile Detention Center.

Some change in spite of the system. Missing a measure of caring intervention, kids are often dumped into a correctional system that's too busy to deal with individuals and too much influenced by gangs. The facilities are often overcrowded, understaffed, and hampered in what they can do to help kids by laws that are increasingly harsh and punitive. In state after state, we now spend more money building prisons than we do building schools. This can leave even the most dedicated police officers and court personnel frustrated.

In spite of being thrown on society's dump heap, however, kids survive, learn to respect themselves, take personal responsibility, and see others not as people to exploit but as fellow children of God—surprising when you know many come from broken, abusive families. With little to emulate at home, they developed little respect for themselves and had no basis for learning to respect others. The people who became their victims were mere objects on which to take out their revenge and greed.

How do these unpromising kids come to see themselves as important, if not in their own homes then in another family—God's family?

Let me answer with an illustration. My friend Charles is an African-American youth of medium build from suburbia. He came into juvenile detention at 16 as a feisty, manipulative street punk who saw other kids as rivals to fight and adults as victims to rob. His home situation was better than that of many kids, with a mother who deeply cared for him and a stepfather who was a respected police officer. Still, just as the prodigal son in the Bible chose to go astray despite having a great father, so did Charles.

"When I had a piece [gun] in my hand, I had power," Charles will tell you. "I didn't even need the money I got. It was just the rush, the excitement."

He was the type of hard-core, young thug the public has in mind when it demands that young predators be tried in adult court and locked up for as long as possible. "His kind never changes," the hardliners insist. But that judgment may not be the last word.

When he turned 17, Charles was moved to the county jail, still awaiting trial in adult court, only now he was in a setting even more conducive to achieving gang status. Gangs have a great deal of power behind concrete walls and barbed wire.

"I had no intention of changing," Charles says. "I knew what I was and wanted to be—none of it good. I figured I'd go to the joint, serve my time, build my connections in the Black Disciples, and come out with even more rank and experience."

Then his gang career path got dramatically detoured.

Charles is glad to tell you why: "I met some people who genuinely wanted to help me—teachers and counselors on the youth wing. Then I got a cellmate who was my age, in deep trouble, but who had really given his life to the Lord. I didn't know what to do with Casey! When you live with a guy 24-7 [all day, every day], you know if he's real or just putting up a front to impress the judge. I could see my homie changing in many ways day by day, a step at a time—falling down now and then, but quickly picking himself up and getting back on the right path. That kind of sincerity can get to a guy; it certainly got to me.

"Casey asked me to go to the Friday night youth service at the jail. He didn't push, just invited. And I knew my mother was praying for me at home." (A Christian cellmate and a praying mother—now, that's a powerful combination!) "Before long, I went to the youth service.

"'About time you came,' Casey said, and when I told my mother, she shouted 'Hallelujah!' over the phone."

I had first met Charles in juvenile detention. His stony face and hard stare betrayed a very different agenda from what I presented in Bible class. But later, when he started coming to the youth service at the county jail, I saw something had changed. He stayed behind one night to tell me he wanted to accept the Lord into his life—a joyous session that ended with me having a new, young brother in the faith.

Charles has grown in his walk with the Lord and eventually made a carefully considered decision to "drop his flags" and "go off count"—leave his gang. It wasn't easy. The potential danger was severe, but he was respected enough by his peers that he was able to walk away unharmed. He looks different now. The cold eyes of a gang zealot have given way to a pleasant smile and eyes that sparkle with warmth. He even manages to look well dressed in his carefully pressed, drab-tan jail uniform. But the major change is internal.

Charles talked with his family, and they all agreed he would not get out on bail pending trial, a choice it's hard to imagine anyone in jail making. Explaining the unusual decision, he said, "The time I'm doing now will count when I'm eventually sentenced. Besides, I don't want a taste of freedom now, only to come back and be locked up again. And frankly, there's some work I have to do here helping some of the young brothers."

While he awaits court dates, Charles keeps busy with school classes, Bible studies, and talking with new young men who come into the jail. Meanwhile, his attorney is trying to negotiate dropping some charges and is seeking a lesser sentence. I plan to be with Charles in court when the time comes. When I respect a young man and know he is sincerely changing, I tell the judge of the progress he has made. If that testimony helps alleviate a harsh sentence, I consider it time well spent.

When asked about his future, Charles says, "I want to get this case behind me and go on to college. Eventually I plan to be a funeral director. But my main business will be serving the Lord. Mr. G, you might as well get used to having me around for a long time as a volunteer worker with the kids."

Today you would find Charles a young man well worth knowing. You might also decide there are ways *you* could influence a
hurting kid's life, just as those teachers, counselors, and jail volunteers did with Charles.

When a caring person enters a troubled youth's life to make
God's love real, modeling how that boy or girl can personally experience it, you have the seeds of a new spiritual birth. That encounter
can move a youngster who's consumed with self-hatred from a world
of indifference and rejection to a genuine transformation.

Do all the kids we work with make it back on the bricks? No.
In the story of the sower and the seeds (Matthew 13:19-23), Jesus
showed that there would be various responses to the gospel. Not all
the seeds took root; of those that did, some had shallow roots and
withered when trouble came. Some young people want to be on the
Lord's team and the world's team at the same time, but trying to
serve two masters is futile (Matthew 6:24). Others try to fake change
and can be convincing liars, perhaps even so slick that they end up
believing their own stories.

And unfortunately, some young people who sincerely want to
change are released back to the community but don't have in their
neighborhood a caring church that reaches out to them or other
resources they need to succeed.

We—the people of God—have what these kids are desperate for:
His life-changing love. If we think these kids are someone else's problem, if we don't get the message out, we'll need to comfort more mothers, build more prison cells, and throw even more kids on the junk
heap. But it doesn't have to be that way. Charles and the young people
you'll meet in this book convinced me years ago that the solution
lies in the hope of God's love—the good news of the gospel in action.

I want to take you with me out on the streets and into the jails
to see this dynamic miracle in action. Our young people are too
young to die. By God's grace, many can be saved. Hope can grow out
of tragedy. Love can vanquish hate. And the Spirit of the Lord can
overcome despair.

Gordon McLean
River Forest, Illinois

One

❖ ❖ ❖

"QUICK, PULL OUT!" 16-YEAR-OLD SAL yelled as I drew up next to him in the shopping center parking lot.

"What gives?" I asked as he jumped into the backseat and slammed the door.

"Don't ask. Just drive! Get moving!"

I spun the car around, squealing the tires, and headed for the street. Dagger, another teenage kid who was already sitting beside me, gripped the armrest for balance as I made a sharp turn, hoping to get lost in traffic. Glancing in the rearview mirror, I noticed a carload of guys coming up on our tail.

"My homies guessed what's up!" Sal yelled from the backseat as we zoomed in and out of traffic. "I was waitin' back there for you when they pulled up and offered me a ride. I told 'em I was waitin' for you, Mr. G, but one of 'em guessed you had someone with you I didn't want 'em to see."

In my rearview mirror, I noticed Sal give Dagger a sideways glance. These two rivals hadn't been all that eager to meet; street rivals rarely do—unless they're fighting. "They said they was gonna wait," Sal groaned. "I told 'em you wouldn't stop if you saw 'em with me, so they took off—but they must've been waitin' outta sight 'round the corner till you pulled up."

"Looks like they're trying to head us off," I said grimly. "Hang on! I haven't done any driving like this since I was a kid!"

I made a sharp turn onto a narrow side street, then raced through an alley, our pursuers still behind us but losing ground. Next I shot down a one-way street in the wrong direction, driving through a busy cross-street just as the light changed and the traffic flow blocked our tail.

"Whew! Where are the cops when you need them?" I said, slowing down and easing into the traffic stream.

"Man, Rev, I didn't know you could drive like that," Dagger said, relaxing his grip on the armrest now that the crisis had passed. My two young passengers calmed down a lot more quickly than I did.

A short time later, the three of us were sitting in a local restaurant, enjoying hot fries and hamburgers with "the works." If the people around us had only known who the two young men were— and that there was an active blood feud between their two street organizations—they might have headed for the doors.

I sat back and listened as these two rivals not only discussed adrenaline-pumping adventures and escapes from each other's gangs, but also ways to help the "shorties" (younger kids) quit warring on the streets. It was clear that both of them were fed up with the hatred and violence that had defined their short lives and had come to respect each other.

Though my efforts to bring gang rivals Sal and Dagger together had nearly resulted in a violent confrontation, this was not my first such experience. Back in 1983, I had a dream of starting a "United Nations" (so named because gang members often refer to their organizations as "nations"). The U.N. was to be a neutral place where kids whom Christ was rescuing could come together as brothers. I had even dared to hope that such a gathering of leaders from rival gangs might ease some of the tensions on the streets.

My first attempt was with two 17-year-old rivals in the Little Village district of Chicago—also known as Little Mexico. Both had been responding to the gospel message. But getting Kent and Bobby even to meet each other took weeks.

"Look, there ain't no way I wanna see Kent," Bobby told me

when I first brought up the idea. He was a solid, husky kid who looked as if he worked out with weights. "We're enemies. His boys shot my boys, and that ain't gonna change." Kent had said much the same thing, so my idea appeared to be going nowhere.

Yet I persisted, holding on to a Bible verse that told me it could be done: "When a man's ways are pleasing to the LORD, he makes even his enemies live at peace with him" (Proverbs 16:7).

Now, either those are just nice words in a pleasant book or they are God's words telling us that, even in the middle of street battles, kids being changed by Jesus Christ can come together in peace. The Bible also says, "We are therefore Christ's ambassadors, as though God were making his appeal through us. We implore you on Christ's behalf: Be reconciled to God" (2 Corinthians 5:20).

With that in mind, I decided I wasn't going to take no for the final answer. My pitch to them was, "Look, you've given yourself over to the Lord and another guy has done the same. So if God is your Father and God is his Father, what does that make the two of you?"

"Brothers," Kent acknowledged reluctantly. He was slim, with a thin face and black hair that hung over his collar—a contrast to his stocky, neatly cropped rival.

"And you won't even meet with a brother?" I challenged.

"But you don't get it, man," Kent said in frustration. "Those guys have taken down my boys, shot at me—and now you want us to meet? You're crazy!"

"And haven't you done exactly the same thing back to them?" I challenged. "But of course *you've* asked the Lord to forgive you. Well, I have news for you. God won't even hear you unless you're willing to forgive the guy who has wronged you."

"That's in the Bible? Where?"

I pulled out my pocket Bible—the only weapon I carry on the streets. "Here it is in Matthew 6:12: 'Forgive us our debts [sins], as we also have forgiven our debtors [those who have sinned against us].'"

Kent mulled that over for a moment. "But look," he protested again, "we're not talking about a one-time thing here. How can I forgive some guy who messed me and my friends over again and again, every chance he got? How many times does God expect me to forgive?"

"As many times as you expect to be forgiven yourself. But don't take my word for it; Jesus already dealt with that issue with one of His boys, Peter. Here, take a look." I flipped the pages to Matthew 18:21-22, which reads, "Then Peter came to Jesus and asked, 'Lord, how many times shall I forgive my brother when he sins against me? Up to seven times?' Jesus answered, 'I tell you, not seven times, but seventy-seven times.'"

After similar discussions with both boys and with many people praying for the success of the effort, the two rivals finally agreed to meet. I was elated! But the problems weren't over yet. I knew they'd have to meet away from their territories, where no one would recognize them. So I enlisted the help of one of our volunteers, a young businessman named Mark Beedle, and we took the two boys to a restaurant away from their neighborhoods.

As Bobby and Kent greeted each other coldly and we all sat down, I wasn't sure it was such a good idea after all. Icebergs were warmer than that session. Their formal politeness appeared to be intended just to get Mark and me off their backs.

But then Kent suddenly looked up and shot a question across the table: "Remember that shoot-out last summer near the park? I thought your boys had me cornered a couple of times."

"Yeah, I remember," said Bobby. "Say, how did you get away from there, anyway?"

Soon they were exchanging war stories, sometimes sadly, but eventually laughing uproariously as they recalled the traps they had set for each other and their corresponding escapes.

Then Kent stopped, suddenly serious. "You've chilled out," he said. "I can tell you're not into that stuff anymore. How come?"

"Because . . . it's a dead end, man," said Bobby. "I've got a girl-friend and a couple kids to think about, a future to plan. And I decided that's not what the Lord wants me doing anymore."

"Same here. I think we're on to something better, and our boys need to know about it."

The last of the fries sat cold and soggy on the plate. I suggested another meeting where each guy would bring one of his key boys with him. They agreed. We closed in prayer for peace and understanding.

I don't know what the people at other tables thought that day. Here were two Latino gangbangers with two white adults, starting out with quiet conversation, then enjoying a good deal of laughter, and finally ending in prayer. What was going on? I'm sure the onlookers would have been amazed to know.

Since then, I've been conducting those meetings regularly—sometimes with 30 or 40 guys from several rival gangs together at the same time. And I still get law-enforcement people telling me it's impossible; it will result in a bloodbath.

"You're a little late with your advice," I reply. "We've been doing it for a long time, and we have yet to experience our first incident." Of course, not all the guys become friends. Some keep their distance from one another, but they've learned basic respect and that their faith must be bigger than the walls dividing them.

Actually, I grant the critics a point. I would discourage a community group from trying a similar meeting except under carefully controlled conditions. Our United Nations meetings work because we come together in the Lord's name, and we take sensible precautions: Kids are invited and come with our staff; the meetings are always on neutral turf; and they're held irregularly. It's really quite prestigious to be part of the group. Instead of problems, we've seen unique solutions where it counts—out on the streets.

Chente, a handsome Hispanic kid, can name one. "It was New Year's Eve," he told me, "and I was out with my boys—Satan's Disciples—when a bus pulled up. When we got on, my boys recognized Vicious, one of our rivals, and were ready to shoot him right then and there. I had to act fast. 'No, not here,' I said. 'You might hurt other riders and bring down the heat [law] heavy on us.'"

It seemed like a minor deflection, but it saved the life of Vicious, and he thanked Chente most sincerely at the next U.N. meeting. Chente, only 16, firmly believed in putting his growing faith to work and later helped his rival get a job at the same store where he worked.

Many more things happen at these meetings, but before I tell you about them, let me introduce you to some of my "congregation." I want you to hear the cry of the streets, where kids who are far too young die almost every day in cities and towns across America.

Two

❖ ❖ ❖

"IN THE SIXTH DECADE OF THE TWENTIETH century the Almighty Latin King Nation was formed," one of the boys read from the gang constitution. New recruits don't much care when the Latin Kings started, however; all they care about is joining. The youths saluted with a fist over their hearts and repeated the sacred words: "I die for you, for you are flesh of my flesh, blood of my blood, son of my mother who is the Universal Nature and follower of 'Yahve' who is the almighty King of kings. Once a King, always a King!"

"*Por vida!* For life!" swore the brothers and sisters in the Nation as they came forward to embrace the new members. Small for his 11 years, lean and wiry, one boy nearly burst with pride. He had a new "family," and he felt accepted and loved as never before.

He now enjoyed the common bond and identity he'd been searching for throughout all his years of being shuffled around to different foster homes by Chicago's Department of Child and Family Services. *I will be a King until my dying day,* he thought fiercely.

This was Chicago Lawn, a working-class neighborhood of small, neat homes on the southwest side of Chicago—and the hub of Latin King territory. After the formalities in the basement of one of these homes, Joker, an older teen, slipped a gun into the boy's hand.

15

"What's this for?" Xavier McElrath-Bey asked, taken aback.

"Who knows, man, you might need it," said the older boy in a hushed voice. The thin, black hairs on Joker's upper lip could almost be taken for a mustache. "You never can tell, man. These days out on the bricks, a King's gotta be ready, *comprende?*"

The piece was heavier than Xavier had imagined, the steel warm from being carried in the other boy's pocket. Xavier slid its snub nose cautiously into his pants, trying not to think what might happen if it went off. He knew this was a test, and he would *not* fail.

"Hey, man," he said with bravado, "let's have some brews and blunts." In a short time, the beer and marijuana being passed around had calmed his nerves and given him the machismo he needed to fit in with the rest of the gang.

When the Kings weren't gangbanging—keeping control over their territory by riding the streets, planning attacks on rivals, and maintaining a monopoly on drug deals—they were partying. All it took to get a party rolling was some girls, some brews, a little music on the box, and, of course, food. The parties—held in a basement, an apartment, or even a tenement stairwell—could get loud, but no one feared that the residents would complain. They wouldn't dare to call the police on the Latin Kings. Long after the police had come and gone, the gang would still be there.

The Kings are the largest Latino gang in the Midwest, with more than 10,000 members in the Chicago area alone—and that's not counting the fringe kids, the wanna-bes and peewees who swell the ranks. According to the Gang Awareness Association, young kids are allowed into the gang, but not into the inner circles of the local chapters, which are run by an elected Inca (leader), Cacique (vice leader), and Enforcer. The top leaders in Chicago are the Sun-King and the Corona, whose policies are implemented by a "Council of Princes" made up of leaders from the local chapters, and a "Crown Council" that functions as a trial court.

The Kings' reference to "Yahve"—an adaptation of the Hebrew word *Yahweh*, meaning "God"—is an attempt to put God's endorsement on their organization and leaders. Some of their holy days—especially their "King's Holy Day" on January 6, when they honor the memory of their slain brothers and sisters by fasting—correspond to Epiphany or Three Kings Day on the Christian calendar. Another major commemoration is the first week of March, which is the Week of the Sun (or King's Week), when they celebrate their founding anniversary. All gangs have holy days that commemorate various things of importance to the gang, such as their gang leader's birthday or the death of a leader.

A detailed constitution and manifesto outline the highly organized structure of the Kings. The young King usually goes through three stages of nation life: The *primitive stage* describes kids like Xavier whose primary aim is to be thought "big and bad." Their actions are often impulsive and thoughtlessly violent. This stage is useful to older gang members for accomplishing certain objectives, because young kids are dispensable when they get arrested. The *conservative stage* describes the gangbanger who tires of street life and settles down with a job and a family, a more-mature stage but still part of the fabric of gang life. In the *New King stage*, the gang member has proved himself and learned "the values of life and brotherhood." Now he puts his increased knowledge to work in leading the organization and seeking to "better" all his brothers and sisters—though it may only be at this stage that the gang member fully discovers the depth of the group's violent and illegal activities.

The other major street gangs in Chicago and around the country have their own names for leadership positions; their own "constitutions," rules, and bylaws; and their own traditions, languages, and codes of honor. But they're similar in demanding total loyalty from the rank-and-file members and providing a social group that offers protection, belonging, recognition, self-worth, motivation, and discipline—elements of socialization and survival that most kids on the street don't feel are available to them from mainstream society.

Even after Xavier learned some of these facts about Latin King structure, he would never mention them to an outsider. The only thing he needed to know about the Kings was that he belonged. It didn't matter whether they were gangbanging or partying—he just liked hanging out with the older members, who didn't seem to worry about anything or anybody. They had respect, money, cars, and girls.

One night when the girls showed up at a party in a block full of apartment buildings, they brought some alarming news. "La Raza's gonna pull a hit on us," the girls said, their dark eyes flashing with agitation. "That old guy who sells us beer said so, and he knows what would happen if he's lying."

The party immediately turned into a war strategy session to strengthen security in the immediate neighborhood against the Kings' rivals. The Kings blocked the surrounding alleys with the big, square garbage Dumpsters that squatted behind every apartment building. Then they closed half of the busy residential street with orange construction cones (conveniently lifted from an unfinished street repair job nearby) to funnel the traffic into a single, narrow lane of slow-moving traffic. No one would get through this makeshift shooting gallery if the Kings chose to stop them. The boys then shot out all the street lights, making the block pitch-dark to protect the snipers they stationed on various rooftops. Xavier got to fire his pistol in taking out the lights, and even though he didn't hit anything, he felt the heady power that flows through the barrel of a gun.

Any "civilian" drivers who accidentally drove down the block would simply think the area was under construction to repair the poor lighting or dig up the sewer. But the Kings' intention was to take total control of their neighborhood against any drive-by rivals. And they had it! Their only vulnerability could come from some desperate enemies willing to creep into the area on foot for a risky walk-by. If they tried it, though, they might well be on a suicide mission.

Meanwhile, the residents recognized gang activity when they saw and heard it and knew the best response was to lock the doors and pull down the blinds.

By 1:00 in the morning, nothing had happened. The street was quiet—so quiet that the Kings began to doubt how good their informant was. "We're gonna get that old buzzard," Mexico swore as he strolled into the middle of the street. "There ain't nothin' happenin'."

"Yeah," agreed Joker, disgusted. "False alarm . . . and nobody gets away with putting us through that much work for nothin'."

Soon the boys were so relaxed that they started passing around some joints and calling the girls outside.

"Hey, Joker," Macho suddenly said in a loud whisper. "I think I heard something in that gangway between those two houses across the street."

"Aw, shut up," said Mexico. "You just tryin' to get us goin'. There ain't nothin' happenin' tonight. That old man was just puttin' us on. But it's gonna be the last time."

"No, man, I really heard somethin'," insisted Macho.

"I think I heard somethin', too," Xavier spoke up. He hoped his voice didn't betray the nervousness he felt.

"Yeah?" said Joker. "Then why don't you go check it out? It'll be your first assignment."

"You guys are just tryin' to scare us," said one of the girls, tossing her long, thick mane of hair. "There ain't no one over there."

The words were no sooner out of her mouth than the night exploded with gunfire.

Xavier dove behind a parked car, but his gun caught on something and flipped out of his hand. He spent precious moments scrambling around in the dark, trying to find it. When his fingers finally touched steel and found the trigger, he had no idea where the enemy was. He just fired in the general direction of the houses across the street.

Suddenly, the back window of the car he was crouching behind shattered, showering him with a thousand pieces of glass, and then there was silence.

A baby in the building behind him began to cry, and a light in an apartment came on briefly until someone in the building began yelling to shut it off.

"Macho, you okay?" Joker said in the darkness.

"Yeah. I think I got one!" came back Macho's boisterous voice.

"Sure, just like last time," Mexico snickered from farther down the street.

"No, man, I really think I did."

"Shut up," barked Joker. "We gotta get out of here before the Five-0s show up." ("Five-0s" is street slang from the old *Hawaii Five-0* TV cop series.) Even as he spoke, police sirens could be heard converging on the neighborhood.

"What 'bout the new kid?" called Macho. "Xavier, you okay?"

Xavier didn't know whether he was hurt. Was it glass or a bullet that had hit him? He could feel bits of glass in his hair, down his neck, and in his shoe. Was he bleeding? He had heard that the pain of a bullet wound sometimes isn't immediately felt.

"Hey, *niñito,* you hit?" demanded Joker.

Being called a "little boy" angered Xavier, and he yelled back, "No, stupid! I ain't hit!"

"Then let's get outta here."

Xavier took off after the dark shadows of his gang brothers as they all fled down the street.

He got over being called *niñito* by the time they got to Macho's house three blocks away. The guys were all slapping one another on the back and bragging about how close they'd come to being hit as they raided the refrigerator for beer. Macho kept claiming that he shot one of the rivals, but no one would believe him.

Then someone noticed a little blood on Xavier's ear. "Hey, man," the gangster called out, "you been hit!"

They all gathered around. It was just a tiny cut from flying glass, but Xavier quickly became the center of attention, the hero of the night. The memory of shooting a gun in an actual street battle was transformed from total terror to a powerful sensation of control. The weapon had been a part of him; it had spoken his thoughts, reaching out and conveying his hatred to his enemies.

What a day! No question about it—he was down for the Kings!

❖ ❖ ❖

A LATE-MODEL CADILLAC ROLLED QUIETLY TO A STOP IN FRONT OF A small bungalow on Chicago's west side, and five young men stepped into the night, guns ready. It could have been a scene from a movie about Chicago gangsters of the 1920s, but the shiny car wasn't square and the boss's name wasn't Al Capone.

"You take the back porch," ordered Walter Davis, a handsome, slender two-star general for the Conservative Vice Lords. In another setting, this intelligent, neatly dressed man in his early twenties, with warm brown skin and a disarming smile, would have belied the image of a gangbanger. Most mothers would take one look at him and tell their daughters, "Why don't you go out with somebody like that nice Walter Davis?" But tonight, Walter's eyes were hard as he snapped a few more orders: "You, cover the alley; and you, the other side. We'll hit the front." There was no other conversation that might alert the sleeping family inside.

It's not a good idea to owe the mob money and be slow to pay. That's as true of today's drug-dealing street gangs as it was of the traditional Mafia syndicates whose collection practices are the stuff of movie plots and television dramas.

At over 7,000 members, the Conservative Vice Lords (CVLs) is the largest of the predominantly African-American organizations that ride under the five-pointed star and belong to the gang alliance known as "People." Vice Lord organizations founded in Chicago's westside area known as the "Holy City" include the CVL, the Unknown (UVL), the Imperial Insane, the Cicero Insane, the Revolutionary, the Renegade, and the Four Corner Hustlers (though the latter now consider themselves independent of the Vice Lords).

Why is the area known as the "Holy City"? Contrary to popular opinion, the "vice" in Vice Lords doesn't refer to evil or wickedness but is used like "vice president." In a religious sense, it means "under God," a quasi-Muslim tradition.

The top-ranking position for the whole organization is a five-star "universal elite." Local areas are governed by "chapter elites," who have up to four stars. As one of the chapter elites, Walter was second in command in his local area, and he and his crew were out to collect. Kenny, a drug dealer for the gang, owed the organization $300,000 and hadn't paid.

On signal, the five armed young men burst into Kenny's home.

Bedlam broke loose. Screams of terror came from women and children startled from a sound sleep.

"Find Kenny!" Walter shouted. "Check the whole house!"

"Don't hurt us!" pleaded a young girl.

"Just stay in your room and do what you're told," Walter ordered. "Nobody gets hurt."

A few minutes later, the young gunmen reported to Walter, who had set up command in the living room, "We checked the whole house. Kenny's not here."

"Figures. I didn't expect him," Walter said. "Let's have a little talk with Momma."

It's common for "Momma" to hold a dealer's cash. "We know you're holding Kenny's money," Walter challenged the woman cowering in her bed. "So hand it over!" The five gunmen gathered around the bed quickly persuaded her to give up all the $170,000 she had stuck in her dresser drawer.

After satisfying themselves that there was no more cash on the premises, the quintet left as quickly as they had come.

"Floor it!" Walter yelled to the driver as they climbed back into the Cadillac. The young gang leader felt a rush of satisfaction as they sped away. That would teach Kenny not to mess with the CVLs. He might not like it, but what could he do?

Much more than Walter Davis could have imagined.

❖ ❖ ❖

Eight-year-old Silviu Spiridon twisted the knob of the bedroom door and opened it just a crack. He and his 11-year-old brother, Tiberiu, crowded their white faces and dark heads close to the sliver of light. The secret prayer meeting that met in the Spiridon home was winding down, and the children strained to hear what was being said from among the murmuring voices in the sitting room below.

"Ow! You're stepping on my foot!" complained Tiberiu. Their younger sister, Emmanuela, was asleep in another bedroom of the "company house" the family occupied as respected employees of Romania's railroad.

"Shh!" hissed Silviu. "I hear Papa."

"Today we have good news," their father was saying, his voice choked with emotion. "After seven years, our application to emigrate to America has finally been approved."

The swell of quiet exclamations from the little Pentecostal group was punctuated with "Praise God!" and "Hallelujah!" Then came a barrage of questions.

Silviu punched his brother playfully as they tumbled back into bed. It was true! They were going to America!

Silviu was too excited to fall asleep. For as long as he could remember, his parents had talked about emigrating to America. They had filled out application after application, but each time the communist interviewers had grilled them with the same questions: "*Why* do you want to leave Romania? You have a good job as an engineer with the railroad. Do you want to make our country ashamed?"

As he lay in his bed, Silviu heard the sound of the front door opening and shutting at five-minute intervals. He knew the people who had come to the prayer meeting were leaving one at a time so as not to call attention to the fact that a religious group had met at the Spiridon house. It was against the law to hold church services in communist Romania. People who did risked being arrested and thrown into prison.

Silviu shivered with excitement. All that would be different now. In America, people could worship God whenever and wherever they pleased—even in public. Even in the daytime! In America, everyone had his own car. In America, people could buy whatever they wanted. In America, they played football and basketball. In America . . .

Still, Silviu could hardly believe it when he and his family stepped off the train in Rome's enormous station a few weeks later. This was the first stage in their long journey. From the railroad station, they would go to Rome's international airport and get on a plane to America. The vaulted station was alive with loudspeakers blaring, people chatting in an unfamiliar language and hurrying to catch their trains, and the ringing bell of an ice cream vendor.

Ice cream! "Please, Papa, please can we have some ice cream?" the boys begged, their eyes wide with excitement.

Their mother's eyes smiled in sympathy as she cradled a sleepy Emmanuela. Papa shrugged. "All right, all right," he told the boys, "but you must share with your sister." To the vendor he said, "Two ice creams, please."

The boys' feet danced impatiently as the woman scooped two ice cream cones and handed them to the brothers. But when Papa reached into his pocket, he came up short. He had more than enough to pay for one ice cream, but not enough for two.

With a snort of disgust, the vendor grabbed Silviu's ice cream out of his hand and tossed it into the garbage.

Stunned, all the joy drained from young Silviu's face. No one would throw away ice cream in Romania! What good would it do anyone in the garbage? Deep down in his heart, Silviu made a vow that once he got to America, he would do whatever it took to get what he wanted—and no one was going to grab it away from him.

❖ ❖ ❖

GULPING THE LAST OF MY ORANGE JUICE, I OPENED THE MORNING PAPER for a quick glance at the headlines. It was Saturday, a glorious September morning, and I was just about to head out the door to pick up some kids from the bricks for one of our United Nations meetings. But the headlines seemed to leap off the page and scream at me:

KIDS KILLING KIDS!
2 BOYS FROM ROBERT'S GANG CHARGED
IN HIS EXECUTION!

My work with the Juvenile Justice Ministry of Metro Chicago Youth for Christ puts me in constant contact with kids on the street, gangbangers, and young drug dealers. After 50 years on the bricks, I'm not easily shocked, but this particular morning I had to sit down as I read the tag beneath the headlines: "Shavon

Dean, killed Sunday, was 14. Her suspected killer, Robert ('Yummy') Sandifer, was 11. Those charged in his slaying are 16 and 14."

Three families had been sucked into a terrible tragedy. I shook my head sadly. I'd attended too many of these funerals, with grieving families crying, "Why? Why?"

Over the next few days and weeks, even national newspapers and magazines carried the story. *Time* magazine's cover photo of 11-year-old Yummy Sandifer—a police mug shot of a little boy with a haunted look, found killed execution-style after an intense, three-day police manhunt—sat grimly above bold, black-and-white letters:

So Young to KILL
So Young to DIE

I saved as many clippings as I could, reading and rereading the story that shocked even Chicago, a city familiar with gang wars and drive-by shootings. I also talked with my contacts in the law-enforcement community. Gradually I pieced together what could be known from the in-depth media reporting.

Sunday, August 18, 10:30 A.M. Robert Sandifer, known to family and friends as Yummy because of his love of cookies and candy, left his grandmother's house to go hang out with friends.

The woman who had helped raise Yummy may have suspected her grandson was spending time with the Black Disciples (BDs) gang, but as with most parents and grandparents, denial came easily. Robert wasn't in a gang. Not her Yummy. Oh, sure, he was hard to handle sometimes. She had to go to school when he got in a fight, and he sometimes acted wild when he was with a group of his friends. But by himself, he could be sweet as sugar. Why, he was only 11, a child.

Sunday, August 18, 6:00 P.M. Police were summoned to 108th and Perry Avenue. A teenager had been shot. Bending over the wounded youth, a Chicago police officer asked, "Who shot you?"

The boy clutched his bleeding stomach and gasped, "Yummy shot me. . . . I think his name is Robert."

Sunday, August 18, 9:00 P.M. Shavon Dean's mother was grilling ribs and chicken in back of the family dwelling when the 14-year-old girl left the house to walk a friend home. As the girls walked past a group of boys playing football on the neighborhood playground, a burst of gunfire shattered the calm. One of the boys hit the dirt after hearing the shots, then realized he'd been hit in the hand. He got up and ran. But Shavon Dean was lying on the ground, a bullet in her head—dead. When the police arrived, the frantic witnesses all agreed: Yummy Sandifer had walked up to the group and opened fire with a 9-mm semiautomatic pistol.

Monday and Tuesday, August 19-20. The police initiated a massive manhunt in the Rosedale neighborhood for one vicious boy who, for reasons unknown, had gone on a shooting spree. Some people weren't surprised when they heard Yummy was the suspect. His mother was a crack addict, and his father was in jail. The boy had been abused, neglected, and in and out of "the system" since he was three years old. A local grocer had banned him from his store because of Yummy's constant stealing. By the time he went on his shooting spree, Yummy had a rap sheet of 23 felonies and 3 misdemeanors. But he had always been returned home because he was too young to send to prison.

As a Black Disciples shorty, Yummy may have been acting on his own, trying to make a "rep" for himself of being big and bad. The BDs don't require new members to commit a violent crime as an initiation rite, but a Chicago gang researcher thinks Yummy had been sent on a mission of revenge against members of the rival Gangster Disciples. *Time* magazine quoted the researcher as saying, "If it was just an initiation ceremony, he'd do it from a car [a drive-by]. But to go right up to the victims, that means he was trying to collect some points and get some rank or maybe a nice little cash bonus." Whatever the reason, the police manhunt put a lot of pressure on the BDs, who were probably hiding him.

Wednesday, August 31, 10:30 P.M. A neighbor woman was sitting on her front porch in the late evening when she noticed a very frightened Yummy standing in the shadows. She called to him, and he came to her, shaking. According to the woman, Yummy begged her to call his grandmother—he wanted to turn himself in to the police, and he wanted his grandmother to go with him.

The woman left to contact the boy's grandmother, but when she returned, Yummy was gone. Her daughter reported that while Yummy was waiting on the porch, another neighbor boy, Derrick Hardaway, had appeared in the gangway next to the house and motioned for Yummy to come with him. The two boys had disappeared. When Yummy's grandmother arrived, she was angry that her grandson wasn't there.

Thursday, September 1, early morning. The next morning, the neighbor woman walked over to the Hardaway home, thinking maybe Yummy had spent the night with Derrick. But Derrick's mother said no, he hadn't been there. Just as the neighbor was getting ready to leave, Mrs. Hardaway suddenly called her back as a news bulletin flashed on TV. In horror, both women watched as TV cameras showed police putting the lifeless body of a young boy into a police wagon. Passersby had seen the body lying in a pool of blood in a pedestrian tunnel under a train viaduct at 108th and Dauphin. He'd been shot twice in the back of the head.

The boy's name: Robert "Yummy" Sandifer.

The neighbor crumpled in grief. "I almost saved that boy!" she moaned again and again. And then she went home and called the police.

❖ ❖ ❖

JOHN JOHNSON DRIBBLED THE BASKETBALL BACKWARD, LAUGHING, ALL the while keeping his older brother, Michael, from making a steal. The Johnson brothers, ignoring the late-afternoon July heat, were shooting some hoops in the alley behind their frame house on the west side of Chicago. At 10 years old, young John was already a lanky kid with a passion for basketball. With a fake and a quick turn, he shot the ball through an imaginary hoop against the brick backside of an apartment building across the way.

A cheerful honk from a battered car nosing its way down the alley broke up the game. "Hey, Dad!" yelled John, running to hang in the window on the driver's side, "how come you're home early? Where'd you get this piece of junk?"

The boys' stepfather grinned and eased the car into the small, concrete space beside the garage where he tinkered on engines. "Glad to see you boys at home," he said with a nod, climbing out of the car and lifting the hood. He was wearing oily, stained coveralls with AJAX MOTORS monogrammed on the chest pocket. "You stayin' clear of those gangbangers hangin' out over at Garfield Park?"

"Sure, Dad," said John, draping himself over the front fender and peering into the fascinating array of wires, carburetor, belts, and gummy, black oil.

Mr. Johnson stuck his head back out from under the hood. "Michael?" There was a warning note in his voice.

Fourteen-year-old Michael rolled his eyes and balanced the basketball on his hip. "Yeah," he said reluctantly. "But—man! Ain't no place we can play if we can't go to the park. Like, it's summer, man—what're we supposed to do? We don't even got no hoop here in the alley, but they've got lots of 'em at the park."

"I know, son," said Mr. Johnson, frowning once more at the ancient engine. "But ain't no son of mine gonna run drugs for those no-good gangbangers. . . . Gee-Gee," he said, using the younger boy's nickname, "get me the five-eighths-inch socket from my tool-box, will ya?"

Next to basketball, John most loved watching his stepfather work on cars. He knew lots of things about engines already. He was going to be an auto mechanic when he grew up, just like his dad—if he didn't make it into the NBA, that is.

"Tomorrow's the Fourth of July," Michael went on, leaning against the car and idly bouncing the basketball. "Everybody's gonna be over in the park—barbecuin', hangin' out. Can't we go to the park tomorrow at least?"

"Umph," grunted Mr. Johnson, trying to twist a stubborn bolt on the alternator. "We'll see tomorrow."

The Fourth of July was even hotter than the day before, and John, his mom, and 12-year-old Marie sprawled in front of the fan in the darkened front room and watched TV. Mrs. Johnson's first husband had walked out just months before John was born, leaving her with three children to support. More fortunate than many abandoned women, however, she soon met and married a good man, an older, steady man who already had kids of his own but was willing to support and raise her three as well. John was just a baby when his mom remarried; his stepfather, whom he idolized, had always been "Dad."

Michael poked his head in the door and asked, "Where's Dad?"

"Went to pick up some food for our barbecue," murmured Mrs. Johnson. "Now don't keep askin', Michael. He's gonna come back and get us when it's time to go to the park."

The daytime TV show was boring, but John lay on the cool floor, letting the moving air from the fan blow over him. He vaguely heard the phone ring and was glad when his mother got up to answer it. He didn't want to move.

Suddenly he heard his mother scream, "No! No!" and then she was crying hysterically.

"Mama! Mama! What is it?" cried John, scrambling to her side. Michael, Marie, and several of their stepbrothers and sisters all converged around the phone.

"Your . . . father!" gasped Mrs. Johnson, slumping weakly against the wall. "He's been shot . . . in the park."

John was stunned. Not his daddy! Why, he had the best daddy in the whole world. No, no . . . this couldn't be true! Why would anyone want to shoot his daddy?

Numbly, the family made its way to the hospital where Mr. Johnson had been taken by ambulance. Two other people had been wounded as well: A woman had been shot in the neck, and another man was hit in the leg. But Mr. Johnson had been wounded in the head. If he lived, the doctor said gravely, he would never be the same man.

"But what happened?" cried Mrs. Johnson, still in shock. "Was it a robbery? A gang fight?"

No, said the police, just a crazy guy who started shooting into the holiday crowd in the park. He had been subdued by bystanders and hauled away to the county jail by the police.

The next three months were a living nightmare. Mr. Johnson was in a coma. The family members prayed and cried. They visited the hospital and held his hand. Then he died.

"Maybe it's for the best," whispered Mrs. Johnson as she helped the kids get dressed for the funeral. "Your father wouldn't want to spend his life hooked up to tubes in a hospital."

Young John's insides felt like coarse sandpaper. Never work on those old junker cars with his dad anymore? Never see his dad's proud smile when he brought home a good report card? He simply couldn't believe it.

❖ ❖ ❖

News travels fast on the streets, and the kids we work with know they can call me or my staff at the Juvenile Justice Ministry any time of the day or night. When I responded to my pager one particular day, a familiar voice blurted, "Rev? Angel's down. His brother, too. They took them to the hospital, but I don't know if they're gonna make it. Can you come quick?"

I got the name of the hospital and headed right over. When I arrived, I found Angel Nieves in the intensive care unit. The 18-year-old Puerto Rican was in shock, and doctors were taking the bullets from his jaw and wiring it shut so he could heal. His kid brother had already been taken to the morgue.

"Don't talk to him now," a doctor advised quietly when Angel finally awoke. "Just let him see you're here, then come back when he's had some rest. Incidentally, we haven't told him yet about his brother. Maybe you can be the one to tell him tomorrow."

I dreaded the assignment. But it was one I often faced, though I was usually telling parents their wounded son or daughter would not survive. In this case, however, it was a while before I even learned the details of what had happened.

Earlier that evening, Angel and his younger stepbrother Roberto had been caught out in a torrential downpour, more like an Asian monsoon than a fall Chicago rain. The winds had tossed traffic lights like pennants. Tree limbs had broken off and cluttered the streets of the neighborhood known as Little Village, alias "Little Mexico," where two- and three-story houses were packed into narrow lots and filled with multigenerational families. Only a few cars and fewer pedestrians were out. Angel and Roberto had thought they could make the few blocks from their house to a friend's before the rains got too heavy, but the downpour had overtaken them, and they were soaked.

Perhaps the rain, wind, and cold explain what occurred next. On a calmer day, it never would have happened.

A car pulled up, and the driver flung open the passenger door and shouted, "Get in! It's miserable out there."

Angel recognized him. They had been in high school together, but they weren't friends. Angel had joined the Maniac Latin Disciples when he was a shorty, before his mom had married Roberto's dad. His stepbrother was a Gangster Two-Six, but that was cool because the two gangs were both in the alliance known as "Folks" and not especially rivals. But the driver, whose street name was Pro, was a rival Latin King, a deadly enemy of both the brothers' organizations.

Pro sensed their hesitancy as the door almost blew shut. "Forget who we are," he said. "I know you guys. It's miserable out. Climb in and I'll drop you off."

The boys jumped into the front seat, glad to get out of the downpour.

"Where you headed?" Pro asked. When the Nieves brothers explained, he said, "No problem. Hardly outta my way."

But when he got to 26th Street, Pro suddenly turned and raced east several blocks past darkened storefronts until he crossed Lawndale and into King territory. Angel and Roberto glanced at each other apprehensively. To the average commuter, Lawndale was just another busy north-south artery dissecting the city. But to gang kids on each side, it might as well have been the Berlin Wall.

Near 26th and St. Louis, Pro slammed on the brakes, jolting his passengers as the car squealed to a stop. Quick as lightning, he drew his gun and began firing. Three bullets hit Angel in the jaw and neck, severely wounding him, and one bullet in the back fatally wounded Roberto.

Pro reached over, opened the door, and shoved the two boys onto the street. "King love!" he shouted triumphantly and sped off.

Angel, severely wounded, crawled along the rain- and wind-swept street to his dying brother and cradled him in his arms. He was blinded by rage, pain, tears, and pouring rain. A car spun by the pair, swerving to avoid them and throwing more water on them. A second car stopped, and the driver got out, saw the situation, and immediately went for help.

In just a few minutes—though it seemed like forever to Angel—an ambulance and police cars arrived and rushed the brothers to Mount Sinai Hospital. Roberto died in the emergency room.

The next morning, when I returned to the hospital, Angel had been moved to a regular-care room. He was sitting up when I arrived; his parents had just left. His jaw was wired shut, so he couldn't talk, but a clipboard and pad with a pen allowed him to write, "My brother. I know." Tears streamed down his face and wet his bandages.

Angel was a tough, young kid—no stranger to violence—who had known the dangerous ways of the streets all his life. Several relatives were in gangs, and he had gotten started at age seven. Soon he knew little else but gang wars and drug dealing.

Trips in and out of the district police station and juvenile detention taught him little, but they added to his reputation on the street. Nothing ever really happened. His parents came and signed him out, and that was that.

But then came a shooting case that wasn't so easily brushed aside, and at age 15, Angel was committed to the juvenile correctional center in St. Charles, Illinois. There he sought out gang buddies, but he was also pulled in a more-positive direction by counselors and teachers who saw him as a bright young man with much good potential.

Gary Camp, one of the teachers, often encouraged Angel about his ability to make a life outside the gang. One day he added a real shocker: "Why don't you go to chapel this week?"

"Church, you mean? Me? You gotta be jokin'!" Angel said. "I don't go in for that stuff, not since I was a little kid."

But Mr. Camp wouldn't give up. After a time, Angel decided that if someone he respected as much as that teacher urged him to go to church, he would give it a try. To his surprise, he found it interesting. The chapel volunteers talked straight. He even came to one of the smaller Bible study groups, which is where I first met him—a feisty, young street rebel with an attitude, yet utterly amazed to hear that God cared about him, knew all about him, and loved him anyway.

In those Bible studies, Angel grappled with the word *forgiveness*. It implied that he had been wrong—not just unlucky enough to get caught, but really guilty. And *guilty* was another problem word. Among Angel's crowd, the word didn't mean being responsible for doing something wrong. *Guilty* was merely what a white man in a black robe downtown said when your luck ran out. (For most street kids, nothing in the court process arouses the slightest sense of shame or responsibility. "If I hadn't shot him, he would've shot me" is the most-common explanation for violence, even murder.)

One night, Angel came to the chaplain's office after a youth service I'd conducted with the chaplain and wanted to talk. "I come from a pretty rough family," he said, peeling back a layer in his tough-guy attitude. "My uncles and some of my cousins have been in gangs and served time. I thought that was just the way it is. But . . ." He was silent a moment, staring at his hands resting on the table. "One thing I learned being here is that I don't want to spend the rest of my life behind bars." He looked up. "But I dunno, Rev. I done some pretty bad stuff. It's one thing to say I wanna make some changes, but I don't really know how. I know it's more than just goin' to church and goin' through the motions. But what it is, I really don't know. Or even," he said with a wry laugh, "if the Man Upstairs would give me a chance."

I handed Angel a Bible. "You can keep that," I said. "But here, let's read something together." As he followed along, I read the Bible story in John chapter 8 about the woman caught in the act of adultery whose accusers wanted to stone her to death.

That caused Angel to sit up and take notice. "Hey, man," he

said, "Jesus really stuffed a rag in it when He said any dude who had never sinned could throw the first stone."

"Yeah," I agreed. "And those were the so-called good guys."

Angel laughed. I could see him thinking that maybe this Jesus did understand how things work.

"But look again at what Jesus said to the woman after her accusers drifted away," I said, pointing at verse 11.

Angel read, "'Neither do I condemn you,' Jesus declared. 'Go now and leave your life of sin.'"

He left the chaplain's office that night with a lot to think about.

It didn't take Angel long to figure out that if Jesus came into this world to die in our place for our sins, then all of us, including himself, must be in pretty bad shape. "Messed up inside" was Angel's phrase, and it fit. Angel finally decided he had blown it on two levels—how he had treated God and how he had treated other people. It stunned him to understand that he hadn't just gotten caught, but that right and wrong are real standards, and he had run up a big debt in the "wrong" department. For the first time, Angel began to experience the true purpose of guilt—to drive us to make things right.

Angel declared that he wasn't going to live "like that" anymore. *Okay,* I thought. But such regret is common among prisoners. "Sounds good as far as it goes," I told him, "but it's a far cry from the repentance of which the Bible speaks. To repent in biblical terms is to not only change your actions and your mind regarding your failures and shortcomings and a few bad habits, but to go further and take a deep, sincere look at God, His love expressed in Jesus, and your need to open yourself to a life-transforming encounter with Him."

Angel listened. It's not every day a hurting kid meets someone who will give him a second chance, let alone a God who will give him a second chance every day. But eventually Angel met God—or, to be more exact, God brought Angel into His eternal family.

But conversion doesn't change everything overnight. A new life takes time to develop, and Angel's was no exception. We talked about what would happen when he got out. I stressed how important it was to be part of a church and the family of faith. He kept coming to our services and Bible studies for a while, but then he was sent home on parole—sooner than the chaplain and I would have liked—back into the real world, where every temptation and test was multiplied.

We knew Angel would now face a lot of pressure from his gang buddies to get back into selling drugs and leading attacks on their rivals. Having been locked up, he had a reputation to live up to. And the boys wouldn't let him forget it.

Going clean wouldn't be easy either. None of the high schools wanted him because of his gang background, and there were few jobs for a young man with a criminal history who had just been released from reform school. Still, Angel came to some of our community ministry events, worked at a few jobs, continued his education through alternative schools, and tried to pull his brother away from the streets. Then came that rainy night and the ill-fated ride.

Several months after the street tragedy, I was introduced to a young man at Cook County Jail who had come to several of our services, showed some interest, and made the effort to get a Bible. He was a pleasant-looking fellow, 5'10" tall, and mature-looking for an 18-year-old Latino, with the first signs of a mustache. Like many of the kids I meet in jail, the most outstanding thing about him was that he looked so ordinary, like a typical teen I might pass in the halls of a high school or college. I asked his name, which was not significant to me, but then he added, "On the streets, they call me Pro."

I froze. I was face to face with the young man charged with killing Roberto Nieves and so terribly wounding Angel. I didn't know what to say or how to react. I was almost shaking.

Pro sensed my discomfort. "You know what my case is about," he said. "I know the victims were your friends, so I won't come to the chapel again. I don't want to put you through any more hurt." And he turned and walked away.

It took me a moment to regain self-control and calm down. He was by the door, leaving the chapel, when I called him back. I waved for him to follow me to the chaplain's office. Inside, I shut the door, but neither of us sat down. "You're right," I finally said. "Angel is very much my friend, and so is his family. But I also have a responsibility here to every guy who wants to come to our meetings. And you've come. You're interested and respectful. You must not stay away. I'll deal with my feelings, but I'm not your judge. It's my job to share God's Word with you, and I intend to do that. I'm very sad over how you got here, but I want you to come any time you can. We'll take it from there."

And we did. Pro became one of our most-faithful, active participants while he awaited his trial. He took part in discussions and brought many of his friends from the wing to the meetings. The school staff came to consider him an eager, excellent student, and the wing officers trusted him with extensive responsibilities.

Meanwhile, I continued to spend time with Angel and often visited his family, who were fine, well-meaning people. They strove to recover from the tragedy of losing one son and having another wounded. There was no doubt that they eagerly awaited Pro's trial. Vengeance flashed in their eyes. They hoped he'd be sentenced to the maximum time behind bars. No one could fault them after what they had been through.

When I briefly mentioned that Pro was active in our chapel programs, they simply accepted the fact without comment.

In court, Pro told his version of what happened. The Nieves brothers had planned to get a gun and shoot at Kings, he said. In his mind, he had acted to prevent more killing.

The trial was hard on Angel's family, as it usually is for victims as they relive the horror in the sterile, unemotional give-and-take of questions and answers from a witness stand. Gruesome pictures of the deceased have to be identified, fine legal points argued, and eventually a verdict rendered.

Many people think the court process brings closure for the victims of violent crime. But over the years, I've found that to be only partly true. The victims may demand long sentences and later tell reporters that whatever sentence was given wasn't nearly severe enough, even if it was death. And they often make statements such as "I'd like to give the lethal injection myself!" However, talk to those same people months and years later and they have a different view. They never forget the tragedy, but quite a few realize that the harsh punishments don't bring satisfaction in the long run.

Yet if revenge doesn't dominate everyone's feelings in the long run, it certainly does for nearly every victim in the short term, and that included Angel's family. They felt real satisfaction when Pro was convicted on murder and attempted murder charges.

The night before the sentencing, I dropped by the Nieves's house. They were hoping for the maximum sentence, and the events of the next day were on their minds as well as mine as we enjoyed nachos and soft drinks around the kitchen table.

"There's something I've got to tell you," I finally said solemnly.

"Well, go ahead, Rev," Angel encouraged.

"I'm going to be in court tomorrow for the sentencing—"

"I expected you to be there," Angel's dad interrupted. "It should be very interesting."

"But there's something you need to know," I continued. "I'll be testifying on Pro's behalf. He's going to get at least 20 years for murder, probably more. I plan to tell the court about our ministry with him and see if we can get the final number of years down to a reasonable figure."

Angel's father put down his glass and stared at the table. Angel's mother got up and walked over to the sink, turning her back to me. The younger kids didn't know how to react. Angel wouldn't look at me.

Mr. Nieves finally broke the silence. "I thought you were our friend, that you shared our loss and hurt," he said. "How can you do this to us?" His measured words revealed his sense of betrayal.

I nodded, understanding how this hurt them. I explained, "I am your friend. But I'm also a minister, and I have a responsibility to all the young men in my jail group, just as I do to you and your family. Angel is not going to be sentenced tomorrow. Pro is. For months he has been one of our most dependable, faithful helpers, a positive role model among the young men awaiting trial. I believe the court is entitled to know that side of him as well as what you'll say as surviving victims. Only if the court knows the good as well as the bad can any of us expect a fair decision. But I wanted you to know before you heard it all tomorrow."

No one moved. Finally, Angel's dad said, "Thank you for telling us now. I don't agree with you, but . . . do what you gotta do, and so will we. I know you're our friend."

Angel got up, walked around the table, and came over to me, and we embraced. Both of us had tears in our eyes. "If I was on trial, you'd do the same thing for me, wouldn't you?" he asked huskily.

"Yes, I would," I replied softly.

I was being forgiven in advance for something I knew they could hardly accept or understand.

Three

❖ ❖ ❖

THE MIDSUMMER DAY WAS HEAVY WITH HEAT and humidity when Xavier and some of the other young Latin Kings decided to retaliate on the La Raza gang for raiding their neighborhood a few nights earlier. It wasn't enough that the Kings had driven off the La Razas without suffering any casualties. They wanted revenge!

"On a day like this," said Xavier, checking his .22 caliber pistol, "they're bound to be kickin' back and not payin' much attention to what's goin' on." He'd quickly learned it wasn't hard to pick up a gun. Older gang members used their connections to the underworld mobs to get weapons, then turned around and sold them on the streets. Sometimes guns were also obtained during house burglaries. And if you kept your ears open, you soon learned which convenience stores sold guns "under the counter" or out of the back room.

"I'm ready," added Lil Man.

"Yeah!" said Macho.

The three young Latin Kings headed up the embankment of one of the railroad tracks that crisscross the city so they could approach their prey from behind.

"We'll have the high ground," gloated Lil Man, "and can split before they realize what's happened or who we are."

39

"Hey, man," scoffed Macho, "they gonna know who we are. Even if they don't see us, they know they got it comin'."

"Afterward, we'll split up and meet at Pito's house," said Xavier. "We can hide there while the heat's on."

The three youthful Kings may have thought it was a good day for a raid, but it was also a good day to be out driving around in a low-rider, enjoying the luxury of air conditioning. And some La Raza boys were doing just that when they spotted the three Kings sneaking along the railroad tracks.

Before the Kings got into position, the La Raza boys were out of their vehicle and heading right for them.

"Look out," yelled Lil Man as he dropped to the ground between the tracks and began shooting. In an instant, Macho and Xavier had joined him, laying down a blaze of reckless fire.

The La Razas fled for the cover of their car when suddenly one crumpled to the ground and began yelling for help as he crawled for the war wagon.

"I got one!" yelled Xavier as he jumped up, oblivious to the possibility of return fire. Fortunately for him, the La Razas were on the run and didn't stop until they had roared out of the area.

The three King boys disappeared nearly as fast when they heard ambulance and police sirens. Soon the area would be crawling with Five-0s.

They made it to their hideout in Pito's backyard between two apartment buildings and celebrated with glee while the cops busily checked out every Latin King they found on the streets. To the three "victors" it was party time, and they reviewed every move, every shot, every howl from the enemy. They had accomplished a major objective and were intoxicated by their success.

"Man, did you see those suckers run?" sang Lil Man as he grabbed Xavier's gun and demonstrated how he had laid down fire on them. He swung the gun around, pulling the trigger: click, click, click, BAM!

Xavier suddenly felt warm blood pouring out of his cheek, mouth, and nose. "What happened?" he sputtered. "Hey, man . . . Hey, man . . . I can't see. What'd you do?"

"Oh, no!" screamed Lil Man, and then he fled.

"Take it easy," urged Macho as he eased his friend to the ground. "You been hit in the face."

"Am I gonna die, man? I can't hear right. Am I bleedin' a lot?"

"Yeah, man. It's comin' pretty fast. Here, hold my T-shirt against your face."

"God, why me?" moaned Xavier. "I can see a little bit with my right eye. You think I'm gonna make it? I feel kinda faint."

"Here, lean back against the fence." And then Macho began yelling, "Help! *Ayúdame!* Somebody help me! We need some help back here!"

"*Callate la voca!*" shouted a woman angrily from an apartment window several floors up.

"No, no *señora*. *Ayúdame!* You gotta help us!"

"What's goin' on down there? You kids get out of here. You're just a bunch of no-good gangbangers."

"No, *señora*. This was an accident. Call an ambulance. *Mi hermano*, he's hurt real bad. *Por favor, señora! Ayúdame, pronto!*"

In a few minutes, Xavier heard the approaching sirens—but only through his right ear. And only through his right eye could he see anything as he tried focusing on bits of trash strewn around the grassless, treeless backyard between the two low-rise apartment buildings. Then the pain began to descend, and he couldn't bring things into focus any longer. It was crushing him. He looked up for Macho, but Macho was gone, and Xavier was alone with the blood still flowing down his face and neck.

❖ ❖ ❖

TWO DAYS AFTER WALTER DAVIS AND HIS MOB RAIDED KENNY'S HOUSE, Walter was out early checking the drug-dealing spots in his neighborhood—a vacant house with plywood windows, a back alley behind a liquor store, a residential street corner a block from a main artery. The streets were quiet. No kids played in the litter-strewn vacant lots. No yuppies lined up in their fancy cars waiting for the boys to take their orders and deliver the goods. No gang sharpshooters watched from the level roofs of the brownstone two-flats and crumbling brick apartment buildings. No police cruised the area.

Early morning as the sun came up was a good time to make his rounds. Walter had never had any trouble at this time of day, and so, although he was alert and cautious, he was without his usual 9-mm handgun.

Suddenly, three minivans filled with young men squealed around the corner and surrounded Walter. The heavily armed crew jumped out and cornered their prey.

Walter immediately recognized them as a faction within the Conservative Vice Lords who were Kenny's friends.

"Sorry Kenny wasn't home when you called the other mornin'," the stone-faced leader snarled, "but maybe we can talk now. And you best be talkin'."

Not waiting for the invitation to be accepted, one of the boys hit Walter in the back with his weapon and shoved the stunned, slumping young man into a van.

Walter was tied and gagged and held on the floor as they sped off. The van careened around corners and bounced over potholes as it wove through the rough streets and alleys of Chicago's west side. Finally it came to a stop. Walter heard a garage door go up, and the vans moved into the dark. The door went down, and the engines died. Van doors opened, and he was yanked out and thrown up against a post as the renegade CVLs gathered around him in the dim light and removed his gag. "We ain't playin' wich ya, chump," said a wiry young hit man as he smashed Walter across the mouth with his gun. "We wants our money back right now, and that means all of it or you be dead! Dig?"

Walter tasted the blood before the jackhammer pain registered. *He's ruined my teeth! My face is cut open!* Walter thought as he probed the side of his mouth delicately with his tongue.

"Go ahead; you take you time," said the hotheaded pistol whipper as he danced around, obviously high on something. "You got 'bout two minutes while we decides how we gonna off ya. We quick. Won't take us long!"

But it did take time as they questioned Walter further. Every so often, two or three of the boys would discuss—loudly enough for him to hear—various tortures they were considering.

"Why not pay a visit to *his* family?" suggested the leader of the group with cold, sober eyes. "Maybe they's holdin' it."

"You know they don't have it," snapped Walter. "That was organization money. That's why Kenny shoulda paid it in the first place."

"Now we's gettin' down to where he's takin' notice," said the hothead. "Seems to me," he continued, addressing Walter, "that you was the first one to bring family into this situation by visitin' Kenny's momma and scarin' her kids. So why you squealin' 'bout yours now?"

The hours dragged on slowly as the jumpy crew waited and questioned and threatened and waited. Walter studied each of the guys so he could identify them if he should get out of this alive: caps tilted to the left, athletic shoes laced in five holes with black-and-gold laces, a Playboy bunny tattoo on this one, a dollar sign shaved into that one's hair—all symbols of the CVLs. But as time passed, he began to realize that something outside the garage was holding them back. Maybe they were waiting for instructions from a higher-up.

Finally a cellular phone trilled and a low voice murmured. The cold-eyed one snapped the phone closed and dropped it into his pocket. "Call's from the leadership," he said. "Gotta let him go."

"What?" raged the hothead. "Who say that?"

The other one shrugged. "The boss say so. We be riskin' full-scale war within the organization seein' how this *punk*"—he jabbed a finger at Walter—"be a two-star general. With that rank, there'd be major complications and retaliations, so we's gotta let him go."

Walter knew "the boss" was in prison, but he still kept a tight rein on the organization. Walter's captors were enraged. On the streets, where reputation meant everything, losing face and having to back down was hard to swallow. But orders were orders, and they had no choice but to obey.

"We still gonna get you!" yelled the hothead. "You just wait. It'll come some night when you not expectin' it."

The leader dismissed him with a wave and pulled Walter to the side. "Look here," he said, "don't pay him no mind. We just doin' business. Know what I mean? We ain't lookin' to carry this no further. Understand? Is that cool?"

Suddenly, Walter realized he was back in the driver's seat. They were worried that he might return with even more of his guys and do them in.

"We could make it right," the leader said as he pulled out a roll of money and started peeling off bills, "considerin' your time and your face and all."

"Eat your money!" sneered Walter. He certainly didn't want this two-bit leader or Kenny to think bygones were bygones. He had been kidnapped, beaten, and threatened for 17 hours; let them sweat a while. "Just get me outta here!" he snapped.

The guy motioned for the door to open, and Walter was put back into one of the vans. Soon the same procession that captured him was returning him to his hood. But the leader was in another van, and the hothead was guarding Walter, who was crouched on the floor. Suddenly the driver said, "There's the signal"—presumably to release Walter. But the hothead, who was still high on drugs and couldn't get anything right, pulled out a gun and put it to Walter's head.

"What'cha doin', you idiot!" said one of his partners as he knocked the weapon from his hand. The van pulled up to a curb on Chicago Avenue, and Walter was shoved out the door—shaken up, worked over, but otherwise all right.

They'll never forget this day, Walter swore to himself, flashing his gang sign—thumb and fingers arched in a letter C for the CVLs—in a show of defiance to the departing vans. *Just wait!*

❖ ❖ ❖

Silviu Spiridon's eyes were big as the car hurtled along the beltway on the outskirts of Houston, Texas. So many cars! And all whizzing so fast! He paid close attention as the driver, a Romanian friend of his father who had picked them up at the airport, pointed out the sky-scrapers of the downtown area in the distance and chatted about the NASA space center and the Houston Oilers. So this was America!

After driving a long way, his father's friend pulled up beside a modest house surrounded by a lot of trees. Silviu was confused. Where was the city? Where were the stores? Where were the buses and trains? Everything was so quiet. This wasn't how he imagined America to be! As the days passed, he could tell his parents were uneasy, too. Every time they wanted to go somewhere, they had to get in the car and drive a long way.

Barely a month later, the Spiridon family boarded another airplane, this time to Chicago. The Romanian Pentecostal Church there had agreed to put them up for a month until they found jobs and a place to live. Their welcome in Chicago was warm. All these people had been refugees, too, and knew what it was like to come to a new country where everything—clothes, food, money, the language, customs, even the way people think—was unfamiliar.

Silviu's parents quickly found jobs, his mother as a cleaning woman and his father cleaning airplanes between flights. They worked hard and soon had their own apartment in the heart of the city. This was more like it! As Silviu and his brother and sister watched the other kids playing on the street from their apartment window, they couldn't wait for school to start. Then they could learn English and make friends. Then they would be real Americans!

School, however, proved to be painful. The other kids laughed at the Spiridons' funny accent and humorous attempts to speak English. Silviu knew they snickered at the secondhand clothes his mother bought them from the thrift store. He looked longingly at the other kids in his neighborhood—some of them foreigners like himself—who nonetheless spoke English fluently and swaggered down the street in the latest fashions. The Asians, Latinos, and black kids—everyone seemed to have a group or "gang" to belong to. Silviu's longing was so strong he could almost taste it.

Silviu and his siblings soon picked up English—much faster than their parents. He couldn't understand why the Romanian Pentecostal Church held its services in Romanian. He didn't want to speak Romanian. He was in America now; he wanted to speak English like the other kids. He felt embarrassed when he was with his parents or other Romanian immigrants, and he ducked out on church gatherings whenever he could get away with it.

Silviu and his brother worked hard to fit in at school. They saved every dime they could and bought the NBA team jackets and name-brand shirts and jeans popular with the other kids, picked up the street language, listened to the popular music, and cheered for the Bulls and the Bears. And as Silviu entered junior high, he realized he had something going for him: sports. Though not very tall, both he and Tib were athletic, with powerful bodies and quick reflexes. Silviu was eligible for junior-high football, and he threw himself into the sport with gusto. Finally he began making friends, and for the first time he felt as if he belonged. Even the girls flirted with him. In eighth grade, he was elected captain of the football team.

Then one day the coach called him into his office. "Your father wants you to drop from the team," he said soberly.

Silviu flushed with anger. His dad was always complaining that football was a waste of time. A 14-year-old should be working after school, making money to help the family, he had said. Usually Silviu just ignored him. Sure, he knew his dad had gotten laid off from his job and things were hard right now. But his father just didn't understand. Silviu couldn't believe his dad had actually called the coach. This wasn't Romania. This was America! Of course he wasn't going to stop playing football!

"Yeah, I know, Coach," he said, exasperated, "but he don't understand—"

"I'm afraid it's not that simple," the coach said. "You have to have your parents' *permission* to play football. And your father has made it clear that he doesn't want you to play ball. I'm afraid I don't have any choice but to drop you from the team." The man laid a hand on Silviu's shoulder. "I'm sorry, Silviu. You have a lot of promise."

Silviu was devastated. Not play football? He felt as though the bottom had dropped out of his new world.

In spite of Silviu's vigorous protests, Mr. Spiridon held firm. "You and your brother need to help the family right now," he said.

"I talked to the manager of the produce store—he'll give both you and Tib jobs. No more arguing! That's the way it is."

Now, after school, instead of practicing football with the team and enjoying respect as its captain, Silviu unloaded crates of lettuce and boxes of bananas. He prayed fervently that none of his school friends or the guys from the team would come by and see him bucking boxes like a common laborer. And as he stocked shelves and filled bins, something deep was churning inside. He wasn't going to let the strides he'd made in this new country be snatched away. Oh, no. If he couldn't play football, there were other ways to belong.

The guys who played sports at school weren't the only ones who were respected. He knew some of the Two-Six Boys—the Latino gang that dominated his neighborhood and numbered in the hundreds across Chicago. They had style. They exuded confidence and demanded respect. You never saw a Two-Six Boy alone; they had lots of friends and all the ladies they wanted. Everyone talked about them—from teachers and cops who denounced them, to rival gangs who hated them, to young boys and hot bloods who admired them. Most important to Silviu, *nobody* made fun of or disrespected a Two-Six. Whether they were loved or feared, *nobody* messed with the Two-Six Boys.

A new determination settled in Silviu's gut. He was going to become a Two-Six, no matter what it took. There was only one problem: The Two-Six Nation was a Latino gang, and he was a white boy.

❖ ❖ ❖

AROUND 8:00 IN THE EVENING OF SEPTEMBER 1, POLICE DETECTIVES converged on the Hardaways' little frame house. Pounding on the door, they flashed their badges and pushed their way in, demanding to see Cragg and Derrick.

"C-Cragg's not here!" cried Mrs. Hardaway, a petite, attractive teacher at the nearby public school. "Why do you want my boys? What did they do?"

By this time, the detectives had discovered Derrick in the boys' tiny bedroom. He was tall for 14, holding his hands up fearfully as the detectives barged in, his eyes wide with fear. "Derrick Hardaway, you're under arrest in connection with the murder of Robert Sandifer," the detective in charge said grimly as Derrick's hands were jerked behind his back and handcuffs were snapped in place.

"But I didn't kill nobody!" Derrick protested. His eyes found his mother, who was standing helplessly to the side as the detectives hustled him out the door and down the wooden porch steps. "Mama, I didn't do it!"

Mrs. Hardaway stood in bewilderment on the small, narrow porch as the police ducked Derrick's head into the backseat of one of their unmarked cars, and then she watched the cars disappear around the corner at the end of the block.

By 10:00 the next morning, the police announced that the Hardaway brothers—Derrick, age 14, and Cragg, age 16, members of the same gang as Yummy Sandifer—had been charged with first-degree murder.

As newspapers reported the appalling news that little Yummy Sandifer—wanted for the wanton murder of 14-year-old Shavon Dean—had been found shot in the back of the head, and that two young members of the Black Disciples—Yummy's own gang—had been arrested for his murder, the nation was stunned. "What has our society come to?" people asked. "Why would an 11-year-old go on a shooting spree? What was an 11-year-old doing with a gun, anyway? Where were his parents? Do gangs really recruit little kids? And why would gang members kill someone in their own gang?" The whole shocking episode had a surreal quality—too ghastly to be true.

Unfortunately, the grist behind this sensational story is all too common. The court system sees hundreds of Yummy Sandifers every year—abused, neglected children from dysfunctional families, with absent fathers and addicted mothers and no one really in charge, who are in and out of trouble with the police and school authorities. The only men in the community who seem to have power and respect—along with nice rides, sharp clothes, great parties, and wads of bills in their pockets—are gang leaders. Kids like Yummy look up to them; they want to be like them. They eagerly leap at the chance to "belong."

In a society that has developed a permanent underclass, where middle-class acceptance and economic prosperity by traditional routes seem impossible goals, gangs provide an alternative society. Kids like Yummy who are desperate for belonging, guidance, attention, and a sense of self-worth are proud to take the oath: "I pledge my soul, heart, love, and spirit to the Black Disciple Nation and will be part of it even in death."

What kids like Yummy don't understand is that the code of loyalty only goes so far. When the actions of one shorty threaten the self-interest of the gang leaders or the gang itself, the youngster is disposable.

The newspapers continued to follow the story closely, and so did I. I knew that sooner or later in my ministry with young offenders, I might run into the Hardaway brothers.

❖ ❖ ❖

JOHN JOHNSON DIDN'T NOTICE MUCH OF ANYTHING FOR A WHILE AFTER his dad died, just that nothing seemed the same. But before long, he realized Michael was hanging out at Garfield Park more and more after school.

"Whatcha hangin' out in the park for?" John demanded.

"Whatchu think, Gee-Gee?" said Michael with a shrug. "Mama needs money, don't she?"

John's eyes widened. "You dealin'? Michael! You know Daddy didn't want—"

"Well, Daddy ain't here, is he!" snapped Michael. "We gotta look after ourselves now, don't we? But you stay outta this. You too young."

John's mind scrambled. Michael could be dealing dope only if he had joined the Black Gangster Disciples—or GDs, as they were known—the main gangbangers and dope dealers in their neighborhood. The gang's six-pointed star surrounding the letter G, with devils' pitchforks sticking out of the top, was spray painted on garage doors and brick walls all over the neighborhood, marking its turf.

The gang's top leader, "King" Larry Hoover—or the "Chairman," as he preferred to be known—was legendary. In prison both for murder and for directing huge drug sales, he probably wouldn't ever see the bricks again. But he still managed to direct his "governors" and "regents" out on the street.

When John confronted his brother, Michael just warned, "Don't you be tellin' Mama now, you hear? She just get worried. But the gang, see, they like brothers. They look after they own. So don't you worry 'bout me."

With nothing else to do, John hung around with Michael and his friends after school—when his brother would let him. He watched as the fancy cars from the suburbs rolled into the neighborhood and out again; he saw the local junkies get their daily supply. He observed as little, plastic bags were exchanged for wads of green bills. It sure looked like an easy way to make money. But it didn't look like as much fun as fixing cars.

"You stay in school and keep your nose clean," Michael warned when John hung around too much. John shrugged. He liked school all right. He was playing junior-high basketball and singing in the church choir. And he didn't really want to get in a gang. His father had made them promise they wouldn't. But he missed hanging out with his dad and brother, tinkering on those old cars. Michael was all he had now, the only one to look up to.

Four years passed after John's stepdad died. John was now 14 and about ready to graduate from eighth grade. He sat on the front porch one day, thinking how proud his daddy would've been to see him graduate. It made the empty place inside him hurt all over again.

Little kids were running up and down the sidewalk, jumping rope, tossing balls, and riding their bikes. *If that one girl don't quit ridin' her bike so fast down the sidewalk, she's gonna hit somebody,* John thought.

The girl on the bicycle suddenly braked to a stop in front of the porch. "Gee-Gee!" she cried, her eyes wide. "Your brother dead! Shot by the police! Over in Garfield Park!"

John took off running, covering the five blocks to the park so fast that he thought his lungs would burst. When he got there, an angry crowd was milling around. Several police cars were parked at rakish angles, their blue lights twirling, and more were arriving. John pushed his way through the crowd . . . and then he saw Michael, lying face down on the grass with two bullet holes in his back and blood pooling around his body.

He dropped to his knees beside his brother. "No, no, Michael!" he screamed. "You can't be dead!" But his brother didn't move.

"Where's that ambulance?" someone yelled. "Why is it taking so long to get here?"

Others in the crowd were muttering angrily, "Shot 'im in the back. Said he had a gun. I don't see no gun."

Suddenly anger seemed to boil out of every pore in John's skin. The next thing he knew, he was tearing into the police officers like a kamikazi pilot, yelling and screaming. The crowd backed the boy up, accusing the police of murder.

"Get back! Get back!" threatened the officers.

Just then the ambulance arrived, and everyone stood aside while the medics worked on the fallen teenager. But it was too late. They took Michael's body away, and eventually the police cars left. John was beside himself. Why did the Five-0s shoot his brother in the back?

The police explained that somebody had given them a tip that a man fitting Michael's description was dealing PCP—angel dust— in the park, and that when they showed up, Michael ran. The police insisted he had a gun; other witnesses said he didn't. No gun was found. But Michael didn't stop running, so they shot him. Eighteen years old, and now he was dead.

John felt he would go crazy with grief and anger. Alongside Michael's gang brothers, he joined in a three-day spree of throwing bottles at police officers and shooting at squad cars. It felt good to be part of the group; it felt good to vent all the hatred and rage churning inside him.

But when the frenzy had spent itself, the pain was still there. His father was gone; now his brother was gone, too. John's world had been shattered.

❖ ❖ ❖

IN MY JOB AS A MINISTER TO KIDS CAUGHT UP IN THE CORRECTIONAL system, I sometimes find myself walking a fine line between being an advocate for kids in trouble and supporting the police, who are trying to do their job to keep our streets safe. I know how difficult it is for the front-line officer to confront the problems of youth violence in our major cities and suburbs, and increasingly in small towns and rural areas as well. If the police are too aggressive in ridding the streets of suspected thugs, they're charged with being brutal. If they're too cautious, not wanting to violate a suspect's civil rights, they're charged with failing to deal firmly with criminals.

Frankly, police officers are often outnumbered and out-gunned by the street hoodlums. Officers risk their lives every time they step out of their car in a troubled neighborhood. Many brave officers have been wounded and even killed combating gangs who often have more-powerful weapons. At times, in a potentially explosive situation, the temptation must be strong to "shoot first and ask questions later." Despite this, the newest direction in policing is to enforce even minor law violations such as curfews, jaywalking, and traffic offenses in order to be visible in the community and to head off problems before they become severe.

Admittedly, this can lead to prejudicial targeting of certain segments of our population, even when they're law-abiding citizens. Just ask any young, African-American male (or *any* African-American male, for that matter) how often he has been stopped by the police on "routine traffic checks" or illegal searches for weapons or drugs. And sometimes frustrated police who "know" gang members are dealing drugs or responsible for a shoot-out, but can't prove it, will plant evidence or drum up other charges just to get the hoodlum off the street. The attitude is: "Maybe you didn't do this, but we know you've done a lot of other things."

Still, the front line in a community's defense against violence is the police, who are often hampered by having jurisdiction only in a particular city or suburb while the problem they confront ignores the lines on maps and reaches its tentacles everywhere. For better or worse, the police are the eyes and ears of the community, and at their best, they are quick to move in and thwart gang recruitment and drug sales.

It has been my privilege to meet many concerned officers who walk that careful line between firm, fair enforcement of the law, investigating and arresting suspected perpetrators ("perps"), and—at the same time—trying to steer young, potential gang recruits in the right direction before their lives are destroyed.

One of these admirable officers is Sergeant Mark Johnson, a 15-year veteran of a suburban Chicago police department. I know his family well; they're active in church and community affairs, and his three daughters are talented musicians. Recently, we had lunch together. Over Chicago's best pizza, he lamented the "conventional wisdom" about youth today.

"I tell you, Gordon," he said, "when suburban folks see 10 teenage males in a group, especially if the kids are minority youth, their first thought is not that the guys are going to play basketball. They think, *Look out! A gang's on the move!*"

"Why does the public have that image of young guys?" I asked.

"The media don't help. Between news headlines and TV dramas, many suburban dwellers are afflicted with a basic fear of kids who may not be just like us."

He talked for a while about how he and his department are dealing with big changes in their population. "I can remember when our residents saw our suburb of 23,000 as a nice refuge from the problems of the inner city," he said, then grabbed another slice of pizza. "But no more. Many people have moved here to escape the problems downtown, but some of them have just brought the problems with them."

Mark sees the role of his department as something more than just investigating and apprehending offenders. "Years back," he said, "we set up a liaison with the local schools. Drug prevention is stressed at the elementary and junior-high levels, and a youth officer is assigned to the high school. That officer is there to be our eyes and ears, but more importantly, to work closely with the teachers and deans to help steer kids toward positive goals. He makes friends with the students, is there to talk with them, and does a lot to give kids a more-positive view of the men and women who carry a badge. He can often diffuse tensions because he's already on the scene. When a law violation occurs, he will take action. But most of the kids see him as being not only firm but also fair."

The medium-sized pizza was disappearing at an astonishing rate. "But one of the complaints I hear," I said, wondering why we hadn't ordered a large, "is that too often the police show up only when there's a problem. So it's adversarial from the start."

Mark nodded in agreement. "Too often the departments are underfunded and understaffed," he explained. "But an important part of police work is to get to know the people in the community we've been hired to 'serve and protect.' I have a session scheduled this afternoon to talk with our patrol officers about the importance of walking their beat, getting out of their cars, and meeting citizens of all ages, from the little guys to the seniors. We're working hard to encourage our townspeople to know and respect people of all races and cultures," he said with firm conviction. "But that's an ongoing process, starting right within our own department."

As I've gotten to know Mark, I realize that he sees his responsibility as a policeman as a vital extension of who he is as a husband, father, and church leader. And he cares about young people. "I enjoy driving down a street and having kids wave to me rather than shouting some profanity and running to hide from my car," he said as we paid our bill and stood outside, reluctant to end our visit. "I want their respect, so I know I need to give them mine."

The sergeant smiled ruefully as we prepared to go our separate ways. "Frankly," he said, "I'd rather get a kid help—refer her to a good agency that can get her on the right track—than wait till she really gets in trouble and has to be arrested. Prevention is the key. Personally, I think it can be done, and my department and I firmly believe in it."

He's right. Prevention *is* the key. But the police can't do that alone. It takes the efforts of the whole community—concerned families, schools, social services, and, above all, the churches who have something all the rest of them combined can't offer—the life-changing good news of redemption in Jesus Christ.

I turned and headed back to my "beat." When all is said and done, this is where our good intentions are tested, day after day—on the streets.

Four

❖ ❖ ❖

DESPITE THE GUNSHOT WOUND TO HIS FACE, Xavier spent only three days in the hospital. The bullet had hit him in the left cheek, shattering the bone and temporarily blinding and deafening him. But his brain was undamaged, and even the eye and ear were recovering. He came out with his head wrapped in bandages like a mummy, and his mother wailed at him, "Have you learned your lesson now? Don't go foolin' around with no guns and no gangbangers! Look what happened!"

But Xavier just looked at her. Didn't she know this was an opportunity to gain a reputation on the streets for being tough? Man, he'd been in two gang fights already, had even been shot—and he was still alive! It made him feel invincible. His King brothers started calling him "Speedy" and considered him a little crazy for the risks he began to take. They supposed that the shot in his face had somehow affected his brain.

Xavier didn't mind this evaluation. It enhanced his reputation as someone who was dangerous, who just might do anything. More than once, his feigned craziness saved him from a disciplinary beating (known as a "violation") in the gang. When he messed up and was in line for a violation, one of his friends would step in and say, "Why don't you let him go? Speedy doesn't got it all *en la cabeza*—

know what I mean?" Only the brothers closest to him knew better and realized Xavier was becoming a good actor.

When he turned 12 years of age, Xavier attended a racially mixed school where rival white, Latino, and African-American gangs fought for power. One day the police came into his classroom. "All right," said the sergeant, "everyone stays in their seats. Officers Flanagan and Brunner here will see that you do. So don't try nothin'! The rest of you—by the row—come up here for a weapons search. Understood? You first, there in the back. I see ya bendin' over. Get up here!"

He was talking to Xavier.

"Why me? I wasn't doin' nothin'!" Xavier insisted.

"Get up here!"

Xavier shuffled to the front of the room, where the sergeant patted him down. "Hey, what's this?" he said. "Flanagan, cover this kid while I cuff him!" The sergeant then produced the .25 caliber automatic Xavier had hidden in his bulky jacket. "What you doin' carryin' this piece?"

"I have to 'cause it ain't safe around here," Xavier said, pleading innocence. "Those gangbangers are fightin' and threatenin' people all the time, and you guys don't do nothin' about it. How's a kid 'sposed to get an education if the school ain't safe?" But the police dragged him out of the classroom. They knew who they were looking for before they ever entered the room.

That ended Xavier's welcome in that school. He was immediately taken to the Cook County Temporary Juvenile Detention Center, where he sat for three weeks awaiting a court date. But when he stood before the judge, Xavier received only a stern scolding. As he walked out of the courtroom, a small smile played on the corners of his mouth. The judge thought he'd given Xavier a warning that he needed to reform his ways. But the judge had, in fact, just convinced this 12-year-old that he was, indeed, invincible.

Xavier's next school was controlled by La Raza gangsters, to whom he was well known—as the enemy. There he probably *wouldn't* have been safe without a gun, but instead of taking the risk of carrying one, he simply dropped out of school in the seventh grade.

His new "freedom" gave him the opportunity to make his gang an all-day, every-day priority. And before he reached the age of 13, he had been arrested 19 times, each event teaching him more about court procedures and giving him the impression that he was the equal of any judge or lawyer.

One judge, however, was not duped by Xavier's scams. He sent him to Maryville Academy, a residential center in the suburb of Des Plaines. All around the academy, people lived on quiet streets, drove late-model cars, and enjoyed modern shopping centers and community activities. He saw garages and walls that just "cried out" to be tagged with gang graffiti, and it bothered him that he didn't have the opportunity.

But that didn't mean he wanted to be there. Xavier's heart was back in his hood, where he'd had to leave behind his wild and crazy life. As far as he was concerned, the only important question was, How soon could he get back there?

❖ ❖ ❖

AFTER THE KIDNAPPING, IT WAS BACK TO BUSINESS AS USUAL FOR WALTER Davis. But he'd lost some of his cocksureness and felt as if he were always looking over his shoulder. Every day was tense. Besides having to guard against cops and rivals who were out to steal the drug-dealing spots under his supervision, some of his own boys wanted to take over his rank and power, always watching for him to make a mistake.

And then there was his stepbrother, Boyce Allen. Just 17, Boyce wanted to make a name on the street and prove he could handle himself without big brother looking out for him. So Boyce had joined a rival mob, the Unknown Vice Lords (UVLs). Boyce's infectious, ready smile disguised the seriousness of his rank in the gang. He soon became the "enforcer" for his section on the west side, assigned to keep the other boys in line and mete out violations to any who disobeyed orders. A violation could be anything from a beating to being shot in the leg.

The two brothers remained loyal to each other, but still they had a sense of rivalry, and Boyce's membership in the UVLs added immensely to Walter's problems. He not only had to deal with the power of the UVLs, but at the same time he also had to make sure he didn't start anything that might target his stepbrother.

Meanwhile, Boyce's crew didn't know what to think of this eager, fiery recruit whose older brother was a key man in the opposition.

To ease the tensions of belonging to rival gangs, Walter and Boyce pulled some independent jobs together. One evening they were cruising down North Avenue, looking for an easy mark, when they spotted some guys parked at a fast-food restaurant. They wheeled in and screeched to a stop. Out they jumped, dressed all in black and pullover masks. "We'd like to borrow your wallets for a few minutes," Boyce declared as "Batman" and "Robin" waved a Tech handgun in the victims' faces. When the wallets were returned, they were considerably lighter.

Sometimes they were so brazen that they pulled unarmed robberies, simply intimidating their victims with the intensity of their demands. Soon this dynamic duo had a reputation for fast, efficient hits. They were moving in high gear. The adventure was great, and the money was even greater. What could top that? As long as they stayed away from the really plugged-in guys in either of their organizations, whoever was out there was theirs for the taking. And they took.

❖ ❖ ❖

"HEY, WHITE BOY, COME HERE."

The handsome young man leaning casually against the apartment building with a group of other Latinos motioned at Silviu Spiridon. Silviu knew him by sight as one of the section leaders of the Two-Six on the southwest side of Chicago. Aware that he was being sized up, the 14-year-old showed no fear or nervousness, but he was careful not to appear overly familiar or disrespectful.

"I hear you want to join the Two-Six Nation," the gang leader said. He was maybe 18 or 19, but he had a confidence forged by years on the street and rising through the ranks.

"That's right," Silviu responded. His heart was thumping wildly, but he kept his voice calm and steady.

"I understand you've been hangin' around with some of the boys, goin' along on some missions. They say you're a pretty smart shorty, down for the gang, and we ought to give you a chance to prove yourself."

Silviu nodded. Everything was on the line here. As a white kid, he knew he'd be watched closely and expected to prove his loyalty two or three times over. But he wouldn't fail. All he needed was a chance.

"You willin' to take the oath? Do whatever you're told by the section leaders and lieutenant governor?"

"Yes," Silviu said simply.

The impromptu gathering took on a tone of seriousness as Silviu repeated the Two-Six oath: "From this day forward, I, Silviu Spiridon, swear to give my full allegiance to our beloved Familia. I shall never dishonor our Familia's beliefs, concepts, or laws, for in doing such I would dishonor myself . . ."

The section leader shrugged indulgently. "Guess you're in, Spiridon—at least for now. But you better prove yourself, and no messin' up, *comprende?*"

The other boys broke out a six-pack of beer to celebrate their new member. But as far as Silviu was concerned, he didn't need to wait until he got an order to prove his loyalty. Within days, he was spraying the gang's signs—the letters T-S, a Playboy bunny with a dropped ear, and the three dots that stood for the gang's slogan, "Our continuous growth"—all over the hood. He was even sneaking into rival territory, marking out their signs and replacing them with Two-Six "tags."

Silviu wasn't given a gun until he'd proved himself in other ways. He had reason to be glad he didn't have one the day a carload of Two-Six boys he was riding with saw some guys they thought were rival Latin Kings using a public phone. Pulling to the curb, the driver popped the trunk, where a .32 Dillinger Special was hidden. "Grab the gun—we're gonna get those guys!" he ordered under his breath.

Are these guys crazy? Silviu thought, staring out the other window. They had stopped right outside the district police station.

Just then he heard a shout from the guy in the phone booth. He was pointing right at them and yelling, "They've got a gun! They've got a gun!"

The next thing Silviu knew, he was staring into the barrel of a police weapon pointed right at his head.

The driver and some of the other Two-Six Boys were arrested and charged with unlawful gun possession, but the police let Silviu go because he was clean.

Still, packing a piece was the only way to do serious business in a street gang. When the rival Ambrose, another Latino gang, jumped one of the Two-Six Boys on his own turf and tried to stab him, the Two-Six pulled a march, walking right into the Ambrose neighborhood, guns at the ready, daring their rivals to mess with them. Silviu walked right up front. As expected, the march ended in a shoot-out. To prove his love for the gang and his respect for the Nation, the newcomer made sure he was not only first on the scene, but also the last one to leave.

Even though he was "in," Silviu knew he was still an outsider. His white skin and European accent were barriers. His determination grew to show his gang brothers that he was down—would take any challenge, do any wild thing—for "the Familia." His opportunity came when some Ambrose shot at a couple of Two-Six Boys at the local Burger King, riddling the car with bullets and busting out the windows. Within hours, word came from the lieutenant governor—the gang chief on the south side—to "take care of it." The command was understood as an order to pull a drive-by. Silviu was hanging out with some of the boys when the order passed through the ranks and a couple of local gangbangers were tapped to do the job.

Silviu didn't hesitate. "I'll go too," he volunteered. He knew the mission hadn't been assigned to him, but a drive-by was serious business. He wanted to show the gang he had what it took.

The other two boys looked at each other and shrugged. The new boy was all right; he had proved himself so far. Let him come. After all, the chief didn't put any names on the assignment. It was a local decision. That way, if the cops hauled in the gang leaders, they couldn't point a finger at the actual perpetrators.

Silviu hopped into the backseat, all his senses alert as the war wagon cruised into Ambrose territory. There—a small number of rivals wearing their gang colors (black and blue) were hanging out in front of a house squeezed between a couple of decaying apartment buildings. The driver slowed. "Two-Six! Two-Six!" everyone in the car yelled defiantly, throwing down gang signs outside the open windows.

"Ambrose! Ambrose!" the rival gang members yelled back, stabbing the air angrily with their own gang sign. But before they could do anything more, the Two-Six car squealed around the corner.

Silviu hated what the Ambrose were thinking: *Just a bunch of Two-Six cowards, representin' and runnin'.* Maybe they were even laughing. But they'd be thinking differently in a few more minutes.

After taking the corner, the war wagon made another sharp right into the alley behind the house where the Ambrose were hanging out. The driver kept the car running while Silviu and the other Two-Six crept silently through the narrow gangway alongside the house. Silviu felt his heart beating in his throat and hung on tight to his gun—a nine-shot .22 revolver with a long barrel and the safety off. His hands were sweaty, but his grip was firm. His partner packed a .38. At the front of the house, a quick glance showed them that the Ambrose were still looking toward the corner where the car had disappeared. *Now!* his mind screamed.

"Two-Six! Two-Six!" they yelled as they jumped out, laying down a spray of gunfire in the direction of the rivals. Taken off guard, the Ambrose dived for cover. For a few seconds, mass confusion reigned. By the time the other boys figured out where the gunfire was coming from, Silviu and his partner were already racing back down the gangway and jumping into the car.

The driver laid rubber as they sped out of the alley—nearly clipping a police car as they turned out into the street. The chase was on—up one street, down another, the police siren wailing behind them. "Get ready to jump and run," the driver yelled as he cut into another alley. He screeched to a stop, swerving the car so it blocked the alley. Silviu's feet hit the pavement, and the three

boys took off running. Tossing their guns into the bushes in a convenient backyard, the trio disappeared into another gangway and
were nowhere to be seen when the police car squealed to a frustrated
stop behind the abandoned war wagon.

Once out of danger, the fear that had been beating wildly in
Silviu's chest slowly faded and was replaced with an adrenaline
high. They had carried out that mission with class and had come
back without a scratch. They even picked up the guns a day later.
As word got around, Silviu noticed the girls were looking at him in
a new way. The gang brothers hailed him and said, "What's up?"
shaking his hand in the solid way that conveyed respect, brotherhood, and belonging.

Silviu felt good. His boys had all but forgotten he wasn't Latino,
the girls were whispering stories of the crazy things he'd done, and
his enemies hated him. It was a solid package.

The feeling faded, however, when he went home and saw the
strained, worried look on his mother's face. Silviu just turned his
back, went into his room, and shut the door.

❖ ❖ ❖

Derrick Hardaway sat in the interview room of the Calumet Area
police headquarters and shook his head as questions were fired at
him. He was scared.

He remembered the look on his mother's face in the doorway
of their little house as the detectives took him away. Now he was
alone—alone in a room full of uniforms and a guy in a suit pep-
pering him with questions. No one told him a 14-year-old kid
should have a parent with him. Even more important, he didn't
know he could request consultation with a lawyer before answering any questions. All he knew was that the Five-0s wanted him to
talk. But if he did, he'd be in trouble not only with the cops, but also
with his own gang. Wasn't that why Yummy Sandifer was killed—
so he wouldn't talk? If Derrick told the police what he knew, what
would happen to his brother, Cragg? Would someone take revenge
on his parents or his sister?

After a long night of interrogation, however, the police had a version of what they thought had happened. It went like this:

Derrick and "CR"—Cragg's nickname—were at a friend's house Wednesday afternoon when CR's pager beeped. The caller's ID belonged to a high-ranking member of the Black Disciples. He wanted to see Cragg—now. The boys knew something was up. Everyone realized the police manhunt for Yummy Sandifer was putting a lot of heat on the BDs.

What happened in that meeting? "Kenny [one of the leaders of the local "set," or "dynasty"] told CR he had to get rid of Yummy," the police said Derrick told them. "Yummy knew too much about the gang, and if he got caught by the police he probably would have told and had all the high-authority members locked up."

The police had already speculated that high-ranking gang members—maybe even "King Shorty" himself, the name by which top boss Jerome Freeman was known—had given orders to dispose of Yummy before the youngster told police who had given him the gun or ordered him to take out some GD rivals.

While Cragg waited in a borrowed car, Derrick went looking for Yummy and found him sitting on a neighbor's front porch. With Derrick's promise that the gang was going to get him out of town, Yummy slipped off the porch, disappeared into the dark gangway with Derrick, and reappeared a block away, where Cragg was waiting. The three boys then drove to a pedestrian tunnel beneath some railroad tracks. Derrick was sent to see if any Five-0s were nearby. When he came back, CR pulled him aside and told him to get in the driver's seat, leave the car running and lights off, and keep the passenger-side door open. Then CR and Yummy disappeared into the tunnel.

A few minutes later, Derrick heard shots, and CR came running. Cragg jumped into the car and said, "Drive!"

When the statement had been typed up by the police, Derrick signed it.

Unknown to Derrick, his brother had also been picked up. According to police, Cragg Hardaway's story was similar to Derrick's, but with one critical difference. When Cragg and Yummy got into the tunnel, the gang leader named Kenny was waiting for them. Cragg left Yummy with the older gang leader and turned to leave. When he heard shots, he turned back and saw Yummy on the ground. That's when he fled the tunnel and jumped into the car.

This version, too, was typed up. But Cragg knew enough not to agree to anything without a lawyer's approval. He refused to sign.

Was Cragg the triggerman or not? As far as the state prosecutor was concerned, it didn't really matter. Nor did it matter that Derrick was just waiting in the car. The prosecutor intended to nail both Cragg and Derrick for first-degree murder under the accountability law: If you "aid and abet" a murder, you're just as guilty as if you did the killing yourself.

❖ ❖ ❖

John Johnson glanced over his shoulder, then slipped down the concrete steps into the basement of the apartment building. Only a few days had passed since his brother Michael's funeral, and he'd received word that the Black Gangster New Breed—a renegade off-shoot of the Gangster Disciples—wanted to see him. He felt a thrill of expectation.

About 30 older teens lounged around the basement room on broken-down furniture. Some wore the gang colors, black and gray. The gang symbol—a circle within a square with three L's outside the circle—decorated the wall beneath the water pipes and electrical wires that crisscrossed the low ceiling. One of the guys separated himself from the group and held out his hand.

"Glad to see you, Gee-Gee," he said politely. He motioned for the other guys to shut up and gather around. "We heard about your brother. Real bad news. Even though Michael was GD, we was cool with him. We just wanted to express our sympathy and let you know we there for you if you or your family need somethin'."

A lump in his throat threatened to keep John from speaking. Michael had said the brothers in a gang were like family. But he wasn't about to show any emotion in front of these street-tough guys.

"I want to join the New Breed," John blurted. There. It was out.

The gang lieutenant looked at the other guys, then back at John. "What you be, 14?" he asked. "You still pretty young to join the gang."

"Michael didn't want his kid brother joinin' up with a gang," one of the other guys said. "We oughtta respect the man's wishes."

"But Michael's dead now," challenged John, feeling a surge of confidence. This was what he wanted, and he was going to get it. "My brother was all I had, and now he's gone. Nothin' out there for me now. You heard what the Five-0s did to Michael. I'm choosin' up sides, and it's with the gang."

In silence, the lieutenant looked John up and down thoughtfully. Then he said, "But why not the GDs, like your brother? Why the New Breed?"

John was ready for the question. He took a deep breath and answered, "I looked up to my brother and respected him. But now he's gone, I gotta make my own way, be my own man."

The lieutenant pursed his lips. "New Breed and GDs been cool lately, but there's bad blood between us. What if we start warrin' with your brother's old gang?"

John shrugged. "That be the way it is, then. I want to build *this* mob stronger—whatever it takes."

The New Breeds around the room seemed pleased with John's answer. "Guess you in, then," the lieutenant said with a grin. "Hey, everybody, welcome Gee-Gee Johnson, our newest New Breed brother."

Every guy in the room walked by and shook John's hand. That was it. No initiation beating; no elaborate ceremony. He was one of them.

They didn't have to explain the gang symbol; John already knew the three L's standing outside the circle stood for life, loyalty, and love. A renegade gang, not a part of either the "Folks" or "People" alliances, the New Breeds didn't use either a six-pointed or a five-pointed star but a square with four points.

The lieutenant gave John some gang literature to read that outlined the gang rules, the gang prayer, and the gang's leadership structure. At the top is a "don" over the 3,000-plus New Breed members, assisted by two princes, field marshals, generals, and lower ranks in the military-style organization. At the bottom are the soldiers, expected to carry out without question the orders from the leadership. There are no physical beatings as a form of discipline for breaking the rules, as in other gangs. In the New Breed, there's only one form of punishment: death.

John was at the bottom . . . but he didn't intend to stay there long. He knew the New Breed—like every other street organization—was at war with its rivals to maintain turf, increase power, and control the lucrative drug sales in its neighborhoods. He was smart and quick to learn; his parents and teachers had always told him that. *Well, I'll show the New Breed leadership I'm down for the gang 100 percent,* he thought.

When word came from the top leadership, "We want this neighborhood; go do it," John was a quick volunteer. Give him a gun and a few guys and he'd do whatever it took to get recognized in the gang, no questions asked.

By the time John began high school at Farragut Career Academy on the city's west side, the New Breed leadership was already taking notice. This young recruit had heart. He was ready for anything. But unlike some of the other hotbloods, he could keep his head and his cool in a tight situation. So they began giving him more and more leadership responsibility, and his reputation on the street grew rapidly, even earning him wary respect among other gangs.

John was keeping one promise to his family, however. His stepdad had always asked him not to sell drugs, and for the sake of his father's memory, he was trying to honor that.

In spite of his new gang identity, John was looking forward to high school. Farragut had a powerhouse basketball team, and he intended to make varsity—early. After all, some of Farragut's graduates had made pro teams. Maybe he had a shot at national fame as well.

Farragut Career Academy was in Latin Kings' territory, however—a fact that the numerous King students never let members of other gangs forget. Just getting to school, John and other African

Americans had to go through King hood, always watching their backs. But even the other African-American organizations on campus recognized a leader when they saw one—not because John was violent and ready to pick a fight but because he was a good thinker and generally could handle difficult situations without tearing up the school.

The Latin Kings, on the other hand, were wary. As one school year went by, then two, they realized John was being given a lot of authority and respect among the African Americans. Was their own power in the school threatened? After all, out on the streets, top New Breed leaders had already handed John gang responsibility for the whole west side. Maybe, the Kings' leaders thought, they ought to do something about John Johnson before it was too late.

One day shortly thereafter, 16-year-old John was hurrying to basketball practice when he suddenly found himself surrounded by a group of angry Latinos. He looked up and down the hall but didn't see any potential reinforcements. "Guess it's me or them," he muttered to himself, coiling both his will and his body into readiness. He wasn't about to wimp out now. Even at 1 against 10 or 15, it became quite a brawl. When school security staff broke up the melee, the Kings insisted John had started the whole thing.

"Sure I did!" John said, his voice dripping with sarcasm. "One guy against their whole clique! I mean, they are *deep*, and I'm going to start somethin' by myself?"

Maybe the school authorities thought it best to maintain the status quo of Latin Kings dominance among the gangs in their student body rather than inflame an intense rivalry into something they couldn't handle. Whatever their private reasons, they chose to believe the Kings' version of the fight and expelled John Johnson from Farragut Academy.

Just like that, John's dreams of a basketball career burst. He was stunned. What was he going to do now? His mind was too active and his ambitions too high to simply accept the slothful life of a school dropout. And then the answer seemed to fall into his lap. His uncle—an auto mechanic like his stepdad—was retiring and wanted to sell his shop.

John's mind began spinning. He had always liked tinkering with cars. What if . . .? Could he . . .? Nah, it was crazy. He was only 16. But the idea wouldn't go away. He'd find a way to buy the shop and go into business for himself!

❖ ❖ ❖

MOST OF OUR WORK AT THE JUVENILE JUSTICE MINISTRY IS WITH YOUNG men, but a growing number of young women are also involved in gangs. A recent news-magazine TV show featured a special titled "Girls in Gangs." Two teenage girls in a Latino street gang in one of our nation's cities agreed to let the cameras follow them around for a couple of days to give viewers a glimpse into their world. It was an eye-opening experience.

Both girls were attractive, with rich, dark hair and bright smiles. Girl A was an older teenager with a serious side. Days, she had an office job (she didn't tell her boss about her gang affiliation, and he didn't ask) and hopes of going to community college. Stuffed animals and posters on the wall decorated her bedroom in her parents' home—but she rarely slept there. She spent her nights with her gang friends, both girls and guys, partying or just hanging out.

It was obvious that girl A was not a drug addict or into hardcore gangbanging. Asked by the interviewer why she didn't get out of the gang and just pursue the job and college, she shook her head. "This is my group, my family," she explained. "I'll always be loyal to the gang."

Girl B, as slim and smooth-skinned as any magazine cover girl, had no aspirations beyond the gang. She had tried a job once, but that meant working "too hard, too long, for too little." So she went back to her "former business," where she made a lot more money and didn't have to work so hard.

"You mean dealing drugs," the interviewer asked.

A self-conscious grin crept over her face. "You could call it that."

Her bedroom wall was like a memorial, with pictures of teenage friends who had died in shoot-outs with a rival gang. The night before the television crew arrived, a young boy in her neighborhood had been killed, caught in the crossfire between rival gangs. "Don't these deaths of your friends, this little boy, make you question your life in the gang?" she was asked.

Girl B shrugged and shook her head. "It's sad, but it's, you know, just part of life," she responded. "I mean, you could get killed in a car accident, or crossing the street, or get hit by lightning. We all gotta die sometime."

"You don't feel responsible? After all, these were gang-related shootings."

"No." Another shrug. "It . . . happens."

"But what about your future?" The interviewer was persistent. "Don't you ever think about what you'd like to be doing 10 years from now?"

"Ten years from now?" The girl laughed as if the concept were totally foreign. She stuck her hands in her jeans pockets and tossed the thick mane of hair. "I don't even know what I'm going to be doing tomorrow, much less in 10 years," she said, then smiled.

Most viewers, I'm sure, were aghast. How do young people like girl B develop such a casual attitude toward life and death? How can our society survive if our youth have no vision of a future? Does gang involvement produce such an "eat, drink, and be merry, for tomorrow we may die" attitude? Or do parental neglect, idleness, and lack of purpose propel some of these otherwise bright, vivacious teenagers into the shallow excitement of gang life?

The answers aren't easy. I've asked some of those questions myself in getting to know Robin, a bright, intense young lady I met in the course of my ministry. She stands out in any group of her peers—and that includes a gang organization. Of Puerto Rican and German ancestry, she lived with her mother and young stepsister. Her father died before she was born. The ups and downs of her life left her disappointed and hungry for love. Since elementary school, she had moved in the fast circles. One of her first boyfriends was a Spanish Cobra, but she soon left him for a Vice Lord.

Robin and her new boyfriend seemed suited for each other. He sold drugs, and they partied. She became a Lady Vice Lord and moved in with him when they were both 17.

Then came an early-morning raid, and police hauled the pair off, along with a supply of drugs and guns. Robin went to juvenile detention but was promptly released. Her boyfriend, who wasn't so lucky, was locked up. He got out quickly enough but was soon rearrested on another drug charge.

Robin shrugged him off as a loser, but she soon met another young man who was even more trouble.

Papito was the youngest of 10 children in a Puerto Rican family on the northwest side of the city. He joined the Spanish Cobras, eager to follow in the footsteps of his older brothers so he could cash in on the good times and excitement. Surprisingly, his brothers didn't want him to join the gang, pointing out all the dangers. But Papito wasn't going to be treated like the baby brother forever. "I can get down as much as you," he insisted, and he pretty much forced his way in.

Gang life wasn't all fun and games, however.

Several months after he and Robin had started living together, Papito, his 17-year-old nephew, Tiny, and another friend—all about the same age—were on their way home late one night after a party. Understandably, they weren't too alert when some white Gaylords confronted them.

"What you guys ride?" demanded one of the Gaylords, asking what gang they identified with.

"We ain't in no gang," mumbled Papito, too wasted to realize the green and black beads he was wearing already identified him as a Spanish Cobra.

As the two groups parried back and forth, one of the Gaylords suddenly pulled out a gun and started shooting. Tiny lurched back, ran 30 feet, and fell to the street. Papito dove toward a parked car, but he didn't reach cover before he, too, was hit. Then the Gaylords were gone.

Papito got up and put his hand inside his jacket. It came out covered with blood. *Oh, no*, he thought, *I've been gut shot!* He lurched to a friend's house nearby and pounded on the door. When the friend opened the door, he said, "I'm shot!" but the "friend" slammed the door in his face.

A girl came out of another house as he staggered down the sidewalk. "I'm shot. I'm dying," he pled, but still no help came. In a few minutes, another friend came by in a car, and Papito jumped in, but the car engine died and wouldn't start again.

Finally, when an ambulance showed up, he staggered over to the paramedics. "For me?" he asked.

"No," they answered. "We're here for that guy on the ground."

It wasn't until the police arrived and asked what happened that Papito was able to get a ride to the hospital. In the emergency room of Masonic Hospital, he kept asking about Tiny. "We're working on him. We're working on him," said the doctors. Four days later, Papito learned Tiny had been DOA—dead on arrival.

The shooter was caught and ultimately sentenced to 15 years, but that was small consolation to Papito and the rest of the family.

When Papito came home from the hospital, his family hounded him to get out of the gang, but it wasn't that easy. He was known in the neighborhood as a Cobra. If he tried to quit, he'd have lots of enemies and no friends. His enemies would never believe he'd dropped his flag, and neither would the cops. As he figured it, "I'd have opposition shooting at me and no one watching my back. That could be suicide!"

So he kept busy on the streets, selling rock (crack cocaine), gangbanging, and especially going on missions against the Gaylords. That felt good. He vowed that every year on August 12, the anniversary of Tiny's death and his being wounded, he'd be back to let the Gaylords know he still remembered.

Papito's aimless, feisty, empty life was getting old to Robin. She was pregnant with Papito's baby by now and longed for some stability. Then one day as she crossed the street, she was struck by a car and dragged facedown. The ambulance came, but where was Papito? At the hospital, the doctors said her injuries weren't too severe, but then she started having contractions. "Where's Papito?" she moaned. That evening, she lost her baby.

When she was finally released from the hospital and returned home, she found out where Papito had been: partying with his boys! And to make matters worse, he was furious with her for losing the baby. The next time she got pregnant, she had an abortion without even telling Papito. He was not someone on whom she could depend.

Realizing she'd have to look out for herself, she determined to stay in high school. Oh, she would party and hang with the gang at night, but every day she was in class.

Then Papito came home with a stolen car. He parked it down the block, intending to abandon it, but he decided he would first take out the radio and sell it. While he was removing the radio, the cops arrested him and took him off to jail.

Good riddance! thought Robin. *Maybe he'll grow up.* Then she moved back in with her mom.

In Cook County Jail, on the school wing for 17- to 19-year-olds, Papito became involved with our Juvenile Justice Ministry. One of our staff members, Glen Fitzjerrell, began working with him because he and his wife, Jane, were responsible for the northwest part of the city in which Papito and Robin live. Papito responded positively to Glen's concern and presentation of the gospel over a period of time, and one day he gave his heart to the Lord. Meanwhile, Jane made contact with Robin on the streets.

Jane Fitzjerrell worked with many of the guys' girlfriends. Some of these young women are mature and caring, a strong and stabilizing influence as they try to get their boyfriends away from the streets. Others are going through severe problems of their own, attempting to recover from family neglect or abuse. They're often afraid to trust men, but at the same time they still reach out frantically to find love, only to catch the attention of a boy looking for a sexual partner but no commitment.

Some girls have been hurt so badly that they shut and lock the door to their feelings. They become gangbangers, either in a branch of a boys' gang or in their own small but intense groups. They carry guns and drugs for the boys, because they're less apt to be suspect. But they fight on their own level as well, and the results can be exceedingly violent.

For example, I heard about a young Maniac Latin Disciple who was killed by some Latin Kings. He was a favorite of the Lady

Disciples, and four of them, ages 13 to 19, set out for revenge—not in the form of a drive-by shooting, as the boys might have done, but with seductive strategy. Two of the girls struck up a conversation with the targeted Kings, and then, with the promise of "a little love," lured them to a secluded place, where their waiting partners shot them in the head at close range.

But some of these girls, Robin among them, aren't so different from their "middle American" counterparts. They want a relationship with a man they can trust, a stable home, and a family. "Will I ever have that with Papito?" Robin wondered aloud to Jane.

"Well, one good thing Papito has going for him right now," Jane told her, "is that he has given his life to the Lord. That could help him make some changes . . . and the Lord can make some changes in your life, too."

When Papito's burglary case came to trial, he was convicted and sentenced to prison for three years. Because the state had to make room for more-violent felons, however, he was released with an electronic ankle monitor after three months.

Once Papito returned home, he tried to do the right thing and asked Robin to marry him. She agreed. The newlyweds then set up housekeeping in a small basement apartment beneath his parents' place. Would things be any different? She hoped so.

The young couple get together regularly with Glen and Jane Fitzjerrell and spend lots of time talking about marriage, budgeting, establishing a home, and respecting each other—basics they had never been taught or seen modeled.

Can Robin and Papito make it? Jane gives a careful answer: "I think so. They're learning a good deal about each other and about how to think before they react. When they can pray together, that will be a good foundation.

"Papito's working now, and he's off the electronic monitoring that kept him tied down. They go to church with us. Papito doesn't hang out with his old gang buddies. Robin has good plans for work, would like to be able to have a child, and she's growing in her own walk with the Lord.

"There are no guarantees. Every day is a struggle. There are plenty of heartbreaks. Ups and downs. But if this couple isn't all they *ought* to be, they sure aren't what they *used* to be. And if the church community will encourage them, they may just turn out better and happier than many people expected, including themselves."

Five

❖ ❖ ❖

AS XAVIER CHILLED OUT IN MARYVILLE Academy, his mind was constantly on the alert. He needed a plan to get back to his hood as soon as possible.

Maryville was designed to rehabilitate kids like Xavier, but it was also run by typical human beings who had developed convenient routines and didn't like any disruption of those patterns. In time, Maryville ended up being run more for the convenience of the staff than for the accomplishing of its stated goals. Xavier quickly figured this out. If he conformed to the rules, didn't make waves, and showed unfailing respect and politeness, he would be considered rehabilitated whether or not he had changed inside.

Already a skilled actor in the game of life, he now began performing convincingly for this new audience. He got good grades, participated in track and field, did his chores, and even volunteered to help the staff and other kids. Soon he was charming the staff and earning weekend passes back to his neighborhood.

Once home, he made up for all his "good time" by being a complete terror, a serious menace to society. After wreaking havoc for a couple of days, he would go back to Maryville and leave others to deal with all the trouble he had caused over the weekend.

The year passed slowly, and finally Xavier came up for review for a permanent home release. He went into the administrator's office with eager charm. "Good afternoon, sir," he said. "I hope you have some good news for me."

"Sit down, Xavier," the man instructed. "We have some talking to do."

No "jivin' and slouchin'" for him today. Xavier walked smartly across the room and took the offered chair. "Yes, sir," he said brightly. "What's the good word?"

"It's not so good," the administrator answered as he shuffled and frowned at some papers. "Seems as though you've been a little two-faced with us."

"Who, me? What seems to be the problem?"

"The problem is, I've got reports that say you've been raising a ruckus every time we let you go home."

Xavier dismissed a small flicker of worry. "There must be some mistake, sir. I wasn't picked up even once when I was home. I knew I had to keep my nose clean, so I didn't even go out with the boys. I stayed in with my mother. After all, she's the only reason I went home. I dropped all the old friends I used to hang with. You know me, I've made new friends here—mostly with the staff."

"Yes," said the administrator as he rubbed his chin. "You've been sly enough to avoid arrest, but the police peg you to no fewer than six burglaries, and . . . let's see here . . ." He studied the papers before him.

"That can't be me," Xavier protested. "You know those Chicago police. They just want to close a case, so they put anyone's name down. I'll admit they know mine pretty well. But that was from the old days. I ain't—I mean, I'm not like that anymore."

"I think we'll just take a little more time to see about that. If all your new friends are here, as you said, you won't mind staying around a little longer."

"But . . . my mama," complained Xavier. "She needs me!"

"That's all," said the administrator, closing the file. "We'll talk again in a couple months."

Two months later, another session ended in much the same way. This time, Xavier stormed out of the office in a rage. *I've played their stupid little games,* he thought, *wasted more than a year, and still they ain't gonna let me go. Well, I'll show them—especially*

DCFS, the Department of Children and Family Services, which was responsible for the disposition of his case.

"They're gonna pay! They're gonna pay big!" he muttered to himself over and over as he stalked back to his room.

Xavier's hatred for DCFS dated back to when he was six years old and its agents took him and his brother and sisters away from their mother. It was true that she had trouble taking care of them, but instead of supporting her and helping the family, Xavier felt they had just torn his family apart. They placed the children in foster homes, where the kids learned firsthand what government-condoned abuse and neglect were like. Xavier believed Maryville was just one more of the agency's attempts to break his family ties and remake him in its image—an image he hated.

He was sick and tired of all his counselors talking about "a good future" and "a new way of life." Rebellion was uppermost in his mind. He needed a new plan, and he needed it *now.*

That night, he snuck out of the dorm with several of his comrades and burglarized three homes on the campus, stole the center's "trust funds" (the kids' money kept in trust for them by the center), started a small fire behind the administration building, and set off fire alarms in the girls' residence. The boys would have done more mischief, but the place filled with police and fire department vehicles so quickly that they abandoned their other plans and ran to a gas station. There they simply called a taxi and rode in style to the depot, where they caught the next train to Chicago.

The mood of the four young men on the train got more jubilant as the miles clicked by. "I'm a Latin King for life!" declared Xavier. "Wait till the boys hear how I left Maryville in style!"

"Yeah, we got some tale to tell!" said another.

"What's better," added Xavier, "there ain't nobody gonna be orderin' us around, tellin' us when to get up or what to do. This here's our freedom train, and we're ridin' it to a bold, new life."

Things didn't turn out so gloriously, however, when Xavier got back to the hood. The cops were on the lookout for him immediately, so he couldn't go to his mother's place. He crashed at the home of one of his King brothers, but his presence soon brought down the heat, and he was told to move on. He got good at running, but moving every night or so and always looking over his shoulder got tedious.

Xavier couldn't admit that he didn't know what to do or where to turn. He just knew he couldn't look back. He had run from everyone and everything until there was nothing left to escape from . . . except himself. And for that, there were always alcohol and drugs.

Xavier's days grew more violent and his nights darker. He didn't let himself think about the kind of person he was becoming. He had no feelings of care or tenderness for anyone. The only emotional relief he felt was when he discharged a pistol or beat up a rival.

But somewhere, somehow, he was heading for a crash.

❖ ❖ ❖

"WHAT'S YOUR BROTHER DOIN' RUNNIN' SOME OF YOUR SPOTS?" ONE OF Walter Davis's gang chiefs challenged. "He don't have no business around here."

"Hey, it's cool," Walter said. "We're tight."

"Why you so tight with him, him bein' a UVL and all?" the young gangster questioned. "Man, that's gonna lead to nothin' but trouble, and you be right in the middle of it!"

But Walter didn't know what to do. To protect his stepbrother, he had to keep him close enough to watch over him.

As for Boyce, he didn't worry much about anything as long as the money was good and there was lots of action. But he did notice when one of his closest friends, a real reckless dude named Princen, began to back off the wild stuff and slow down. One day Princen said he had a friend he wanted Boyce to meet, a really different guy.

"Yeah, different in what way?" asked Boyce.

"For one, he's older." Boyce didn't react, so Princen continued, "And he's a minister on the streets."

Boyce closed his eyes and let his head roll from side to side. When he looked up at Princen, he said out of the side of his mouth, "Yeah, like I need some jack preacher on my case. Whasamatter wichyou, man?"

"That ain't all," said Princen with a sly smile. "He's white, too."

Boyce looked at his friend a few moments, then burst out laughing. "Now that's what I like about you, Princen," he said. "You make me laugh. God knows I got little enough humor in my life these days."

"I ain't jivin' you, man," said Princen. "He's a minister, an older white guy who helps guys like us . . . guys on the streets. I want you to talk to him."

"*How* old?"

Princen shrugged. "He's not that old. He's a little . . . ," and Princen patted his stomach with both hands. "And his hair is . . ." He brushed the top of his head. "But he's not too old. I want you to meet him."

"No way. I don't have time for that."

I'm the minister Princen was describing, Gordon McLean, and I'm kind of like the guy who doesn't mind what people call him just so long as they don't call him late for dinner. My guys call me "Rev" or "Mr. G" and describe me the way they see me, but at least we have a relationship.

A few days later, Princen had me in tow—Bible and all—when he showed up at Boyce and Walter's home. Walter was gone, and Boyce's first impulse was to walk away, but he was curious about why Princen would have time for an older white dude. I had a nice "ride"—car— so Boyce asked if I would drop him off in the hood where he had to meet his boys. I said sure, but just before Boyce got out, I told him, "It was good to meet you, Boyce. Maybe we can get together sometime. Here, I've got something for you." And I handed him a Bible.

Boyce had no idea what to do with it. It was too big to fit in his pocket, and he certainly couldn't carry it on a night selling drugs with the boys. Of course, I knew exactly what I was doing by giving him that book when I did. It put Boyce on the spot. That's the way I wanted it.

Boyce got out of the car, thanked me for the lift, and then decided to stash the Bible beside a nearby porch. From then on it was a typical night, but, funny thing, before he went home in the early hours of the morning, he went back and picked up the book.

A few days later, Princen and I returned to the Davis house. This time Walter was home, too. "Yo, Walter! Come on down here,"

Boyce yelled from the bottom of the front step. But Walter didn't come. Boyce called again; he didn't want to face me alone. If his stepbrother was around, that might deflect some of the attention off himself. Finally, he went inside and insisted Walter come out.

"Should we offer him a brew?" asked Walter as he grudgingly came downstairs.

"Better make it a 7-Up," said Boyce. "I don't know 'bout this Mr. G, though I'd sure prefer some beer on a day like this."

On the front step—there was only one and no porch on the decaying four-flat in which they lived—we passed the time with some small talk, and then I asked matter-of-factly, "What are you guys going to do with your lives?"

"With our lives?" said Walter. "Whatcha mean?"

"I'm just wondering where you want to be in a few years—taking care of a family? having a job? or callings the shots for a gang on the main line at a prison like Stateville? What are your goals?"

Both young men shrugged and looked down at the hot cement.

"You know what they say," I said. "If you aim for nothing, you're gonna hit it. The problem is, in your line of work, that'll be the joint or an early grave."

"Yeah, we know," Boyce admitted. Maybe I made sense, but neither he nor his stepbrother was ready to turn from what he considered an exciting, profitable lifestyle to sit in some church pew or get a nine-to-five job just to collect "a few dead presidents," as the kids call small bills. Instead, both guys still had big money to make, wars to fight, and parties to attend. But what I said that day did plant a seed they couldn't forget, especially when their luck began to change. Or was it, as I sometimes tell my boys, "When God sets His sights on a person, He locks in the most persistent pursuit imaginable"?

Walter and Boyce were two of His number-one targets.

❖ ❖ ❖

Silviu Spiridon swaggered through the halls of Hubbard High School on the south side of Chicago and relished the looks he got. He combed his black, straight hair in the sleek Latino style. He walked like the Latino kids. He talked like the Latino kids—had even picked up a Latin accent to his English. In the eyes of the kids on the street, the teachers at school, and the police, he was no longer a white kid from Romania; he was a rising star in the Two-Six Nation. And that's just the way he wanted it.

He had quit attending his parents' Romanian Pentecostal Church back in junior high. He had not only left the old country behind for the United States, but he had also left his family behind for a new family: the "Familia" of the Two-Six Nation.

Even after proving his loyalty to the gang, however, Silviu still wasn't satisfied. Why should he continue taking orders when he could be giving them? He didn't just want the respect of a few guys; he wanted everyone's respect. He liked the way his friends made a big deal over the gang leaders when they walked into a party or came down the street. So soon after he had finished his initiation phase, Silviu set his sights on a new goal: leadership in the Two-Six.

His dedication to the gang and reputation as a quick-tempered shooter who took no disrespect from anyone began paying off. He was 15 years old and only a freshman when the Two-Six made him second in command at Hubbard—a key position because the Two-Six was the largest and most powerful gang in the school. He treated all "his boys" with the respect due them as fellow gang members, but he couldn't help smiling inside when he gave orders to older and more-experienced guys.

School officials weren't smiling, though. Soon after Silviu walked through the front door, they pegged him as a troublemaker. Whenever problems or disruptions arose, it seemed as if Silviu were in the middle of things. Even more frustrating, he managed to avoid any major violations of school rules that would allow them to expel him permanently. They were stuck with Silviu Spiridon—at least until he turned 16.

Silviu didn't care. The deans thought he was a troublemaker? He worked hard not to disappoint them. He was bright and could have been a good student, but he did only enough work to get by, prevent his parents from asking too many questions, and keep the teachers off his back.

Silviu still looked up to his big brother, Tib, and the siblings often hung out together even though Tib wasn't interested in joining a gang. But that was okay; Silviu had plenty of friends in the gang—crazy Cholo, Fat Folks, Puppet, Troubles, and Loco, to name a few. It was a game—keeping one step ahead of school officials and the police—played by some of the brightest kids in school.

One evening, the police pulled over a whole group of Two-Six Boys out for a joy ride. "Out! Out! Move away from your car," one of the cops ordered.

"Why, what did we do, officer?" Silviu asked with exaggerated politeness. His tone was a signal to the others to cooperate and avoid trouble. The boys moved over to the squad car.

The police ignored his question and proceeded to check IDs and search them one by one for weapons. Silviu wasn't worried. He was clean, and he was used to being hassled by the police. He submitted to the pat-down and patiently showed his student ID. But as the cops moved on to Cholo, Silviu noticed out of the corner of his eye that Fat Folks was trying to pass something off to Puppet. A gun! He didn't know Fat Folks was packing. Man! If the cops found that gun, they were all in big trouble.

Puppet didn't want the gun and shoved it back at Fat Folks, but it fell to the ground. Silviu winced and glanced at the police. There was just enough noise from passing traffic so the officers didn't hear it hit the pavement. But they were working their way through the group and would soon find it. Silviu caught Fat Folks's eye and signaled him to move it under the squad car with his foot. Slowly Fat Folks moved his foot and slid the gun back, back . . .

"You!" the officer said to Fat Folks. "You got ID?"

Silviu watched Fat Folks pull out his wallet. The gun was sitting by a tire, barely out of sight.

"Arms on the squad car!" the police ordered. Fat Folks meekly complied as the cops patted him down. Then it was Puppet's turn; ID okay; no weapon.

"All right, you can go," said the cops gruffly, disappointed that they hadn't found any reason to detain the group. "Keep your noses clean." Without waiting for the boys to return to their car, the officers got into their vehicle, turned out, and disappeared into traffic.

Almost in disbelief, Fat Folks dashed into the street and retrieved his weapon. Silviu shook his head, torn between getting angry at Fat Folks and laughing in relief. Then someone snickered and they all cracked up. That one was close!

Not that Silviu always acted smart. One day after school, two Ambrose made insulting remarks about the Two-Six, and Silviu took off after them. No way were they going to get away with disrespecting him or his gang! But the two rivals looked as if they were pulling ahead and might get away. Without hesitation, Silviu grabbed the gun he packed in his belt, in the small of his back, and fired.

That's when he saw the cop he'd just run past.

Now the chaser was being chased. "Stop or I'll shoot!" yelled the officer. But he weighed more than 200 pounds, and the athletic teenager easily gave him the slip. *Too many doughnuts,* scoffed Silviu, leaping over fences and taking shortcuts through people's yards.

The next day, however, he was called into the dean's office. The man was livid. "A police officer was just here to see me, Mr. Spiridon," he sputtered. "He wrote up a report about you firing a gun at two of our students. Why he doesn't just haul you off to jail is beyond me—says he knows what you did but can't prove it." The man took a breath, and Silviu managed to give an unconcerned shrug. But the dean leaned forward over the desk and stabbed his finger toward Silviu's chest. "He doesn't have to prove it to me!" he challenged. "I know your kind, Spiridon. Nothing but trouble. This report goes in your file. It's a big, fat file—more than we need to get rid of you when you turn 16."

Silviu acted nonchalant, but the dean's words nagged at him. What if he did get kicked out of school? His parents would be devastated. They had sacrificed so much and worked so hard to bring their family to America. Maybe he ought to cool it for a while, do some schoolwork and polish up his charm. After all, an effective gangbanger could move smoothly between his different worlds.

He'd seen it: older guys with a wife and kids and a steady job—leading the organization on the side, passing down orders to the street warriors, letting others do the dirty work.

Fooling his parents was getting harder and harder, however. One night, for instance, he was heading out for a party but was low on cash. *I'll get that bottle of Wicki-Water I've got stashed in my room and sell some of it,* he thought. Wicki-Water was a form of PCP, a potent hallucinogen. The Two-Six weren't organized for selling drugs in a big way yet, though individual members did so on occasion when their funds were low. But the bottle of PCP wasn't where he had left it. Anger flushed through his body. That bottle was still half full, worth a lot of money. Who . . .? He noticed his clean clothes folded on the bed.

"Mama!" he yelled.

"Keep your voice down, young man!" snapped his father sternly as Silviu stormed through the apartment. "The little ones are asleep." The Spiridon family had increased since they'd come to the United States.

Silviu ignored him. "Mama!" he yelled. "What did you do with that bottle you found in my room?"

"W-what bottle?"

"You know what bottle I'm talking about! What did you do with it? Give it to me!"

His mother looked frightened. "It smelled evil. I . . . . I got rid of it. I don't want you to get in no trouble."

"What do you mean you got rid of it?" Silviu hissed through gritted teeth.

Mrs. Spiridon looked at her husband, then took a breath and looked back at her angry son. This time her voice was steady. "I poured it down the sink."

"You what?" Silviu smacked his head with the heel of his hand. There went $200, maybe $250, down the drain. Now what was he going to do for party money?

He glared at his mother, his eyes hard. "You owe me $250," he demanded. "That's how much that bottle was worth. You owe me. Give it to me—now!"

His parents stared at him incredulously. They argued. He threatened. His mother cried. But he left the house with the money in his pocket.

❖ ❖ ❖

A WEEK OR TWO AFTER THE YUMMY SANDIFER MURDER, I WALKED INTO the Cook County Temporary Juvenile Detention Center (JDC), a stack of Bibles tucked under my arm. "Hi, Reverend McLean," said the attendant on duty as she buzzed the door open into the main hallway. "Is it Thursday already?"

Thursday night is a Bible study night at "Juvie," as the kids call it. I and several other men and women on our ministry team meet with small groups of kids and talk to individuals on the different wings. All the attendants at the JDC give me a friendly greeting and seem genuinely glad that we're there.

In the chaplain's office, the ministry team prayed together, then spread out to the different wings: girls, boys, younger teens, and older teens. The JDC is an impressive, modern building of glass and steel. There are no bars, but the thick safety glass and locked doors between the units and hallways and of the individual "cells" betray the reality: This is a jail for juveniles. The competent, caring professional staff work to prepare the young people for return to the community. Many of them are being tried as adults, however, and won't make that trip for many years.

As I walked down a hallway, I looked out onto the asphalt courtyard—actually the roof of the first-floor classrooms and offices, surrounded by the dormitory wings rising several stories on all four sides—that serves as the recreation area for these young offenders. A baseball game was in full swing at one end, a soccer game at the other, divided by a concrete wall. *Ouch!* I thought as I saw a soccer player take a dive after a ball. I knew some of the boys I'd come to see might be out there, but recreation time was almost over. I'd catch them later.

I checked in with the attendant on duty in one of the wings, then raised my voice to the boys milling around the common room in white T-shirts and gray pants: "I'm Gordon McLean, and we'll be going to a counseling room in five minutes for a Bible study. Anyone can come."

Several of the boys greeted me with "Hey, Mr. G!" and helped set up chairs. About 10 guys indicated they wanted to come, and we got down to business—God's business. These boys needed to know that God loved them, that whether they were first-time offenders or had a rap sheet as long as their arm, Jesus died for them.

During the study, I noticed a new African-American teenager in the back row—a tall youth with guarded eyes and tension in the set of his mouth. He didn't enter into the discussion, but he was quiet and listened.

When the group broke up, the newcomer held back. I went over to him and extended my hand. Even before he opened his mouth, I knew what he was going to say: "I'm Cragg Hardaway."

I motioned him back into a chair and introduced myself. "I'm a minister," I said carefully, "not a lawyer or an investigator. I'm not here to discuss your case."

Cragg relaxed visibly.

He seemed to want to talk about himself, about who Cragg Hardaway was besides a front-page headline and a sensational spot on the evening news. "My mother's a Christian," he said, "my older sister, too. Our family always went to church when I was younger. My mother especially—she always did right by us, taught us to do the right thing. But then . . ." He shifted uncomfortably. "Well, 'bout the time I hit eighth grade, we had some problems at home. Things weren't goin' well with my dad. Me, it just seemed easier to be out in the street, hangin' with the guys. I was doin' okay in school—had some good teachers who tried to encourage me. But school wasn't half so excitin' as hangin' with the BDs. I knew it would upset my mom, so I tried to keep my involvement quiet, but pretty soon I was in deep with the gang."

He was silent for a moment. Then he continued, "My kid brother, Derrick, got involved, too—he's two years younger'n me and liked to hang out with me. We kinda looked out for each other."

I studied him for a few moments, then said, "The commitment you make to the Black Disciples is serious business, isn't it?"

"You got that right," he said solemnly. We both knew what that commitment meant: You're loyal to your guys, obedient to the leadership, and willing to put your life on the line for the gang.

I handed Cragg a Bible and said, "Keep it; it's yours. You probably know something about it already if you have a strong church background like you say. But"—I leaned forward—"keep in mind that this book isn't about religion. It's about a *relationship* with a person: Jesus Christ. Jesus had disciples, too, when He walked on this earth. When they signed on with Him, their whole lives changed. And He's still making disciples. Forget just going to church on Sunday and doing whatever you want the rest of the time. Check out what a commitment to following Jesus means."

Cragg took the Bible and nodded. "Thanks," he said. "I'll read it."

I stood to go, but Cragg stopped me by asking, "Say, Rev, would you do me a favor? Go see my kid brother, Derrick. I feel really bad he's caught up in this mess, too. He—he needs somebody to talk to."

The urgency in his voice compelled me to check my list for Derrick's location. A few minutes later, I was asking for him by name in another wing.

I was expecting a little kid, but Derrick Hardaway towered over me at six feet tall. He was thin and gawky and looked older than his 14 years. I'm sure he wondered what this aging white guy in a suit wanted with him.

"Your brother asked me to come see you," I said simply.

"Yeah?" he said, perking up. That seemed to make it all right.

We sat and small-talked for a while. Derrick didn't have his brother's calm bearing. For all his six feet, he was just a nervous kid. He seemed bewildered and anxious, his eyes wary, still checking out the other guys as they passed, wondering what gang they were in and how he was going to fit in among his peers here in Juvie.

As I'd done with Cragg, I assured him I wasn't there to discuss his case. "I'm a minister," I said. "I'm here to share God's Word and God's way with you." It wasn't time to push it; he wasn't ready to talk. I handed him a Bible and asked if I could see him again.

"Again? Okay, sure, that's cool."

As I left the wing, I wondered how long I'd have to discuss God's Word and way with the two Hardaway brothers. Cragg, at 16, had already been charged as an adult and would be moved out of the JDC when he turned 17. Derrick had been charged as a juvenile, but the prosecution was trying to get him tried as an adult as well.

The distinction was critical. If convicted under the juvenile system, Derrick would be released when he turned 21. In the intervening time, he'd be able to finish high school and benefit from the juvenile system's counselors. If convicted in adult court, however, his sentence for murder would be anywhere from 20 to 60 years in adult prison—a heavy future for a kid as young and confused as Derrick Hardaway.

More than two years would pass, however, before either brother got his day in court.

❖ ❖ ❖

JOHN JOHNSON'S UNCLE WAS PLEASED THAT SOMEONE IN THE FAMILY wanted to take over the auto shop. And John's stepbrother Don, who was five years older, got interested, too. A partnership was a good idea, John decided. Don could do the tire work, leaving John free to work on motors and transmissions, which was what he enjoyed most anyway. The shop already had much of the necessary equipment and some regular customers. With a few helpful loans from family members, John and Don were in business.

The shop was located in Vice Lords' and Four Corner Hustlers' territory. But John wasn't too worried. He'd just keep his New Breed boys out of the area. He intended to run this business separate from his gang activity.

One thing did worry him a little, however. "How 'bout that big car repair shop across the street?" John asked his uncle. "Don't they take away some of your business?"

"Aw, they were there before we even opened our shop, but we managed all right," said his uncle. "They've got their regulars, and we've got ours."

We'll see about that, John thought. *I'm gonna make this the best auto shop in the area. Ain't gonna be room for two shops on this corner.*

The two youthful entrepreneurs—tall and good-looking at that—attracted a lot of attention, especially among the young people. The guys brought their rides for a tune-up or a brake job, and the girls just hung out and flirted. Something was always happening at the little auto shop, and soon John and his stepbrother had more work than they could handle. They hired a few extra guys to help with the increase in work, and John felt good. *If this keeps up,* he thought, *we'll be able to pay off our loans and start making a profit.* His dad would have been proud.

The shop owner across the street, however, was definitely not happy with the two young upstarts and said so. "What do you punks know about running a business?" he scoffed. "You gonna fall flat on your face."

John shrugged off the comment. They must be doing something right if it made the man mad. But running a business was tougher than he thought. It wasn't just the hard work and 12 hour days, though those were challenging enough for a 16-year-old. It was the paperwork and bookkeeping and having to fire an employee who didn't work out. John was determined to make it, though. His uncle and other family members kept up the encouragement: "Be the best, Gee-Gee, whatever you take a hand to."

"Hey, Gee-Gee," Don said one morning, wiping his hands on a rag, "know that guy we fired the other day? I think he be workin' for the man across the street now."

John shrugged. They could have him; the guy was a loser.

Each morning, the alarm dragged him out of bed. He had to open the shop by 7:00 because people wanted to drop off their cars before work. *Man, this is worse than gettin' up for school,* he thought more than once. But drag himself up he did.

One morning as he unlocked the shop and slid open the big garage door, something didn't seem right. He looked around, puzzled. And then it hit him: The tire-changing machines and a couple of air compressors were missing. Had Don stored them someplace new? But a quick look around turned up nothing. Alarmed, John began a thorough check of the equipment and discovered a lot of tools were gone. *Why didn't the security system go off?* John thought angrily. *There should have been Five-Os crawlin' all over this place.* It was one of the few times he would have been glad to see a cop. But a closer look at the security system showed that the wires had been cut— inside the shop.

This was no random burglary. Whoever did it knew his way around this shop. John had a good idea who that someone was. But he had no proof, and the police never arrested anyone. At least the insurance company came through and replaced the expensive equipment and tools.

Then it happened again—another break-in; more equipment missing. John was really mad now. They were being targeted, and he could think of only one reason: The shop across the street wanted them out of business.

Well, he wouldn't be run out. Gritting his teeth, John filled out all the insurance forms a second time. An insurance adjuster made a careful tour of the shop and interviewed—grilled—John and Don at length. "They think we settin' up these robberies," Don muttered under his breath. But to their great relief, the insurance company once more covered their losses, and after a couple weeks of lost work, the brothers were back in business.

"Hey, man," Don said to his younger stepbrother, "you in tight with the New Breed. Why don't your mob get us some protection?"

It was tempting. But John shook his head. Bringing his boys into this neighborhood would set off a major conflict with the Vice Lords and Hustlers, and he didn't think those rivals were the problem here. No, he would have to handle this on his own.

As soon as the shop was up and running again, however, it was burglarized a third time. This time the insurance company said "No way" and dropped the policy. John and Don looked at each other and knew it was over. They couldn't possibly replace all that expensive equipment on their own. And without the equipment . . .

John seethed. He had tried to make it in high school and was booted out for gang fighting when he was only one kid defending himself against an army. He had tried to set up a legit-

imate business, only to be brought down by professional hench-
men. His father was gone, his brother was gone, basketball was
gone, and now working on cars was gone. Everything he cared
about had been taken from him.

Life had handed him a stacked deck. Forget fairness. Forget justice. Now he had only one choice: get ahead any way he could.
And he knew the fastest way to get there.

Selling drugs.

❖ ❖ ❖

DOWNERS GROVE IS A PLEASANT SUBURBAN COMMUNITY. THE DOWNTOWN
area hasn't been taken over by all the national merchants; those are
bunched together on the south side of town. The people have pride
in their schools and consider themselves to be immune to the violence
a few miles away among the inner-city kids.

When I finished speaking about our Juvenile Justice Ministry
at a prosperous church there one evening, however, several young
people and a few adults gathered around me. "Reverend McLean,"
a tall boy said, "do you know Antwaun Cubie?"

I didn't know him, but I knew of him through my regular
review of local newspapers. Antwaun was the star basketball player
at Downers Grove South High School who had recently been
arrested in a bizarre shooting incident. When I explained this, the
young man said, "I played with him on the team, and we've been
praying for him. I was wondering . . . could you go see him? I think
he needs someone."

I agreed, as I usually do when a kid's friends ask me to make
contact, and that began my involvement in one of the most tragic
cases I've ever worked with—tragic in part because Antwaun had
had everything going for him—until it went down like this:

Graduation week was as exciting at Downers Grove South as at
any other west suburban high school in the Chicago area, and it was
to climax a hugely successful phase in Antwaun Cubie's first 18
years. He was an unusually gifted athlete with an active social life
and a host of friends both on and off the basketball court. He shone

as the star and captain of the Mustangs, the school's regional championship team. His mother had collected several scrapbooks of glowing reports and pictures of this "athlete of the year." A box packed with hundreds of invitation letters from some of the nation's best colleges sat in Antwaun's bedroom. Eager recruiters kept the phone ringing in the Cubie home.

The one shortcoming in this glowing picture was Antwaun's mediocre academic record. He had the ability, and teachers liked him, but with all his athletic prowess and social life, he tended to let his grades slide.

Dick Flaiz, Downers Grove South basketball coach, wouldn't let them slide, however. He knew that if Antwaun were to make it a.b. (after basketball), he had to have the grades. Almost grudgingly, Antwaun accepted the need to study and finally brought his grades up to C's and B's. "It was better than I had done," remembers Antwaun, "but not nearly what I was capable of. I knew it, and so did Coach. That's why he never let up."

Flaiz was not only a coach but also a counselor and mentor to Antwaun—in many ways, a second father. He so believed in Antwaun and cared about this rising star that he postponed his retirement in order to coach Antwaun through his senior year. The bond between coach and athlete was strong, and graduation was to be a climax for both of them.

But four days before the ceremony, it all fell apart.

Antwaun and 16-year-old Jeremy Bruder were lab partners in an electronics class. Investigators, piecing together what happened, believe Antwaun had offered to help Jeremy get a special deal on some fancy tire rims for his car. The pair drove to Oak Park, another Chicago suburb where Antwaun had lived earlier, and there they picked up 21-year-old Kevin Jackson, a friend of Antwaun's. After driving around a while, they pulled into a clean, fairly well-lit alley between two modern apartment buildings. Then, police say, Antwaun robbed Jeremy of the $1,100 he had with him to pay for the wheels and shot him seven times in the chest, arms, and legs with a 9-mm semiautomatic handgun.

Neighbors in the apartments heard the shots and called the

police. Antwaun and Kevin Jackson left the scene but apparently came back to see how Jeremy was. Police apprehended the pair on foot about a block from the scene. Apparently no drugs, alcohol, or gangs were involved. Neither of the two accused had a criminal record.

Jeremy died in the hospital the following day.

Shocked, Jeremy's and Antwaun's classmates were left asking, "How could this have happened?" That was my question, too, when I went to visit Antwaun at the county jail, but I held off asking while we got acquainted. As far as I could tell, everyone's evaluations of him had been accurate. He was as nice a kid as you'd ever want to meet. And that made the question even more burning. Parents want to know how to keep their young people out of trouble. If it strikes like lightning out of the blue, what can anyone do?

As I earned the right to get to know Antwaun, I learned he had been born in a Chicago housing project, surrounded by gangs and violence as an everyday part of life. Hopelessness and despair were rampant.

When Antwaun's father left the family, his mother dedicated herself to giving her son a new opportunity. She worked hard and finally moved to one of the suburbs.

Ten years later, Antwaun was far removed from the projects, 20 miles in distance and light years away in lifestyle, respect, and open doors. His mother had been able to maintain a home in the affluent suburbs so that Antwaun could attend the better schools of the area. She tried to keep track of his goings and comings to make sure he didn't fall in with the wrong crowd. It all seemed to be working until . . .

"So, what happened?" I finally asked.

His answer was long, careful, and thoughtful.

As successful as he had been, he always feared he was climbing a shaky ladder, and the higher he went, the harder he would fall. "What is a kid from the inner city doing with cheering fans, hosts of admirers, lots of friends, two cars, and the best schools wanting me—if I could get decent grades?" he told me. "It's the all-American dream come true, but I wasn't sure I deserved it or at times even wanted it.

"I never took time to stop, think, and ask what my purpose in life was, what I should be doing. I was busy running everywhere but really going nowhere and getting there fast. My mother wanted me to slow down and set my priorities, and so did the coach. But not me.

"What I settled for in two words is *more . . . now.*

"My mother wanted me to keep her informed of where I was and call when I would be out late. But I thought I was too big and renowned for that kind of kiddy care."

Antwaun paused and looked down at the desk in the jail office. "Now I live for the time when it's my turn on the phone so I can call my mom. Funny how things change. A phone call home, a quiet walk outdoors during rec time, looking out the jail fences to the free world—that's important now."

"What about God?" I asked.

"I grew up believing He was up there, and my mother really took her faith seriously."

"Nothing wrong with that, but it's not enough," I told him. "God doesn't offer a family plan to heaven."

"What's that supposed to mean?" he asked, looking at me quizzically.

"Airlines let kids ride free or at half price when an adult pays full fare, but God doesn't operate that way. We all need our own ticket. It's a personal thing."

Antwaun nodded. He got the message.

"Tell me," I continued. "You've been to church many times. You probably know more about the Bible than most kids. How far is it from heaven to hell?"

That stumped him.

"It's the distance between having a good dose of religion in your *head* and a real relationship with the Lord in your *heart*. I'd say, about 18 inches. You've got enough religion to be comfortable in church on Sunday, singing the songs, following the service, maybe even praying if called on. But you don't have enough to change your life out on the streets. There's something you're missing."

I opened my Bible to Luke 18, and we looked up the interview Jesus had with a successful young man. This fellow thought he could inherit eternal life. But Jesus pointed out the one thing that kept him from coming to God: his wealth.

"This was the last thing the young man expected to hear," I said. "He was very rich, and Jesus' words left him frustrated and speechless. He was holding on tight to many material things and wasn't about to let them go. Now listen to what Jesus said." I read verse 24: "Jesus looked at him and said, 'How hard it is for the rich to enter the kingdom of God!'"

I closed my Bible. "If ever a high-school student was rich—in things like talent, friends, and opportunities—you were, Antwaun," I said. "But it wasn't enough. Great as it was, all the acclaim, sports, success, and good times didn't really satisfy you, did they? And now you're here, with your world collapsed. You needed the Lord before, and you really need Him now."

His reply was hesitant but honest. "Look, Mr. G," he said, "if I accept the Lord now, people will say I'm just trying to cop a plea with God or win my case. And that's not it."

"I know that's not it," I assured him. "Nowhere in the Bible does it say God will get us out of the messes we've gotten ourselves into. He promised to save us from our sins, but not from our stupidity. He'll forgive us for what we've done wrong, but we still have to face the consequences in court and in life. However, He did promise to be with us no matter what. We won't be alone; He's there guiding and guarding us all the way. And then there's the promise of a life with Him that never ends."

"Would you say the Lord is like a good coach?" he asked, reaching for a comparison he could understand.

"More than that," I explained. "You've had some fine coaches, but God is inviting you to something far greater. He gives you the official rule book to follow, but He doesn't just stand on the sidelines, shouting orders. Through His Holy Spirit, He offers to step inside your life to strengthen you and face every temptation with you. Now, that's a great way to live this life and the only way to live the next."

I was in no rush. Antwaun wasn't going anywhere, and the Lord was pursuing him far more diligently than I or anyone else ever could. The prayers of his mother and many people of all ages who knew him were going to be answered.

A few sessions later came the harvest.

People find the Lord in all sorts of places: sports chapels, big cathedrals, little churches, summer camps, hotel or hospital rooms, behind a closed office door, at home, and in McDonald's parking lots (one of my favorites—thanks Ronald!). And yes, it happens in jail cells and chaplains' offices. People who pray there are no less sincere than those who pray in more-comfortable surroundings. Only God is the judge.

To those who have told the Lord, "I need You. I want You. Come in and take over my life. Forgive me, and make me Your child," I now add Antwaun Cubie's name. Yes, even a young man accused of murder can be forgiven.

As for Antwaun's legal case, the prosecutor and the judge believed it was a carefully planned robbery and killing. Antwaun's companion, Kevin Jackson, was convicted and sentenced to 40 years in prison. But not everyone agrees. How could someone like Antwaun, with so much going for him and no criminal record, calculate and commit such a violent, senseless crime? Maybe he just snapped.

"No," say two psychiatrists working for Cook County's Forensic Clinical Services. "He was sane at the time of the alleged offense." However, they agreed that he is now severely depressed and therefore temporarily unfit to stand trial. The trial was postponed for a year at the time of this writing while Antwaun received treatment and evaluation in the state mental health facility.

In jail, Antwaun was able to open a Bible and accept forgiveness from its Author. Forgiving himself continues to be a torturous and elusive goal. Still, he continues to show himself among his peers in confinement to be a caring, helpful, and positive person.

That will matter little or not at all when he's finally ruled mentally competent to stand trial. Only the sad events of a June summer evening will count, and they're likely to cost Antwaun the rest of his life behind bars. The investigating police officers have done a thorough, careful job preparing their case. They also have a declaration from the dying victim naming Antwaun as his assailant.

Following one of the last court sessions, the mother of the victim reached out to Darlene Cubie, Antwaun's mother, expressing her sympathy. Two mothers, grieving for their lost sons, unable to make sense out of what happened, and yet they were able to share some measure of reconciliation. However, there's an enormous difference in their circumstances. Antwaun's family and friends will be able to write to him, speak with him on the phone, and visit him in prison. And there's the hope—however remote—of an eventual release. But Jeremy Bruder's family has only painful memories. They can't see, talk to, or embrace their son. Their grief is ongoing. Both families need prayer.

When I hear people clamor for harsher, less-flexible sentences in order to deter would-be criminals, I think about Antwaun. It's hard to imagine anyone with more to lose. Could he have considered the consequences and still proceeded to plot Jeremy's murder as the police allege? The only conclusion is that he didn't think about the consequences at all. He didn't even try to flee the vicinity of the crime. So how could the knowledge of stiffer penalties have prevented Jeremy Bruder's murder?

One of these days, Antwaun will stand trial and face the consequences of what he's done, as he should. But I join other people of faith who believe that some who are guilty of serious crimes—especially young defendants—can seek genuine forgiveness, change, build positive morals and goals, rehabilitate themselves, and eventually become good citizens. People like Antwaun.

Six

❖ ❖ ❖

LIFE ON THE RUN OFFERED LITTLE RELIEF FOR Xavier apart from the drugs, drinking, and the excitement of gangbanging. But the police hadn't picked him up, and that made him feel all the more powerful.

On a still-warm October evening, Xavier was hanging on the porch with Joker, Killer, and Mando when Sly, one of the gang leaders, came cruising by in his ride. Xavier wasn't eager to see Sly. Though Xavier had done some crazy things to build his own reputation, this dude was the devil himself. The only good thing Xavier could say about him was, "At least he ain't *my* enemy."

Sly curbed his car, the music still throbbing from the enormous speakers. "Come on down and pop some brews," he called as he and his girl got out.

They all gathered around as Sly opened his trunk to reveal an ice chest nearly full of beer. "Watch this," Sly said. He grabbed his girl and began to dance.

It was all Xavier and the other guys could do to keep from laughing. "Here goes *hombre boracho,*" sneered Mando, not loud enough for Sly to hear over the music. Sly was no great dancer, and, half tanked, he made a comic character staggering around in the street, holding on to his girl's hand. Soon all the guys were

101

laughing in spite of themselves.

"What you think you're laughin' at?" Sly shouted into Killer's face as he tried to snap sober. "You makin' fun of me?"

"No, man," said Killer. "We're laughin' at your ugly girl."

The scene grew suddenly tense, throbbing with the thundering music, as Sly glared at Killer. Then he looked at his girl. "Yeah, she is an ugly babe, ain't she?" he said. "Come on, babe. Let's see you dance some more."

Her expression dropped ever so slightly as she looked from one boy to the other, and then slowly she began to dance. With good reason, she feared her "old man" more than the worst humiliation. Sly had followers but no friends—not even a girlfriend. She was just his lady.

Joker inadvertently saved the girl when he said above the beat, "Hey, look what we got comin' down the block." It was a Mexican boy in a sloppy T-shirt outside a pair of huge shorts hanging nearly to the tops of his untied Nikes.

Sly stood up and signaled Xavier to follow him, knowing Xavier carried a weapon. They strolled casually toward the young man. The closer they got, the younger they could see that he was, only 14 or so.

"You some kind of gangbanger or somethin'?" called Sly as he strutted along, working his head back and forth like a rubber-necked chicken while casually throwing down King signs with his hands. "We don't want no gangbangers in our neighborhood, ya know."

"Hey, man," said the kid, forcing a scared smile. "I ain't in a gang. I'm one of The Nasty Boys, a party crew, ya know? We can fix you up with a good time."

"Now, that's cool," said Sly, changing his tone. "We was just thinkin' about some fun. We got some beer. You want to join us?"

"What you sayin'?" Xavier whispered to Sly. "I was gonna pop this guy!" He wanted to punch the kid out and chase him away from the area.

"Just play along," muttered Sly, his voice masked by the car's music as they returned to the others. In a few minutes, the newcomer was drinking one of Sly's beers and talking with the others on the porch.

"He ain't no Nasty Boy," sneered Sly's girl in an undertone. "He's a rival."

"I know that," murmured Sly. "We gonna cure him of lyin'. Don't worry 'bout it. Psst, Killer, go get that big knife of yours."

Killer disappeared. When he returned, Sly turned to the newcomer and asked, "Hey, you want to smoke some dope?"

The kid shrugged. "Sure, why not?"

"Let's go across the street to that abandoned building," urged Sly, motioning Killer to join them.

Joker, Mando, and Xavier stayed on the porch with Sly's girl and drank more beer as evening softened the jagged edges of the neighborhood. A short time later, as the darkness descended, Killer came out of the gangway across the street with a look of startled horror. He couldn't speak. He was staggering and vomiting.

None of the others spoke to Killer or tried to stop him as he lurched into the night. Finally, Xavier crossed the street and went through the gangway out of which Killer had come. An empty apartment door stood open. At the entrance to the gutted kitchen, by the dim glow of the alley lights, he saw their "party guest" lying on his back in a puddle of blood. The boy was still struggling to breathe as the life oozed out of his wounded body. Xavier suddenly felt sick and very sad. It even crossed his mind to kill the kid as an act of mercy. He knew the boy was dying a slow and painful death, but he couldn't force himself to go into the room.

As he turned away, Sly came down the gangway, snickering. "'Oh, no. I ain't in no gang. I'm just a Nasty Boy,'" he mocked. "Hey, Xavier, what's the matter with you? Come on in here with me. I dropped that knife somewhere in here and gotta find it."

Xavier just shook his head and stood rooted in place as Sly passed him and went into the kitchen.

In a moment, he heard Sly rummaging around in the apartment. Then Sly said, "What's the matter with you, sucker? Ain't you dead yet?" Next came the sound of several blows as if the older boy were using a baseball bat or table leg to finish off his victim. Finally, Sly came out and said, "Some people sure got hard heads."

❖ ❖ ❖

"We got some money missin'," said Walter Davis's chief, "and word's goin' 'round your brother's been dippin' a little deep. You want to explain that?"

"You know it ain't him," said Walter. "I'd never let that happen. I know no one messes with the mob's money. Didn't I get that $170,000 back from Kenny for you?"

"There was $300,000 missin', and your gettin' some of it back wasn't without some problems. Or have you already forgotten what we went through to keep Kenny and his boys from takin' you out of the box?"

"I haven't forgotten," said Walter, "but you can be sure Boyce don't have his hand in the till."

"Yeah, well then why don't you make it your job to find out who *is* rippin' us off!"

Walter knew an assignment like that from his usually understated chief was a serious threat. That night, he raised the problem with Boyce.

"Well, my boys ain't too thrilled with you, either," countered Boyce. "Every time they see me hangin' with you and your crew, they figure I must be leavin' the Unknowns and flippin' CVL. I try to tell 'em blood's thicker than water, but all they say is, 'Yeah, and you two gonna think the rain comes down red one of these days, too.'"

This wasn't the only problem Boyce was facing. In addition to fighting the Conservative Vice Lords, the Unknown Vice Lords were also at war with the Four Corner Hustlers—and Moltice, a Hustler, had specifically targeted Boyce.

In response, Boyce's chief had approved a plan to take out Moltice—or Tice, as he was called. Both young men had been looking for the right time and place to finish their deadly business.

Tice had grown up on Chicago's streets, where his father and uncle had been founding leaders of the Four Corner Hustlers. His family had been plagued with tragedy from the beginning. His uncle, father, a cousin, and a brother had all been killed. His mother and a grandmother had passed away. His younger brother had been arrested and convicted in a robbery-murder case.

Tice had chosen to follow the street code in response to all these tragedies: "Don't get mad, just get even!" So he had lots of motivation to settle his scores with Boyce—a rival leader of similarly high rank—even though Boyce wasn't directly responsible for his tragedies. Time was running out, and a confrontation was due soon.

"I don't know," said Boyce after he and Walter had gone over all the pressures closing in on them. "This is all too tense."

"Yeah, but what can we do?" asked Walter glumly. "It's like bein' on a roller coaster that's outta control. If we tried to get off, we'd go down."

It seemed as if every time Walter and Boyce had one of these conversations, I—the street-preaching Mr. G—showed up and started discussing how futile their life was, and this time was no exception. As we talked, they slowly began longing to get out of the gangs. At first they just wondered, "What if . . . ?" Then they started to wish, "If only . . . !" But there still didn't seem to be any way out. They were in too deep.

The next day, Walter began asking around about who was taking the gang's money, but his inquiries met with major hostility. There was already too much suspicion about Boyce to get any cooperation in fingering someone else for the missing cash.

"This ain't workin'," Walter told Boyce.

"Well, I know what *I'm* gonna do," announced Boyce. "I'm gettin' outta the hood till things cool off."

"Man, they'll think you're guilty for sure if you split. Besides, what about Tice?"

"What else can I do? You 'bout to go down for me, and you can't get no help. And I ain't ready to face Tice just now. It's better this way. Besides," continued Boyce, "this whole scene is a sickenin' drag, borin' beyond words. I been hangin' 'round the crib too much.

How many soap operas can you watch? How many times can you mow a little patch of lawn?"

The next day, he was gone.

Boyce Allen may have left the hood, but it didn't take me long to track him down. I found him at his father's house in Humbolt Park.

"I didn't expect to see you here, Mr. G," said Boyce when he opened the door to find me on his stoop. It worried him. If this middle-aged, white minister could find him, so might someone else—someone far more deadly. "You must have some kind of a mega-intelligence network," he said nervously, fishing for what went wrong with his cover.

"You're right there," I said with a grin. "My Chief sees everything, and He sent you a message. I'm just the delivery boy."

Boyce froze. *What's the dude talkin' about?* he wondered. He began to worry. *What's Mr. G doin' runnin' errands for some chief?*

Then I stuck a Bible in his hand and said, "Here's the message. I figured you might not have brought the one I gave you earlier."

With relief, Boyce took it and thanked me. "You must be some kind of Robo Christ or somethin' to find me here," he said, shaking his head.

The next Sunday morning, he went out for a walk and came to a small African-American church where the service was just getting under way. He walked past once, looked up and down the street, and then returned to go inside. As he reached for the door, he realized he was actually sweating. He had done a lot of crazy things in his life and never gave any of them a second thought. So why was going into a church one of the scariest experiences of his life? He was certain the people would stare at him, know instantly that he was a gangbanger with rank, and tell him to get out. But finally he went in and sat in the back.

What a service! The choir really got into its music. Scripture and prayer followed, along with some moving testimonies, and then a message that Boyce felt was aimed right at him. *This is weird,* thought Boyce. *I wonder if Mr. G figured out where I'd be goin' this mornin' and slipped the preacher a note about me and my problems.*

The pastor talked about empty lives that only God could fill with Himself.

Then the preacher let fly with a stunning question: "Where will you be when you get where you're going?" Boyce knew where he was headed: prison or the grave, and after that . . . he didn't want to think about it.

Next the man said, "Come on home to the Lord; you've been a runnin' too long!"

Suddenly, Boyce felt tired and disgusted with his life, and he knew he needed what these people had. When the preacher gave an altar call for sinners to come up and pray to trust in Jesus, Boyce made his way to the front.

Hearing about Boyce's decision, I felt like whooping and hollering. But I knew he needed to get connected with a good church right away. Fortunately, when he returned to his neighborhood some time later, he got hooked up with Rock Church in the Austin neighborhood, where Raleigh Washington was the pastor and where some caring people began to help him grow in his new Christian life.

But back there in the hood, Tice was still looking for him.

❖ ❖ ❖

IN MY WORK ON THE STREETS OF CHICAGO FOR THE JUVENILE JUSTICE Ministry of Youth for Christ, I often meet with officials from the different junior highs and high schools when we're trying to help a kid in trouble. I let these overworked, underpaid administrators and social workers know we're interested in cooperating with them to guide gang kids in a new direction.

"Reverend McLean?" said a woman's voice on the phone one day. She identified herself as a teacher at Hubbard High School on the city's southwest side. "There's a boy in one of my classes I'd like you to meet. His name's Cholo—he's a Two-Six Boy. He got in some trouble and came to talk to me."

That's unusual, I thought. Most gang kids isolate themselves from adult input outside the gang. They see the world of their parents, teachers, and the rest of society as irrelevant. The gang has its own laws, its own power structure, its own goals, its own discipline, its own support system.

"This boy is very intelligent and has some good potential if steered in the right direction," the teacher went on. "He even expressed interest in talking about his future apart from the gang, using his talents in a positive way."

Either this guy's a put-on, I thought, *or this is getting more interesting.* I knew what was coming next: She wanted me to see him. But I'll go see a kid only if the kid himself wants to see me or a mutual acquaintance requests it.

"I told him about you," she said, "and he seemed willing to meet you. Would you go see him, Reverend McLean?"

With that much to go on, I called Cholo at home, and we set up a time to get together.

"Hey, Rev," said the boy as we shook hands. He was Mexican-American, with dark, close-cropped hair, about five-foot-ten, and husky. He looked a bit nervous until I told him I wasn't there to put him down or give any lectures. I just represented Someone who had a message that could turn a guy's life around if he wanted to listen. He seemed relieved.

We talked for quite a while. His brother, Enrique, was the number-one Two-Six leader at the high school; a friend of his, Silviu Spiridon, was number two. Cholo had a reputation for being handy with a gun, though he confessed to getting hit twice by rivals. Then he grinned. "And once I shot myself playing Russian roulette!"

In shock, I chuckled. The humor in my line of work can be grim, but I was glad he could laugh at himself.

"Cholo," I said after we'd been talking a while, "from what you've said, you've got a lot going for you. You went to church with your family when you were younger, and you've got decent, loving parents. If you wanted to, you could really make something of your life. You don't really fit the 'gang profile.' Why did you join the Two-Six? Were you pressured into it?"

He shrugged, but a small smile played on his lips. "Nah, that ain't the way it is, Rev. Why, *most* of the boys come from good homes. It's just . . . well, belongin' to the gang in your neighborhood is *the* thing to do. The gang, now, they got respect, they got easy money, they got style, they got ladies. That's where it's happenin', man! Out on the bricks, you gotta be in the gang if you wanna be somebody around here. And it's for protection, too. Why, if I didn't have my boys backin' me up, I'd be a sittin' target for anybody who wanted to mess with me—Ambrose, Popes, Latin Kings. The gangs don't have to go out recruitin'. Most of the shorties can't wait till they're old enough to join. They're willin' to do any wild thing just to prove they're good enough."

I had anticipated his answer. Many well-intentioned parents are dumbfounded when they discover their son or daughter is in a gang. They don't understand the subtle—and not so subtle—currents that lure kids into the fast, exciting gang lifestyle.

"But where is it taking you, Cholo?" I challenged. "Not many gang members end up retiring with a fat pension. In fact, most of the gang kids I know do time in prison or end up in the morgue. It's a high price for a little excitement."

He nodded, thinking. Then he said, "But not too many people willin' to give us gang kids a chance. Ever'body give up on us already. Police hate us; school can't wait to kick us out; if we get a job and they find out we're in a gang—or even *been* in a gang—out we go."

I agreed. Once caught up in the gang lifestyle, it's a downward spiral. "But there's Somebody who won't give up on you," I said. "That's Jesus Christ. He came to this earth and gave up His life for people just like you. He already paid the penalty—the death penalty!—for your sins. He wants to be your friend and your Savior. If everybody else gives up on you, if your friends turn against you, Jesus will stick closer than a brother."

Cholo nodded again, still deep in thought. "Yeah, I been thinkin' about this brotherhood business. In the gang, we supposed to be brothers, we supposed to be friends. But sometimes I wonder. It don't seem like real friendship despite all the talk of brothers together because, bottom line, each guy is lookin' out for himself. We supposed to be loyal to the gang, but . . . loyalty only goes so far. You know—fightin' back, gettin' revenge if someone disses another gang member, that kind of thing. But a guy will dump on you in a second if he can get himself out of a jam."

It was time to go.

"Hey, thanks, Rev, for stoppin' by," Cholo said, shaking my hand. "You want to come by and meet some of my boys? I'd like them to meet you."

"Absolutely," I said. I was hoping I'd get to see Cholo again. Meeting his friends would be icing on the cake.

Not long after that, Cholo gave me a call. When I entered the living room of the small, brick bungalow typical of the row houses on Chicago's southwest side, I was surprised to see that one of Cholo's gang brothers was white—eastern European, I guessed. But I wasn't sure he knew he was white, because he dressed Latino, talked Latino slang, and had all the Latino mannerisms down pat. I wasn't half as surprised to see him as he was to see me, however. When Cholo introduced me to his boys and said I was a minister, this white kid—whose name, I learned, was Silviu Spiridon—did all but roll his eyes. I was probably the last person on earth he expected to come around and hang out with a bunch of gang kids. In fact, I clearly felt he didn't want me there.

But it was Cholo's house, and I was there by Cholo's invitation, so I chatted with the boys, asked them about school and sports, told them some of the things we do in the Juvenile Justice Ministry, and just got acquainted. The soft drinks Cholo passed around ran out, so I made myself at home and went into the kitchen to get refills for the boys.

Silviu collected some empty cans and followed me to the kitchen. To my surprise, he blurted out, "Funny thing, Cholo takin' a likin' to you—you bein' a minister, I mean, and a white dude at that!" He shook his head. "Can't imagine the pastor at my parents' church comin' here and just talkin' to us like we were regular guys— or if he did, it'd be to pour fire and brimstone on us all. He thinks I've sold my soul to the devil."

I popped the top on a diet soft drink and waited.

"We come from Romania, ya know," he went on. "I was only eight. But, man, my folks don't understand what it's like here in

America. They want us to keep doin' things just like back in the old country. Wouldn't let me play football . . ." The muscles in Silviu's jaw clenched and unclenched for a second. "So . . . I joined a gang." He shrugged. "That's been my ticket. Been down for the Two-Six ever since, doin' some heavy gangbangin'." He popped his own soft drink and stood thinking a moment. "I know it hurts my parents. Sometimes when I come home, there's my mother on her knees, cryin' and prayin'. And the school is about fed up—always threatenin' to expel me. But . . ." He shrugged. "I'm in pretty deep. Don't think I could get out even if I wanted to."

"That's okay," I said. "I have a Friend who can help arrange it whenever you're ready."

He looked startled. "A friend? Who's that?"

"Just a minute," I said. I went back to the living room, where I'd left my briefcase, and returned with a modern-language New Testament. "Here," I said. "Read this. It'll tell you all about Him."

He stared at the Bible I'd shoved into his hands, then mumbled, "Yeah, okay . . . well, thanks."

As we rejoined the others, I had to smile to myself. Not only had Silviu ended up talking to a white, middle-aged minister at a gang session, but now he was about to go out into the hood with a Bible under his arm! How mixed up can things get?

Strangely enough, Silviu wasn't offended or turned off by my giving him a Bible. I dropped over from time to time and continued my friendship with Cholo and Silviu and their gang brothers, though none seemed ready to buy the message that gang life wasn't taking them anywhere and that God stood ready to help turn their lives around. But they listened to me respectfully and were always polite and friendly.

Sometimes I picked up Silviu after school, and we'd go somewhere to get a snack and talk. Once when I pulled up, I saw a security guard at the school pointing at me and giving Silviu the business. When Silviu finally hopped into the car, I said, "What's up?"

"Yeah, well, he just wanted to know who that white guy is who picks me up."

I raised an eyebrow. "So what'd you tell him?"

"Just told him, 'He's a minister.' But man, that dude got angry. Said, 'Quit lying to me! You don't know no minister, and no minister would waste time with trash like you. If he's your big dope connection from the 'burbs, just say so!'"

I laughed. "I've been called a lot of things," I told him, "but never that."

❖ ❖ ❖

I HEADED FOR THE COUNSELING ROOM AT THE JUVENILE DETENTION Center (JDC) and looked forward to seeing Derrick Hardaway. I chuckled a little to myself at the prospect. This tall, lanky kid always made me feel like the short half of a Mutt-and-Jeff cartoon. Funny thing, though—he always gave me the feeling that he was looking *up* to me with respect.

Two years had passed since the Hardaway brothers had been arrested for the murder of Robert "Yummy" Sandifer. As soon as he turned 17, Cragg had been transferred to the youth division of Cook County Jail to await his trial; Derrick remained at the JDC. I tried to see both boys as often as I could in both facilities—usually every week.

I was looking forward to seeing Derrick today. The wheels of justice seemed to turn agonizingly slowly as the prosecution and defense both prepared their cases. But a lot had been happening in the lives of the two brothers. As the months had gone by, I had observed a steady maturing in young Derrick. When he first came to the JDC, he had seemed very immature, a young gangbanger jockeying for position in his new environment. But the cockiness had worn off, and underneath was a young man who did a lot of thinking about what had landed him in custody. According to his teachers and social workers, Derrick had settled down and gotten serious about his schoolwork. He was respectful to his instructors and the attendants, obeyed the rules, and participated in many of the programs and activities offered.

He was also a regular at our Bible studies, always interested and asking serious questions. I was deeply moved—but not too surprised—the day he asked me to pray with him as he turned his life over to the Lord.

One day when I dropped in to see Derrick, he was wearing a bright yellow T-shirt with lettering on the front and back instead of the usual white JDC shirt. The JDC has different "levels" as a kid progresses through the system, designated by the color of T-shirt he or she wears. I immediately knew by the yellow T-shirt that Derrick had reached level 4, the top level, which meant both more responsibilities and more privileges. "Hey, man," I said, "let me see!"

Derrick grinned and turned around slowly. The front of the T-shirt read: "The Best and the Brightest." The back of the T-shirt read: "And in Control."

He was 16 by the time his trial date was finally set. The state had decided to try Derrick first, even though he wasn't accused of being the triggerman. The prosecutors felt they had the stronger case against him, based on the statement he had signed. The state's case against Cragg was largely circumstantial. They had no witnesses; they had no signed statement. But if they could convict Derrick first . . .

"Hey, Derrick, my man!" I said, grasping his hand warmly as the gangly youth eased himself into an orange, plastic chair in the chaplain's office. "How ya doing?"

"All right, Mr. G," Derrick said politely, but immediately I sensed that he was under tremendous pressure—and I soon learned why.

"You know my trial date is comin' up," he said.

I nodded.

"Well, the state has offered me a deal."

I waited. Whatever it was, it was weighing on him. His speech was much slower and more deliberate than usual.

"They want me to plead guilty to the murder charge, and then they'll let me take the 20-year minimum sentence, or even 15 on a reduced charge. But . . . there's one condition." Derrick took a deep breath. "I have to testify against my brother at his trial."

Now I understood. Brother against brother. It was a terrible dilemma. But I didn't interrupt him as he laid out one of the most crucial decisions of his whole life.

"They say the state needs me to convict Cragg. Without my testimony against him, he may walk, so the prosecutors want my help. I think my attorneys want me to testify because their first concern is what happens to me. Cragg isn't their client. I'm not sure I could help the state if I wanted to. I don't even know the answers to the main questions they want to put to me. If I take the stand, I've got to know what I'm talkin' about, and I don't think I would. But if I plead 'not guilty' and go to trial and lose"—he shrugged helplessly—"it will probably be 55 years or more."

Fifty-five years. Almost my entire lifetime at that point. Those are huge numbers of years for anyone to serve in prison, especially a 16-year-old.

Derrick put his head in his hands. "I'm sure my family doesn't want me to testify," he groaned. "At least then there's the chance my brother could go free. But . . . that means I'd serve a lot more time." He looked up at me, his eyes full of anguish. "It's all on me. I don't know what to do."

The enormous pressure on Derrick engulfed the room like a storm cloud. I've been with the dying and sensed more calm. *This is a terrible situation*, I thought—but then, so was the whole situation, going back to the death of an innocent 14-year-old girl and the execution of 11-year-old Yummy Sandifer under a railroad viaduct.

I didn't know what to say to Derrick. It didn't really matter, however, since there was no way I could advise him. He understood the issue clearly; it wasn't my role to clarify or explain. Any questions he had were handled by his attorney and family. That had all been carefully done; now the dreadful decision was his.

"I wish I could help you, Derrick," I said gently. "You're a young man I've come to appreciate. But this is your life, and only you can decide what to do. I'll pray that the Lord will give you wisdom and then peace, knowing you chose what you believe to be right, or at least the lesser of two appalling alternatives."

We prayed together for that wisdom and peace.

"Thanks, Mr. G," he said huskily, and then he was gone, back to his unit. I didn't know what he would do. He had a couple of weeks to decide.

❖ ❖ ❖

WHEN THE AUTO SHOP FOLDED, JOHN JOHNSON'S UNCLE BOUGHT IT back. John didn't waste any time taking the small amount of cash he had and buying a supply of drugs from an old friend. He immediately broke the stash down into small packets, sold them on the street, and made back his investment with a profit. Next time he bought a little more, sold it for a larger profit, and bought even more. John's natural charm and quick wit made him a born salesman. People trusted him to deliver. He established himself over one hot corner, then another. It didn't take long to build up a nice business. Big business.

Man, now this is makin' money! John thought gleefully, counting his take on a good night. After making back what the drugs cost him, he cleared $10,000. *Ten thousand dollars in one night!* Of course, he then had to pay off his workers. He had two runners taking the drugs to the different spots, a pack man who broke down the supply into small packets, a pat-down man to make sure a customer didn't have a gun, two young guys on bikes looking out for police, and for a hot spot, three guys on a nearby roof with guns.

After paying them off, John still took home $6500 to $7000. That was on a good night. A good week had maybe four good nights plus the weekend.

First came the nice apartment. Next he bought the gold chains and gold rings. Then came the baby blue Bonzo (Mercedes Benz), a really bumpin' ride. (In plain English, that means it had a powerful stereo that, when turned up full blast, literally shook the car.) All of it was paid for in cash.

"Didn't the car salesman look at you kinda funny?" some of the New Breeds wanted to know. "I mean, man, you only 16! With a wad like that?"

John just shrugged and grinned. "Money talks," he told them. "All they asked was, 'What color?' Drove it home that night."

John was making money faster than he could spend it. Like many young drug dealers, he kept his cash at his mama's house. "Go ahead, Mama," he told her, "buy what you want. Get what you need." The abundance of money was enough to make Mama look the other way and ask no questions. But with upwards of $35,000 under the mattress, John stationed some of his boys around the house "to look after Mama."

John's customers came from all over the city and suburbs and from as far north as Milwaukee and Kankakee. The local junkies got their hit and faded into a nearby gangway or headed straight for the local crack house. But a regular parade of late-model cars from the suburbs found its way to some of John's spots as well.

"Who was that white dude?" one of the runners wanted to know as a pearl-gray Lexus pulled away from the curb and disappeared around the next corner. "Man, that's three nights in a row he here buyin' an eight-ball o' coke and four grams o' heroin. That's one hefty habit."

"He's a dentist," John said, contempt in his voice.

"A *dentist!*" snorted the runner. "Man, I wouldn't want that dude workin' on *my* teeth."

John didn't use drugs himself. He was no fool. He had a rule for himself and his boys: "You work for me, you're clean." Clean meant no cocaine. Smoking a few joints was okay, as was drinking beers and getting drunk now and then. But he absolutely couldn't trust anyone who was "using," especially blows (heroin) or crank (speed).

Soon John's business had expanded to the point where he didn't have to stand on the corner selling drugs himself. All he had to do was drop by to pick up the money and pay off his workers.

In fact, John never carried drugs or weapons in his own car. He loved the incredulous look on the faces of the police as he drove by in his baby blue Mercedes. He knew they'd find some pretext to stop him—going 35 in a 30 miles-per-hour zone, failure to signal a turn soon enough, or some other dumb reason. They knew a 16-year-old in a Mercedes was doing some serious dealing. They knew he knew they knew. But he always politely showed them his driver's license (forged by a "lady friend" who worked at the secretary of state's Chicago office) and refused to give them permission to search the car. Even when they searched it anyway—illegally—they never found anything. "Sorry, officers," he'd say, grinning. "Better luck next time." It gave him a heady sense of power to calmly watch them drive off, frustrated and mad because they couldn't nail him.

In the meantime, John's girlfriend was driving a secondhand Chevy Nova he'd bought her, with a few rust spots and a baby seat in the back—and thousands of dollars worth of cocaine in the trunk. Cops didn't stop cream-colored Chevies with baby seats to look for contraband.

The police weren't the only ones who knew John was dealing and didn't like it. The Gangster Disciples—his brother Michael's old gang—watched him driving around town in his blue Mercedes with the gold trim and thought Gee-Gee Johnson was getting too big for his own good. But knowing his rivals were jealous just made John's pleasure in his honey of a car all the sweeter.

Life was good. Life was fine. Life was his for the taking. He swaggered around the west side with an attitude: "I'm chief around here, and nobody goin' to mess over me. If you get in my way, you gone." He got a lot of respect, as well as a reputation for being trigger happy, a person who "don't care about nothin'." This was his feeling the night he bought a six-pack, parked the Mercedes in front of his apartment, and got happily drunk.

Bam! Scrunch! John's fuzzy brain heard the noises outside and wished they would go away. His head hurt. *Screeeeeech—bam!* There it was again. Some poor fool's car was in big trouble. Why didn't someone—

Car! *His* car was parked out front! The fog in John's head cleared suddenly as he rolled off the couch and made a flying leap for the front window. He got there just in time to see a late-model car—*Crash!*—ram the rear of his pretty little Mercedes, back up a few feet, and then drive up onto the sidewalk, heading straight for the passenger door.

Bam! Scrunch!

In a fury, John grabbed his gun and took the stairs three at a time. He came out the door shooting, but the hit-and-run car was already roaring halfway down the block. With a squeal of tires, it rounded the corner and disappeared from sight.

Gun hanging down at his side, John circled his "baby" in disbelief. The Mercedes had been rammed from the front, the rear, and both sides. Tears of rage and frustration boiled to the surface. The other car must have suffered major damage as well. A couple of GDs must've been in a stolen ride, saw his Mercedes parked like a sitting duck, and figured they had nothing to lose.

When the rage and blustering about revenge finally subsided, John was heartsick. He had no insurance. The car was a total loss. For two weeks he looked at the wrecked hulk sitting in front of his apartment and considered what to do. He knew several good nights of drug sales could buy him another one, but he hesitated. What was to keep the same thing from happening again? In this lifestyle, it was easy come, easy go. He even got philosophical. Deep down, he knew that what comes from wrong, goes by wrong. *That's just the way it is, Gee-Gee,* he told himself, *so get over it.*

A little wiser, John picked up a used Nissan Sentra and drove it for a while. When it needed an oil change, he simply junked it and bought a secondhand Pontiac Bonneville, five years newer. His time was too valuable to spend under the hood of a car. After all, he was raking in tens of thousands of dollars per week. For the most part he was making a profit, though he wasted a lot of money bailing out his workers, who kept getting busted.

Not John, however. He had no arrests, no priors. It took smarts to oversee his operation and keep two steps ahead of the Five-0s.

❖ ❖ ❖

MY FRIEND JOE AND I GOT ALONG WELL OUT ON THE STREET, EVEN though when I kept urging him to make some changes, he dodged the issue. But he knew I wasn't going to let up.

He was a colorful, dynamic person, normally full of fun and laughs like any happy-go-lucky 18-year-old. He could also be violent with the business end of a gun, and he pulled some of the wildest, craziest escapades in the street wars. But he was smart; he had to work harder to fail at school than most kids have to in order to pass.

Not long ago, he called me at my office. "I want to talk with you," he said, "but let's not meet in my neighborhood. How about at the Boston Market over by your place, just you and me? Six tomorrow night?"

"I guess I can do that," I said, wondering what was up to require such an odd arrangement. He had usually been open to meeting me on the streets. But I didn't question his request. "See you there," I concluded.

The next night we met, got our food, and found a table away from the other customers. Soon we were talking.

"Look," Joe said in a low voice, "I need to explain somethin' to you. You're out in the hood, and you've been really comin' at me to get my life together. You probably don't think you're makin' much progress. Right?"

"Well, that's true," I said with a shrug, not knowing where he was headed. "I think you've got lots of potential, and you ought to invest in something better than being the craziest gangbanger and dope dealer in the hood."

"That's just it," he said, leaning closer over the table. He glanced around the restaurant as though afraid of getting busted on the spot. "Out in the hood," he continued, "you've probably noticed that the essays roll deep. You know what I mean?"

I'm usually pretty up on street jive, but he could see that I wasn't reading him, so he filled me in. "You know . . . most Hispanics move in large numbers." When I nodded, he went on, but in a confidential tone of voice. "But I'm different. I'm not what you think or see. You're a lot further ahead with me than you realize."

My head was spinning as he stopped and looked around again. Then he added, almost in a whisper, "I'm a narc, an informant with the ATF."

"The feds?" I blinked and stared. "You mean the Bureau of Alcohol, Tobacco, and Firearms?"

He nodded and inched closer. "Yeah. They've got me in there to get to the suppliers of some heavy guns and also drugs in the area. And I'm makin' good progress. The job is about done. They've got their case. Some high rollers are gonna take a big fall, and soon."

He leaned back, took a big breath, and shoveled some potato salad into his mouth.

"Then I can get out of here—heck, I'll have to," he said with a grin. "I want to get on with my life, get more schoolin'. Me and my lady are gettin' married—she's a Christian all the way, and you can believe we're goin' to be in church."

I was still so shocked I could hardly respond. I've known a number of agents and informants, but Joe was the most unlikely choice I could have imagined. I was sure he was an antisocial, go-for-broke street warrior. From his past, the role was a natural, and he played it to the hilt. "Flipping," as they call it when someone switches sides (in this case to work with the police), is very risky. But as I thought about Joe, the idea spun through my mind that probably for him it only added to the challenge.

"But why? I mean . . .," I stammered, not wanting to suggest for a moment that I disapproved, "how did you get started with the feds?"

Joe turned and looked out the window as though he were gazing back through history. "The feds were on to what some of us guys were doin', and I got busted. I took the fall for one of our chiefs. At the time I didn't mind, because I was certain the boys would look out for me: provide a lawyer, bail money, commissary funds at the jail—that kind of thing. I expected them to visit me, write letters, keep in touch. But none of that happened. It was as though I didn't exist anymore. They completely forgot me. I got no help, nothin'!

"Now, to me, loyalty has to be a two-way street. I did everythin' for the organization, but they didn't back me at all. The feds saw I was hurt and angry, so they made me an offer: 'We'll look out for you if you'll help us.' 'You got a deal,' I said. I wasn't going to prison for guys who'd forgotten they ever knew me. So I flipped. The feds arranged bail, and soon I was out."

Joe took a big bite of chicken. I let him chew a minute, and then I asked, "What happened when you got back on the street?"

"Oh, the boys were glad enough to see me. Maybe they felt a little guilty, 'cause they went all out assurin' me that I was one of them again. We partied, made some money, and all the rest. But I had learned in jail what they really thought of me: I was a nothin'. The organization just used me for a while and threw me away. No thanks. So I decided now it was my turn."

He glanced around the restaurant again. There were only a few other customers on the far side of the room, so he leaned across the table and offered, "Feel under my shoulder. That's a wire. I'm wearin' it for my contact later tonight. I'm also packin'."

It didn't surprise me that Joe was armed. That wouldn't get him hurt among his gang. But to go out on the streets wired to record some kind of drug or weapons deal—that could get him instantly shot.

"Why are you telling me all this?" I asked, still adjusting to the news.

"As I said, the case is almost over. When it is, I'm outta here and won't be back to testify in court. You might never see me again. But I wanted you to know that I've been listenin' to what you've had to say. You don't know how hard at times that made my work out there, because I wanted to say yes and begin my new life openly with Jesus right now, but I had a specific job to finish."

I just shook my head. Sometimes I have no idea how God's working. Finally, I recovered enough to say with mock serious-ness—though it was entirely true—"You've just handed me your life, man. One word in the hood and you're history!"

Joe laughed. "I know better than that. You and your YFC guys don't leak. Your work is built on trust or you couldn't do anythin'. If just once you let loose with somethin' a guy told you, it would be all over the city in a few hours, and you'd be finished. You might not even be alive."

Stalemate! We both laughed.

"No," he said with a grin, "you won't say anythin'. You and I both know that. If the guys haven't made me yet, they won't before we're done."

He was right. Joe's confidence was safe with me. I'm telling the story here because his work is long since completed, the arrests made and the cases closed. He's far away from the area, working at a much-less-dangerous job. But I'm sure he'll never forget those scary, tense days and nights on the streets. And I can't forget him. His is one of the greatest turnaround stories I know. When his boys let him down, what an amazing way he found to get even! And he proved there's more than one way to repay your debt to society.

Seven

❖ ❖ ❖

WHEN XAVIER AND SLY JOINED THE OTHERS on the porch, no one showed any outward concern for the dead boy across the street in the abandoned building. But Xavier knew what he was feeling—deep regret and shame. The feeling was new to him. As a hard-core gang member, however, he acted indifferent. When that horrifying night finally ended and everyone headed for home, Xavier wondered whether any of the rest felt the same.

He couldn't sleep. Visions of the dying victim haunted him. He hadn't struck the boy even once, but he had participated in the deception that lured him to his death. And he had known all along what Sly intended. In his heart, Xavier knew he had killed the boy before the kid ever stepped into that abandoned building.

Thoughts of God drifted through his mind as he tossed and turned on a friend's couch. Could God forgive him? He felt like crying out for forgiveness, but all he really wanted was relief from his own discomfort rather than the kind of repentance that would change his life.

That stupid kid! thought Xavier as he flopped into a new position on the couch. *He shouldn't have been there with our boys around. He was an enemy! He probably would've done the same thing to me if I had taken a stroll in his neighborhood.*

The troubled young warrior tried another angle of rationalization: *That kid chose to be a gangbanger and died. It was his own fault. I didn't even touch him.* Slowly Xavier's emotional discomfort subsided.

The next day, the gangsters realized they still had an undiscovered body on their hands. "We could take him down to the lake at night and drop him off the rocks," said Killer.

"Sure, but not in my car you don't!" said Sly. "You ain't gonna leave any evidence in my car."

"Hey, did you hear about that woman's body they found up in Evanston?" said Joker. "She was stuffed down the sewer, and they didn't find her for months. Might never have found her."

"Yeah, but they did," Xavier pointed out angrily. "Besides, where we gonna do that? If we use one of the sewers here in the hood, then when they do find him, they sure are gonna come lookin' for us." He felt agitated, eager to wipe this whole thing out, as if it had never happened. "We gotta erase any connection to us, and the only way we can do that is to make sure no one can identify him."

"What? You *loco*?" said Mondo. "How you gonna do that?"

"No, he ain't crazy," said Sly, picking up on Xavier's direction. "There's a way to do that. We'll set the building on fire. It's abandoned anyway. The cops will just think some homeless person was trying to keep warm and accidentally burned the place down. Even if they find the kid's body, the fire will destroy all recognition."

Everyone agreed it was a good plan, but they waited a few more days until Halloween night to carry it out. All the trick-or-treaters were off the street when Joker and Xavier made their way to their own haunted house. The smell of the body kept them at a distance as they splashed gasoline at it. Xavier thought he had the whole body fully doused when Joker suggested that they make a trail of gas out of the kitchen, down the steps, and to the back gate. "That way we can light it and be down the alley before the building goes up," he said.

Xavier tried to ignore the feelings of horror churning in his stomach at the thought of burning the kid. But the moment they struck the match, those feelings evaporated. How could they hurt a dead boy?

As the flames whooshed up the gasoline trail, Xavier beat a fast retreat to his mother's house, where he had been staying off and on whenever he thought he could risk it. Now seemed a time when it was worth the risk. If something went wrong with the fire and the police came asking him questions, he could claim he'd been home that night. Getting caught and shipped back to Maryville was better than being charged with murder and arson.

The sirens of the fire trucks wailed sooner than he had anticipated, though. He peeked out the window and saw that it didn't take long for the firefighters to douse the flames.

He got up late the next morning. "Hey, Xavier, it's good to see you," said his mother, giving him a hug as he came into the kitchen. "When you get home?"

"You, too, Mama," he said, pecking her on the cheek. "Came home early last night—needed a good night's sleep."

"Didn't those sirens wake you up last night?"

"No, didn't hear a thing," he said innocently, slathering some peanut butter on a slice of bread. "Did someone have a heart attack or somethin'? I was sound asleep."

"It was a fire. That abandoned building down the street burned, and this mornin' they found a body inside. It's just awful."

"Really? That's sad," said Xavier. "Who was it?"

"They don't know yet. Nobody from around here's missin'. Probably some homeless person. They're still investigatin'."

Xavier shivered and tried to swallow his bread and peanut butter.

In the days that followed, the police asked the closest neighbors whether they had seen or heard anything unusual on the night of the fire. No one had heard a thing apart from the usual trick-or-treaters, and apparently the officers didn't think to ask about any unusual noises from the nights before. Finally, the police presence in the neighborhood subsided, and things quieted down.

The cops hadn't found Xavier, but he still felt jumpy and became more and more paranoid out on the street, finally moving his weapons and gang activity right into his mother's house. Everything seemed cool, except for his older brother. "Big brother" didn't like

Xavier's gang involvement and kept complaining about the kinds of guys Xavier invited over all the time.

Then came the day when his brother found Xavier's arsenal under the bed. "I'm gonna tell the cops what you got under that bed!" he yelled.

"Yeah, right, you rat," Xavier said with a laugh. "Get outta here."

Fifteen minutes later, the police were at the door. After digging a 12-gauge sawed-off shotgun, a .410 shotgun, and a .38 caliber handgun out from under Xavier's bed, they grabbed him. "You're under arrest for murder," they said.

"What? How come? Hey, wait a minute!" said Xavier, jerking back from the handcuffs. He had expected an illegal weapons possession charge and most likely a warrant to take him back to Maryville. But murder? How could they know about that?

The cuffs snapped in place. "You hear about the body we found in that burned-out building?" they answered. "Well, Speedy, seems it all comes back to you."

His mind was tumbling frantically, trying to figure out how the cops knew. The officer was saying something else. He was reading him his rights. His mother was crying, "No, no! Xavier, how could you! What's happenin'?"

This was for real. This was the big one! Instantly, he realized he had been wrong. He had put his whole family at risk by bringing guns home. He had taken part in a murder. He had . . . he had . . .

When the police threw him in the paddy wagon, a strange sense of relief washed over him. He could stop running. He could stop hiding. He could stop lying. He had the strongest feeling he wouldn't see the streets again for a long, long time. It was finally over!

He was just 13 years old.

❖ ❖ ❖

WALTER DAVIS WAS SURPRISED THAT HIS STEPBROTHER WAS DOING THE church thing, and he certainly wasn't ready to buy into religion for himself. Too much was happening in the streets; too much money was waiting to be made.

But God has a way of getting people's attention when they have other things on their minds. Walter had a regular big client. The man never seemed to be short on money and never hesitated to make a drug purchase. Then one day when the money and drugs had changed hands, the guy said, "Sorry, Walter, you're a nice guy, but you're also under arrest."

Walter looked around in panic.

"Don't try it!" the narc said. "My backup has every escape blocked. You'd only get yourself into more trouble by trying to run."

They had him cold with a big-time indictment, and Walter was suddenly in jail looking at upwards of 30 years in prison.

On the jail deck, Walter quickly came to respect one gang leader he knew from the streets by reputation. The man was a no-nonsense dude, and no one dared to mess with him. But to Walter's surprise, this brother had a Bible, and Walter saw him reading it. One day the man saw Walter watching him, looked Walter in the eye, and said, "You need this. There is no other hope, man, no other answer. You and I been out there and done it all, and it's not worth it."

Walter nodded and walked away. He knew some guys turned to God in jail to calm their nerves, begging God to help them with their cases. But when they got out, they went right back to the same old mess. Walter wasn't about to do that. Whatever he did—good or bad—he went for broke.

That night, Walter heard quiet sobs in the cell next to his— some guy hoping no one would hear him release the accumulated tension of fear and hurt. Walter just lay on his bunk, staring into the dark, thinking about how he had ended up in the joint. As a young teenager, he had lived in Oak Park, a Chicago suburb, and attended one of the finest schools in the state. He had been into sports, social life—all the good things. Then his parents split up, and he went with his mother back into the city, to a world of dangerous streets where he could survive only by his wits. At first he got into a gang to give himself protection, but he soon gained a "rep" (reputation), made good money, and became a leader. He knew even then that the situation wasn't ideal, but he'd rationalized that he was making the best of the hand he'd been dealt.

In any society, it doesn't take long to see what the smart, capable people do to thrive. In the suburbs, with their better schools, safer places to live, and more-abundant job opportunities, smart kids apply themselves to education, athletics, and legitimate jobs and businesses. Following this path often has more to do with being intelligent than with being morally good or bad. But the streets of Chicago and other cities constitute a completely different culture. There the really smart guys, the natural leaders, rise quickly to prominent positions in the gangs. Again, this isn't primarily a moral decision. But with gang leadership come the rewards of "success"— money, respect, power, and girls—the same things the suburban kids get from their more-traditional pursuits.

As for the threat of prison or death—the tragic destiny awaiting most gangbangers—it has never deterred the brave ones any more than such risks have kept other young men, from the beginning of time, from going to sea or risking life and limb to work the mines, fall timber, climb mountains, or join the military. They've all done what they thought they had to do.

Walter was no different. He hadn't joined a gang because he wanted to become a criminal or was too lazy get some other job; he had joined because that was the way to get ahead in his society— or at least it had seemed so at the time.

Lying there on his jail bunk, he did some heavy thinking. He got past feeling sorry for himself and blaming everyone else for his problems. Something had gone wrong! There was a world larger than the streets on which he lived and fought, and that world had taken charge of him, demanding accountability to its rules. Walter had come up short.

Thinking ahead was hard. He'd always lived one day at a time. But if he ever got out of the joint, what then? Some action, more big bucks . . . but he never knew in the morning if he'd be dead or in prison by nightfall.

There had to be more to life than this! "O God," he cried silently into the darkness, "if You can take the mess I've made of my life and turn it into somethin' worthwhile, You can have it!"

The next morning, when the call went out on the deck for

anyone who wanted to go to a Bible study, to everyone's surprise, Walter announced, "I'm goin'." He looked around at their open mouths. "Don't just stand there starin'," he said. "You heard it right. I signed on with Jesus for the duration last night, so I'm gonna see what He has to say."

"You gotta be kiddin'," said one of the brothers.

"That's all right," Walter answered with a shrug. "I find it pretty hard to believe myself. But it's happenin'!"

"You think gettin' religion's gonna do your case some good?" mocked one of the other gang members in the unit.

"I know better than that," said Walter. "I'll serve my time, but I've decided that I'll be servin' the Lord while I'm in prison."

Walter's straight answers earned him grudging respect on the deck, and he held fast to his new decision, even though he was convicted of drug dealing. Then, on the night before his final court date—his sentencing—he was praying in his cell when the Lord impressed on him, "You're going home tomorrow."

Immediately he pushed the thought away. He was probably just projecting his own wishful thinking. Nothing like that could possibly happen! The case against him was rock-solid. But . . . still the impression was there. In fact, it was so strong when he got up the next morning that he told a couple of his buddies.

"Get a grip, man," one of them said. "You may be leavin' us pretty soon, but it won't be for the hood. They have you hangin', and the only place you be goin' is downstate to Joliet, maybe even Pontiac. You best face the music."

When Walter went to the courtroom, he took his Bible. And when the guards didn't take it away, as they were supposed to do, his hopes rose even higher. The arguments before the judge went just as expected, with the state demanding a long prison sentence. Still, he felt calm. Something—or Someone—was in control far beyond his doing.

Finally, the judge leaned forward, elbows on the bench and chin resting on his clasped hands. He stared a long time at Walter, then cleared his throat. "I've considered your case very carefully," he said, "and I'm not quite sure why, but I've decided to take a chance with you. You'll be on intensive probation for a year and then regular probation. But you'd better make good!" He banged his gavel, and that was that. Walter was not going to prison.

More shocking to Walter than the judge's decision was the deep sense that his release came from a higher power. Later, as I do with all my guys, I emphasized that while God promises to save us from our sins, He doesn't promise to save us from paying the consequences of our choices. Walter understood that. *There are a lot of guys who've done far less than I did—some who aren't guilty at all— who are locked up for a long time,* Walter thought as he left the courtroom. *If God is givin' me a second chance, in spite of the life I've been leadin', He must have some special plan for my life, and I'd better find out what it is and get with the program.*

❖ ❖ ❖

I STAYED IN CONTACT WITH SILVIU SPIRIDON, BUT THE STORIES I KEPT hearing about his exploits made me realize that working to see him change in the Lord would be a long-term project. Somehow, though, I believed that day would come, even if I had to admit there wasn't much supporting evidence at the time.

When I met his parents, I was impressed by this hardworking couple and their deep faith. The mother told me their Pentecostal church prayed regularly for their wayward son.

"That's great," I encouraged. "Don't give up praying."

Silviu's opinion was that church and God were for weaklings, old people, and babies—and maybe occasionally for guys like him in a pinch. But the time was coming when this tough, young gang-banger would find that the Lord can neither be controlled nor manipulated. God had His sights on Silviu.

The police had their sights on him, too, but for different reasons. While attending a community gang awareness meeting one evening, I noticed several youth officers at the program. During the break, one of them came over and talked with me. She was a dedicated police-woman, often out in the neighborhood, visiting families, keeping up with the happenings on the streets, putting in a lot of volunteer time, and, and, as with a number of officers, often reaching into her own pocket to help a kid who needed a pair of shoes, a schoolbook, or a pair of glasses. As far as I was concerned, she represented the finest and best on the force.

"I've seen you several times with Silviu Spiridon," she observed. "Are you getting anywhere with him? He's still out there messing up. In fact, I think he's getting worse. Do you believe a guy like that can really change?"

It was a reasonable question, but I didn't hesitate to answer, "Yes, he can. The question is, does he want to? He isn't ready yet, but I think the time will come. He's got many good people concerned about him. Something may happen yet."

"Listen, Reverend," she said, "there are lots of young guys out there you really can help. Put your time in on them. Silviu has run the course—he's ours. We're going to get him, and when we do, he'll be gone for a long time. Do yourself a favor: Don't waste your time on him."

"You may be right," I agreed, "but it wasn't my idea to take him on. We'll have to see how he does tangling with my Boss." I'm not sure she knew I was referring to God.

The administrators at Hubbard High School were even less encouraging. They not only considered Silviu hopeless, but they were downright eager to hasten his downfall. "That boy has a sixteenth birthday coming up," one of the deans told me gleefully. "Then by law we can wash our hands of him, and don't think we won't. In fact, I have the date circled on my calendar. We're planning a faculty celebration!"

❖ ❖ ❖

"WILL THE DEFENDANT PLEASE RISE?"

Derrick Hardaway and his attorney rose to their feet. Derrick had refused to testify against his brother and had taken his chances with a jury trial. The prosecution had relied heavily on Derrick's signed statement, whereas the defense had argued that no statement from a 14-year-old should be allowed when he had not had the benefit of counsel, nor even a family member present during the questioning. But the prosecution asserted that while the law requires that a parent be *notified,* the police can continue questioning until the parent shows up, and Derrick had never asked for a lawyer that first day in custody.

The judge ruled that his signed statement was voluntary and admissible.

Now the jury had returned, and the foreman stood to read the verdict: "We find the defendant, Derrick Hardaway, guilty of first-degree murder."

Under the accountability law, Derrick was as guilty as if he had pulled the trigger himself. But I wondered . . . without Derrick's testimony, would Cragg go free? And what about the adult gang leaders who allegedly sent two youngsters to do their dirty business? When all was said and done, was Derrick Hardaway going to take the rap for all the guilty parties?

A few weeks later, I sat in the same courtroom for Derrick's sentencing. The media interest in the case was still at high pitch. Cameras weren't allowed, but several artists sat in the jury box and sketched the various courtroom players as they took their places: the black-robed judge, the attorneys for both sides, and, of course, Derrick, sitting quietly across the room in a white T-shirt and pants, his hands folded on the table in front of him. The Associated Press was there, as well as reporters for Chicago's major newspapers. When one of the reporters discovered that I had a file folder with me of all the clippings on the case so far, she asked to borrow it. Soon the folder was being passed around to the other reporters as they boned up on their "facts" of the case. I shook my head. So much for doing their own research.

The rules in a sentencing hearing are quite different from those in a trial. In deciding what to do with the newly convicted person, the judge will hear not only facts but also rumors, of arrests that didn't result in convictions, as well as stories both good and bad about the person's character. The session often becomes a free-for-all that the judge must sort out.

For Derrick, the benefits of remaining as long as possible in the juvenile system hung in the balance. If he had been tried and convicted as a juvenile, he would have stayed in the juvenile system until he was 21. But since he was tried as an adult, even a minimum sentence would send him to adult prison eventually. Many times in such cases, the overloaded juvenile officials ask the judge for an order to pack the kid off to adult prison as soon as he turns 17, a request that's usually granted. The juvenile department can make the transfer itself on an 18-year-old inmate.

Derrick was only a few weeks away from turning 17. Was he strong enough to withstand the gang pressures in an adult prison? Unfortunately, gangs virtually run adult prisons, and gang affiliation is almost a necessity for protection and survival.

As the hearing opened, the prosecution concentrated on Derrick's school history the year before his arrest. That record portrayed a disruptive and profane youth who had to be disciplined regularly. Two police officers testified to arresting Derrick for illegal possession of a semiautomatic handgun six months before the murder of Yummy Sandifer. The prosecution's conclusion: This was a "coldhearted kid" who should be put away for a long time.

Then it was the defense's turn. As their first witnesses, the lawyer called two psychiatrists who were familiar with the case. One noted that Derrick's troubles began later than most young people's. Up until age 12, he had been a good student and well liked. Then relations with his father had become stormy, and Derrick had begun acting out at school and seeking gang identification on the streets. "He has responded well to positive intervention so far," said the psychiatrist. "If he continues to have positive input, his prognosis for rehabilitation into a productive citizen is quite favorable."

"Are you saying it's not *whether* Mr. Hardaway should be held accountable," the defense attorney asked, "but *how* he should be held accountable?"

"Exactly," said the witness. "He should continue in a program where he can learn social skills, where his academic deficit can be corrected, in an environment where he doesn't fear for his life and where he has appropriate role models. A long prison sentence, on the other hand, can actually be counterproductive because of what he will learn from negative influences in prison."

The other psychiatrist testified that Derrick had expressed remorse for what had occurred, had not continued gang behavior in the detention center (though he was still a member), had clearly improved in his academic performance, and had responded well to all programs in which he had participated. His conclusion: Derrick Hardaway had a "high potential for rehabilitation."

By now, my stomach was rumbling. Courtrooms function on a timetable from a different planet. The judge declared a brief recess for "lunch" at 3:15 P.M. The hearing didn't resume until 4:30.

The next defense witnesses were teachers, social workers, and staff who had worked with Derrick over the past two years at the JDC. They spoke of how he had matured, learned, and become a positive leader among his peers. One attendant's comments were typical: "I've been an attendant at the Juvenile Detention Center for 10 years. This is the first time I've testified for one of the kids, but I'm doing so because I want Derrick to get a chance."

It was almost 7:00 when the defense called me as the last witness. I stated my name and ministry role as one of the chaplains at the JDC. Then I told the judge, "This is a young man I respect. I hope the sentence of this court is one that encourages all the progress he has made and adds to the incentives for him becoming a good citizen. It would be a tragedy to simply warehouse him for years in prison and wipe out all the gains he has made. There's no question he was a problem on the streets. But there's also a unanimous agreement among the people responsible for him every day now that he has turned around and become a positive person."

The prosecutor asked sarcastically, "Don't you think renouncing his gang would be the first step to becoming a positive person?"

I acknowledged that Derrick's gang involvement had been a serious problem—but not all that surprising considering the community in which he grew up. "However," I said, "it's not that easy to just go off count in lockup. It's especially hard to quit his gang since he's looking at going for some years into the adult penal system with its strong gang presence and power. From my experience working with gang kids, leaving the gang lifestyle and identity is the result over time of maturing rather than a prerequisite to becoming a genuinely positive person."

It was late. I was tired. So were Derrick's mother and sister, who sat anxiously through the long day of testimony. So was Yummy Sandifer's grandmother, who sat impassively in the back of the courtroom. Everyone had hoped for a conclusion to the waiting and wondering, each with his or her own private hope—or desire for punishment. But the judge abruptly called it a day. The sentence would have to wait.

❖ ❖ ❖

"D—!" JOHN JOHNSON SAID WHEN HE SAW THE BLUE-AND-WHITE POLICE car half a block behind him. A sixth sense told him they'd pull him over on one pretext or another within two blocks, and this morning he hadn't been able to find his forged driver's license, so he'd taken a chance on leaving the apartment without it. If they stopped him and he didn't have his license, they'd use it as an excuse to put him in the slammer so quick—

With split-second thinking, John pulled to the curb and parked, got out of his car, and started walking. If he was walking, they couldn't ask to see his driver's license. He was just congratulating himself on outsmarting the Five-0s when the squad car pulled alongside him. "Hey, Johnson," called the officer riding shotgun, getting out of the car, "we want to talk to you."

Be cool, John told himself, gritting his teeth. He knew better than to run or even keep walking. These cops were just looking for an excuse, any excuse.

"You clean?" said the other officer, motioning for John to step wide and hold out his arms. John knew the routine. He also knew the police had no legal right to frisk him, but it wouldn't do any good to resist.

"Well, well, look what we have here!" said the officer, fishing in one of John's pockets and coming out with a plastic bag of white powder.

In two seconds flat, they had the cuffs on him and were escorting him into the backseat of the squad car.

John cooled his heels in the county jail while he was fingerprinted and charged with possession. Then, since the arrest was for a nonviolent crime, he was allowed to bond out after three days. Bond was no problem. He just sent one of his boys to his mama's house to collect $1,500 from the stash he kept there.

When he hit the streets, he got word that one of his boys had taken advantage of his being in jail and absconded with $8,000 in drug profits. John was already mad about getting burned by the police; now he was furious. "Bad enough gettin' done dirt by the police," he muttered to himself, stopping by his apartment long enough to pocket his 9-mm blue steel before hitting the street again. "That brother gonna die."

John cruised in his car up one block and down another, looking for the culprit. And then he saw the little thief, hanging out with some guys down at the next corner.

Parking curbside, John took the safety off the gun and stuck it in his belt. Then he started walking calmly and casually. *No rush,* he thought. *But I'm gonnna get that sucker—*

Just then, a police cruiser pulled over to the curb in front of him, and a couple of Five-0s got out. Instantly, John knew he was in big trouble. If they caught him with a gun . . . As clearly as if it had happened yesterday, John remembered seeing his brother on the ground, shot in the back, and the police explaining, "We thought he had a gun."

Thinking quickly, John pulled the gun out of his belt, threw it toward the police, and took off running.

Cutting through a gangway between two buildings, over a fence, and through a backyard, John congratulated himself on outsmarting the police. By throwing the gun at them, he virtually ensured they wouldn't shoot when he ran, since now they knew he didn't have a piece on him. And he'd lose them soon enough. By the look of those two, they'd stopped a few too many times for coffee and doughnuts.

After zigzagging in the alleys and gangways for a few blocks, John slowed down and strolled out into the street. "There he is!" someone shouted. With a rush of adrenaline, John spun around and ran back through the gangway at full speed, but not before he saw at least four or five cops on his tail. *Man!* he thought. *They must've called in backup.*

Taking a dive behind a garbage Dumpster, John tried to still his heavy breathing as shouts and footsteps ran past. He gave them five minutes to disappear, and when all seemed quiet, he unfolded himself from a crouch and peered down the alley.

A police car was sitting at the far end.

For the next 45 minutes, John ran through gangways, cut through a park, hid behind the stairs on people's porches, jumped over fences, and took refuge in basement doorways. But every time he thought it was safe to come out, he saw more cops on foot, looking for him. *There must be 13 or 14 of 'em by now,* he thought. His only hope was getting back to his car and getting out of there for good.

Finally the coast seemed clear. He had circled around so that his car was only about five blocks away. He walked down one block, all senses alert, but he didn't see any uniforms or cruisers. Two blocks . . . then three . . . now four. So far, so good. He turned a corner, and there was his car, just where he'd left it.

He looked up and down the street. All clear. With a weak sense of relief, John headed for his car, took a casual glance around, and opened the door—

"Freeze, Johnson!" ordered a voice. "Keep your hands where we can see 'em."

John's shoulders sagged as three men in blue surrounded him, guns drawn. He was too tired to protest.

This time there would be no bond. The gun he'd thrown at the officers had held five live rounds with the safety off, ready to fire. He was charged with unlawful use of a firearm.

The system had him now.

❖ ❖ ❖

THE CALLER ON MY PHONE WAS ABRUPT AND TO THE POINT: "REVEREND McLean? We got your message on the street. You want to meet with Angelo. He says it's okay. Is tomorrow afternoon at 3:00 all right?"

"I can do that. Where does he want me to meet him?"

"There's a parking lot at 9011 South Stony Island. Do you know where that is?"

"Of course I do. That's Vernon Park Church of God. I know the pastor."

"We figured you'd know it. Be there at 3:00." The line suddenly clicked to a dial tone.

The next day, I pulled into the lot just before 3:00. The pastor was away or I would have stopped in to greet him. Right on the dot of 3:00, two cars pulled in next to me, one on each side of mine, a late-model blue Cadillac and a more-utilitarian Chevy. Ours were the only cars at that end of the lot. Several young men rode shotgun in each vehicle. Two of them got out of the Cadillac and signaled me to come over.

"Angelo is in the backseat. Climb in," said the taller man, his neck roped with gold chains and his face a stony mask behind dark shades. I slid into the car while the duo strutted over to the Chevy to wait with their buddies.

Angelo Roberts and I were face to face and alone. We hadn't met in six years, and this was a decidedly different circumstance and setting. Our last meeting had been in a counseling room at the JDC. The relaxed friendliness he had displayed there was gone, replaced by a wariness and the hard lines that come from harsh years on the streets. Even at the age of 16, Angelo had been a respected leader in the Four Corner Hustlers, an offshoot of the Vice Lord organizations. I had found him polite and courteous in that previous meeting, but he had expressed little reaction as I had talked with him about the direction his life was going. I had given him a modern-language Bible, for which he had thanked me, and I had told him I would like to see him again on the bricks. He had nodded agreement.

When he was released from the JDC, however, Angelo returned to the streets and an increasing place of leadership in his gang. I tried to contact him from time to time but was rarely successful. Setting up a meeting was equally difficult. He had a squadron of gang associates and bodyguards who kept me and everyone else from getting too close—a matter of security, they said.

Now, at my initiative, we were finally having that meeting. I didn't have a particular purpose, but I wanted to make contact. Maybe the Lord had something in mind.

In the intervening time, Angelo had climbed to the top of his gang organization by the age of 22. He was a power on the street with both friends and enemies—those who cheered him, those who were jealous, and enemies who wanted him dead. He could be charming, but to those who wronged him, he was a young man to be dreaded.

Some of his enemies, even those in his own organization, were ready to "take him out of the box" (kill him) if they had the chance. Such a leader never travels alone; armed bodyguards go with him everywhere. These were the guys who sat in the Chevy while we talked; Angelo had made a slight motion with his head for them to stay a few feet away to give us privacy.

I knew those bodyguards meant business. One day on the street, I had approached another gang leader whose name was Nose, the now-deceased leader of the Mafia Insane Vice Lords. His bodyguards had instantly reached into their pockets. Their weapons were about to come out until Nose smiled and greeted me, signaling them away.

"Hey, Mr. G," he had said, "you ought to come up on me a little more slowly. You made the boys nervous. I wouldn't want them to make a mistake and take you out." I couldn't have agreed more, and I've been more careful since then.

Angelo's arrangements for this meeting had been made with care, and his bodyguards were alert as we conversed.

After making small talk and asking about his family, I said, "Ever think about getting away from all the pressure and headaches of gang leadership, Angelo?"

A rueful smile tugged at the corners of his mouth. "There are times I'd really like to," he admitted. "But life on the street is like a merry-go-round goin' faster and faster, Mr. G. It's hard to stop."

He was right, of course. Nobody would let him just walk away—not his boys, not his rivals, not the police.

"I still have the Bible you gave me at Juvie," he said. "Every once in a while I read some of it. To live like that book describes must be really somethin'."

Maybe this was why we were meeting. Maybe God wanted me to give this young man another opportunity to receive Him. "Angelo," I said, "God wants everyone on His team, and He doesn't make an exception for you. You could do a lot of good out on the bricks, if you would."

I paused, and he looked down and pursed his lips as he slowly shook his head.

"Well," I continued, "I'm praying for you, and I'm going to keep doing that. Here's my number. Give me a call any time we can talk again. I'll be there for you."

He shook my hand warmly, and I got out of the car. His guards immediately reappeared and slid into the front seats, and we all left the church parking lot.

Three weeks later, late one night, my phone rang. I've been around the streets long enough to know nothing good happens after midnight; the late calls are always word of tragedy.

It was one of my contacts in the Four Corner Hustlers. "They just found Angelo stuffed in the trunk of his car on the south side," said the young caller, panting in shock. "Shot and with his throat slit. None of his boys were around."

Stunned by the news, I finally recovered enough to ask, "What do you make of it?"

"Dunno yet. If his guards weren't with him, it was a setup. He don't go anywhere alone unless it's with somebody he trusts completely. Dunno. Maybe his own boys killed him . . . maybe his rivals. Some even say the cops—but I doubt it. Tell you when we know somethin'."

A profound sense of sadness swept over me as I hung up the phone.

The next day, I saw some of Angelo's buddies standing on the street and pulled my car to the curb. As I got out and greeted them, I expressed my regret at the loss of their friend and asked them to assure the family of my prayers for them.

"Man, that guy was a real success at a young age," one boy commented, still in awe of his fallen hero.

"Was he?" I wondered out loud. "I know he was your friend, and I liked him, too, though we disagreed on his lifestyle and activities. But a success? I wonder. How about the question in the Good Book: 'What good is it for a man to gain the whole world, yet forfeit his soul?' The man who dies with the most toys—still dies."

None of the boys could answer that one. Unfortunately, neither could Angelo. The only thing he "gained" was a batch of rumors that still circulate over how and why he was killed.

Eight

A T THE POLICE STATION, XAVIER WAS CHARGED with first-degree murder. The cops "Mirandized" him, informing him of his right to remain silent, but then they went to work demanding that he confess. Though the police later denied it, Xavier maintains that they hit him with a phone book several times and went through their "good cop/bad cop" routines. He claims that they said he didn't need or deserve an attorney—all he needed was to tell them the truth.

"You're in big trouble, Speedy!" one cop yelled in his face. "The only thing that's going to help you now is cooperation—full cooperation *before* speaking to a lawyer. Once you lawyer-up, we're not gonna deal with you. It's gonna be hardball after that."

"Besides, look here," said the "good" cop calmly, "we got four signed statements from your gang buddies naming you, so we know you did it. You might as well own up to it. It'll go a lot easier on you."

The police didn't bother to tell Xavier that those written statements were worthless against him in court. The statements did give the police information about what had happened, providing a lot to go on in their investigation. But by themselves, statements of others can't be used as evidence against anyone but the people who sign them. The reason? Only a witness on the stand can be cross-examined—a piece of paper can't. The other guys *might* take the stand

and testify against Xavier in court, but they hadn't yet. Their signed statements were *their* confessions, not evidence against anyone else.

The police, however, told Xavier it was all over. They had him cold. His only hope was to make their paperwork easier by confessing. Then they'd see if they could help him out.

Xavier shrugged. They *did* have him, he figured. He might as well tell them what they wanted to hear.

Later in court, the police and prosecutors denied any improper conduct while questioning Xavier at the station. The judge agreed, and Xavier's statement was admitted into evidence as having been freely and voluntarily given. But it was *his* statement, not those of his fellow gangbangers, that nailed him.

Ironically, Sly beat the case against him because no witnesses came forward to testify and he gave no statement. In a later case, however, he was convicted of home invasion and attempted murder and sentenced to serve 14 years.

Even though Xavier was still only 13, his long and violent criminal record got him tried as an adult. For two years, he waited in the JDC while his case meandered through the courts.

It was there that I, Gordon McLean, met Xavier through our Bible studies and programs. Other Christian workers and I talked with the bright, young Latino frequently. He listened politely, but he wasn't ready to change. I could tell that somewhere inside him he clung to the possibility that the old ways might still work, that he might beat his rap and return to the streets.

Finally, a deal was struck between Xavier and the prosecutors. The best he could do was to plead guilty in exchange for a 25-year sentence. He would *not* be returning to the streets.

Twenty-five years! At 15 years of age, and with time off for good behavior, he might get out before age 30—if he lived that long in the joint. (Before the truth-in-sentencing law, prisoners could earn a day-for-day reduction in their sentences for "good time"—days when they didn't break institutional rules, took part in academic and vocational training, and were generally cooperative. However, a rule-breaker, fighter, or "problem to staff" could have good time taken away.)

To a 15-year-old, age 30 seems a lifetime away, hardly an achievable goal for someone who hasn't learned to delay his gratification even a few hours. When Xavier was sent to the Illinois Youth Center at Joliet, a maximum-security prison for violent kids, he picked right up with other Latin Kings and got involved in every fight and riot he came across. The immediate returns were status, reputation, protection, and the various privileges he could extract from weaker guys. The institution, however, responded with its own brand of immediate "gratification": Xavier was segregated from the general prison population for a month.

That got his attention.

With nothing much else to do, he and his cellmate started reading the Bible I'd given him. Xavier was especially taken with Psalm 51: "Have mercy on me, O God, according to your unfailing love; according to your great compassion blot out my transgressions. Wash away all my iniquity and cleanse me from my sin." Could God really do something with the mess he'd made of his life? He and his cellmate even prayed together every night on their knees when no one was looking. Apparently, the seeds that I and the other Christian workers had planted back in the JDC started to grow in that cell. God was still after Xavier, and He wasn't about to give up. But the seeds were slow growing. Xavier didn't want the other inmates to think he was getting weak. He couldn't humble himself—not in prison—so he didn't tell anyone else about his new interest in the Lord. Other cons still thought he was the young, tough gangbanger.

So did the institution. As soon as Xavier turned 17, he was transferred to adult prison.

❖ ❖ ❖

WALTER DAVIS AND BOYCE ALLEN, THE "DYNAMIC DUO" OF THE WEST side, were now both Christians, and word of their change spread quickly on the streets.

One person who hadn't heard, however, was Moltice, Boyce's rival from the Four Corner Hustlers. But some things had started to change for "Tice" as well. In spite of his rough start in life, he had completed high school and taken up his talent for writing and performing rap music as a way to counter his losses and disappointments. In getting to know some of the Four Corner guys, I'd had a chance to meet him and present the gospel to him. Over a period of time, I saw him begin to settle down and try to find a more-meaningful personal dimension to his life.

"But you know, Tice," I said one day, "it's not just about settling down to a less-crazy life. That's all well and good, and certainly gangbanging's no kind of existence, but you need more."

"Whatcha mean, Mr. G?" he asked. "I thought you'd be glad to see me gettin' civilized."

"I am, but it takes more than being good. When Jesus was on earth, He told Nicodemus, a prominent community leader, 'You must be born again,' because neither he nor anyone else could be 'good enough' in and of themselves to make much difference—certainly not good enough to please God. Ever hear that term, 'born again,' before?"

Tice nodded noncommittally.

"Well, it's got a lot of meaning," I said. "You see, we need God's Spirit to make a new life in us. We can't do it on our own."

"I guess I do know that much," admitted Tice. "I've tried, Mr. G, and I just can't do much to make a new life by myself."

That day was the beginning of a brand-new life for Tice, as he finally invited Jesus to forgive him and take control. In the months that followed, Tice's rap tapes turned from a hostile, crude celebration of gangster life to a positive message, and he liked visiting church youth groups with me to encourage other kids to follow Jesus.

Then one day I asked Tice if he knew Boyce Allen.

"Yeah, I know Bo," he said. "He's really plugged into his organization. We're old rivals, sworn to off each other next time we meet. But that was before I met Jesus," he quickly added with a grin when he saw the shock on my face. "Now I guess I'll just stay clear of him."

"You might not need to," I said, recovering. "He's had a change in his life, too. As a matter of fact, how'd you like to get together with him . . . on TV?"

"TV? Whatcha talkin' 'bout?"

I told him about a program hosted by James Cantelon of Canada's "100 Huntley Street." Cantelon wanted to interview members of opposing gangs who had laid aside old rivalries when they met the Savior.

Tice shrugged and said, "Why not?"

When I put the idea to Boyce, he accepted the plan as well.

A few days later, these two old rivals came together before cameras in the studios of Channel 38. As the cameras rolled into place, they shook hands.

"Hey, how ya doin'?" Boyce said. "I hear you've come to know the Lord."

Tice, the more retiring of the two, simply smiled and nodded.

"I'm really glad to hear that," Boyce said with a big grin. "This get-together would never have happened without it."

"You're right about that," Tice replied. Then, turning to host Jim Cantelon, he explained, "On the bricks, we had hits out on each other. I wanted to take him out, and he was determined to do the same to me."

"Our gangs are rivals," Boyce explained. "And I knew he was a key leader, so he definitely was in my sights." Then, unable to hold in his curiosity any longer, he turned directly to Tice and asked, "Tell me, what got you to change?"

"I've got the answer in a rap I wrote. Want to hear it?"

Everyone on the set nodded in agreement, and, using music and rhythm, Tice told his story of growing up on violent streets, his father and relatives getting killed in gang wars, starting out to follow in their footsteps, being disillusioned with thug life, and finally coming to the Lord. The impact was powerful.

When Tice was through, Boyce led the applause. In turn, he reviewed the highlights of his own life, from street warrior and drug dealer to servant of the Lord, reaching out to redirect other young street brothers.

"Where do you two go from here?" asked Jim, raising the question his audience surely wanted answered.

"We've been enemies," Boyce acknowledged. "But now it seems clear we both have God as our Father. So that makes Tice my brother, and I'd like us to work together to help the young shorties. How 'bout it, bro?"

"You got it, man," Tice quickly responded. "With us teamin' up, we'll have a lot of eyes poppin' in the hood, and we just may get some of the guys from both our organizations to listen. Let's do it, man!"

They stood up and embraced, starting and sealing a commitment to help each other in serving the Lord. Then they left the station together.

Their friendship lasted several years. The two often met, visited each other's families, and took part in a series of United Nations meetings for gang kids on how rivals can change. But one night, as Tice was heading home on his bike after working on his Christian rap tapes, he passed through a part of the city where the Conservative Vice Lords were strong. They were at war with an outlaw crew led by a guy nicknamed Puff. As some of Puff's crew drove past Tice, they apparently assumed he was CVL and started blasting. Tice went down, shot in the face. He was DOA at the hospital.

When Boyce heard the news, he knew it could just as easily have been himself getting shot. The shooters don't have to have a personal grudge against you. If a gang is itching to waste a rival, and someone even *thinks* you *might* belong to the opposition, you're gone. No place on the streets is ever really safe.

Even in that environment, however, God's work goes on. One day when Boyce was home visiting his family, his sister's boyfriend came over. "Name's Tyson," the 16 year old said boastfully. "You know, after the big man, 'cause no one messes with me."

Boyce ignored the swagger and said, "Yeah, well, how ya doin', Tyson? I'm Boyce." He stepped forward and offered his hand.

"You oughta know no Gangster Disciple would shake hands with a lowlife Unknown Vice Lord," sneered Tyson, turning away and flashing his gang sign by extending his thumb and two fingers upward in a "devil's pitchfork."

Boyce shrugged. "That's cool," he said. What he'd heard about and now seen in this young dude sure didn't warm his heart, but this was no time for a confrontation.

Tyson had grown up as Antwane Douglas in Cabrini Green, one of Chicago's roughest housing projects, where he took the name of the famous and hard-living boxing champion. It was his announcement to the world that he was now a cold, mean street warrior for the Gangster Disciples, determined to reach the rank of regent or governor in that huge drug-selling organization.

At the age of 13, Tyson was charged with three counts of attempted murder. In court, he shouted at the judge, threatening that he would be back to get him, too. Finally, the deputy sheriffs removed him from the courtroom.

Tyson continued his feisty, gangbanging ways in the JDC, and before long he was sent to the maximum-security prison for teens at Joliet. That was just fine with him. It would add to his reputation back on the streets . . . if he ever got back there. He wasn't actually paroled until he was 16. Then he hit the streets at full speed, with all the sophistication he had learned in the joint.

He wouldn't have lasted long on the bricks except that he met a nice girl and quickly found that if he wanted to be welcome in her home, his manners needed an overhaul. That slowed him down, at least on the surface.

Boyce knew most of this history, so instead of raising the tension level in the room, he calmly told Tyson he wasn't into street madness anymore. "I found somethin' better," he said, "somethin' a guy like you might dig."

"Whatcha' mean?" said Tyson, both suspicious and interested. He knew of Boyce and Walter's reputation as the Dynamic Duo and figured they might be into some new scam he could cut in on. So he listened.

What he heard was an entirely different message. Over the next few days, he and Boyce met several times. Boyce gave him a Bible and explained how Tyson could get his life turned around. Tyson finally admitted he had sometimes wanted to do just that but didn't know where or how to begin. Thus, what started out as a cold encounter between two enemies ended up several days later with

Boyce praying with his new friend, who opened his life to the Lord and became a brother in the faith.

"I got to this thing pretty late," Tyson told me when Boyce introduced us, "so I have a lot of catching up to do, and quick." I suppressed a smile at the idea that coming to the Lord at 16 was "late." But he'd done some hard living early, and his life following his commitment to Christ showed that he was serious.

Boyce lined up a job for Tyson, and the young man was thrilled at the thought of earning honest money. Channel 38 heard about Tyson's story and arranged to do an interview with him the following week. As his mentor, I wanted to make sure Tyson didn't get carried away on an ego trip, but he just seemed eager to tell his story, so I had no problem with the doors the Lord was opening for him.

A few days after the interview was arranged, my phone rang early one morning, awakening me. The piercing bell filled me with dread. It was Boyce, not noted for being an early riser himself.

"Tyson was on his way to work this mornin'," began Boyce, emotion choking his voice. "First day on his job. He was ridin' with a friend and stopped at a service station on North Avenue and Kedzie." He paused and took several deep breaths. "I guess he didn't realize he was in enemy territory. A car passin' the station had passengers who recognized him. They swerved into the station, and some rivals got out with guns blazin' and drilled Tyson."

"Is he gonna make it?" I pleaded.

"He's dead."

A few days later, Boyce and I conducted the funeral service in a chapel filled with young people who came to pay their respects. The TV crew scheduled to interview Tyson that day instead reported on his funeral.

In speaking that day, Boyce and I offered a message of hope and change through the Lord—something Tyson had modeled so powerfully. But we were both left with the bitter question, "Why?"

As we struggled together with our grief, I said, "We may not know the answer to that until we see Jesus. But Boyce, that's why we're in this ministry. It's easy to think these young men have a long life ahead of them. We forget how short that time can be. Tyson is with the Lord now, and I'm awfully glad you shared the gospel with him. We certainly enjoyed him the few weeks the Lord gave him to us as a brother."

❖ ❖ ❖

THE DAY SILVIU SPIRIDON TURNED 16, HE WAS EXPELLED FROM HUBBARD High School. Now there was one more gangbanger, a natural leader, out on the streets all day with time on his hands—more time to organize his territory and get things going with the other guys as soon as school was over.

His older brother, Tib, was by now also a Two-Six, though Tib was content to hang out on the fringe and drive the other guys around because he had his driver's license. Tib had also quit going to church, but he hadn't rejected their parents' faith in the same "in your face" way Silviu had. In fact, their parents regarded Tib as the "good boy" in contrast to "bad boy" Silviu.

The Spiridon parents' work ethic was still an influence in Silviu's life, however, and he got a sales job at Montgomery Ward in the Ford Center Shopping Center. Nattily attired, he was helpful to customers and well liked by fellow employees—the exact opposite of the gang-leader role he played after work. He even enjoyed the duplicity, playing both sides of the cards—a way to show he could get what he wanted without playing by society's rules.

Yet it was a life that could turn ugly at a moment's notice. One day, Silviu, Tib, Vamp, Troubles, and Loco took their ladies for an outing at a beach on Chicago's north side. The boys went barefoot and ran in the sand, teased the girls by pretending to throw them into Lake Michigan's frigid waters, and consumed numerous 40-ounce bottles of Old English beer. As the party wound to a close and they were getting ready to leave, several cars suddenly roared up beside them, cutting off their path.

"Kings!" Loco gasped.

Silviu sucked in his breath. Dressed in gold and black and flashing the five-pointed crown gang sign of all five fingers extended, these were undoubtedly bitter rivals—Latin Kings, eager for battle.

"They got weapons!" one of the girls screamed.

As if reading Silviu's mind, Tib suddenly floored the accelerator of their car, spun onto the grass, and roared around the Kings and down the street.

Adrenaline was high when the party-goers got safely back to their home base on the south side. And as they drove down one of the main streets, they noticed a Latin King driving alone in his van. "This is his unlucky day," Troubles said gleefully. Tib followed some distance behind the van until the driver pulled over to the curb and got out. In a moment, the Two-Six Boys were all over him, hitting him with clubs and beating him to the ground.

"That's one score settled," muttered Silviu, walking away from their bewildered rival, leaving him badly bruised, cut, and bleeding.

As mean as Silviu could be one day, he could be gentlemanly the next. The rain was really pouring down one night when his shift ended at Montgomery Ward. "Hey, Silviu," said one of his co-workers, an attractive young lady with an engaging smile, "could you and Tib give me a ride home tonight? The weather's really nasty." Her brother belonged to the Insane Popes, but that hadn't affected their friendship on the job.

"Sure," Silviu said. It wasn't far out of their way. Why make her take a bus?

A short while later, Tib and Silviu pulled up in front of the girl's house. "Thanks, guys, I really appreciate it," she said and dashed to the door in the downpour.

"Nice girl," said Tib as he pulled up to the stop sign at the next corner. Just then a bullet shattered the glass right by Tib's head, quickly followed by another. "Down!" he yelled, crouching behind the wheel and stomping on the accelerator. The car careened wildly around the corner and out of gunshot range.

"Man! That was close," Tib muttered. He was visibly shaking. Silviu stared at his brother in horror as he realized how close Tib had come to being killed. A bitter thought was forming in his mind.

"Man, what happened?" Tib said a couple of minutes later, pulling the car over until he could stop shaking.

"It was a setup, that's what," said Silviu grimly. "Those Popes had to have been waiting by that stop sign. They knew I was coming. The girl . . . "

Anger replaced the heart-stopping fear, and the two brothers dropped by Cholo's house to tell him and some of the other boys what had happened. Then they were all angry. Anger in gang terms means retaliation, the sooner the better.

"I'll take care of this," Cholo said.

"I'll go with you," Silviu replied. "After all, I was the target."

"No, you're too shook up. Let me and my brother handle it. This is one night the Popes will regret. They missed; we won't."

They didn't.

For some reason, however, the revenge mission didn't make Silviu feel any better. Something was happening that he couldn't understand. He should have been at his peak—he had power, plenty of action, respect, and no schoolwork to worry about. But not only was he not happy, but he was getting more miserable by the day. Maybe he should try to get back into school and earn his diploma, he figured. Hadn't his parents always said education was the key to success in America?

Soon thereafter, Silviu went with his mother to register at Bogan High School, another public school with a strong element of Two-Six in it. The principal looked hard at Silviu and said, "We don't want any more gang members in this school."

"Aw, man, I ain't in no gang," Silviu protested. "I just want to get my diploma and go on to college."

The principal regarded him thoughtfully. Then he excused himself and disappeared into his private office. A few minutes later, he came back. This time he didn't look at Silviu but turned to his mother. "I just called the principal of Hubbard High School," he said. Silviu's spirits sank. "Mrs. Spiridon, did you know your son is a member of the Two-Six gang? Not just a gangbanger, either, but one of the leaders! Hubbard didn't want him, and neither do we."

Mrs. Spiridon started to cry. Silviu didn't know which made him feel worse, the fact that no school would accept him as long as he was in a gang or that his mother was crying with disappointment—disappointment with *him*.

Adding to Silviu's worries, he heard from a Two-Six girl who was dating a Latin King that the Kings had a contract out on him. They wanted him out of the way.

Silviu couldn't shake the miserable feelings inside. Maybe Mr. G was right—he was heading nowhere fast. How long could he keep this thug life up? One of these days it was going to end, and he'd either be dead or in jail.

"God, You need to help me!" he cried out, unaware that God was beginning to answer the faithful prayers of his parents and the people in their church.

❖ ❖ ❖

MAYBE THE STATE'S ATTORNEY WAS RIGHT; MAYBE THEY DID NEED DERRICK Hardaway's testimony to convict his brother. But Derrick refused to testify, and after 17 hours of deliberation, the jury was deadlocked 9 to 3 on whether Cragg Hardaway was guilty in the slaying of Robert "Yummy" Sandifer. The judge was forced to declare a mistrial, and a second trial date was set.

Derrick, on the other hand, knew he was going to prison. Now the only question was, for how long?

When the sentencing hearing resumed the following week, Derrick took the witness stand and was allowed to read his own statement to the court.

"Your Honor," he began, his quiet voice directed to the judge, not the rows of spectators straining to hear, "I'm sorry we had to be here for the death of a young man. I'm sorry about what happened to him, and it shouldn't happen to him or anybody else."

Remorse. Derrick had to publicly express his sorrow and regret for what had happened to Yummy. But as I had pointed out in my own statement to this court, real remorse goes much deeper. It means an offender has turned his life around, becoming a positive person and a good influence and example to his peers—even in a correctional setting. Many witnesses had already testified that Derrick had consistently shown this kind of remorse while in the JDC. But would the judge hear it?

"Your Honor," Derrick went on, "I would like to tell you that I have changed from the boy I was."

That was certainly true. The Derrick Hardaway sitting on the witness stand that day was very different from the nervous, confused 14-year-old I'd met more than two years before.

Reading from his statement, Derrick said that his stay in the JDC had given him an opportunity to turn his life around. "I had a lot of time to think and grow," he said.

Two years is a long time when you're a teenager. And a lot had happened in those two years. For the first time in his life, Derrick played soccer. He also competed in other sports (basketball and softball); helped with the production of two plays for parents and visitors; became proficient in computer skills and tutored other students; participated in a program called "Project Build," designed to teach life skills and offer alternatives to gang involvement; and enjoyed the role of disc jockey at a talent show put on by the inmates.

"Being involved in all those programs has taught me how I can use my own talents and experiences to help and work with other people," Derrick told the judge. "I know how to think for myself now, and I'm using my head more than I did two and a half years ago."

Reporters scribbled furiously as Derrick admitted the negatives of the life he'd been living. "I know my downfalls," he read from his handwritten paper. "The people I was hanging around with and the things I was doing were part of my own downfall, because sooner or later I would have got killed or been in another courtroom. I was a person hanging out with the wrong crowd, getting into the wrong things."

No one was going to argue with Derrick about that! But not many young people caught in that downward spiral admit it.

Now, Derrick concluded, "I just want people to think of me as a man, not a killer or a criminal—a man who has changed his life for the better. I made a decision to be part of the answer and not the problem. I am truly sorry for what happened. I want to get a job and go back to school because street life is not for me."

It was a good statement and, I believe, an honest one. But would it make any difference?

The defense argued passionately for the judge to give Derrick the minimum sentence of 20 years, since the Hardaway brothers had been acting on the orders of higher-ranking gang members and Derrick had already demonstrated he was capable of being rehabilitated and becoming a productive citizen.

The prosecution argued just as passionately for the maximum sentence of 100 years "to deter others from the same crime." The state's attorney thundered, "In today's society, where everybody wants to escape responsibility, we cannot allow an 11-year-old boy to be executed."

The arguments were over. The judge turned to Derrick and said, "You said you want to get a job, go on to school. You'll have an opportunity to do these things. Mr. Sandifer will not. He will not have an opportunity to do anything again because of the actions of you and your brother."

The black-robed figure raised his gavel and pronounced his sentence: 45 years. *Bang.*

❖ ❖ ❖

DAY AFTER DAY DRAGGED BY AT THE COOK COUNTY JAIL, BUT NONE OF John Johnson's boys showed up during visiting hours to slip him any money. *Man! What's going on out there, anyway?* he wondered. He knew his drug spots were pulling in several thousand a night. Had someone else moved in and taken over? Or were his own boys giving him the shaft?

A guy had to have money in the jail, whether he wanted some smokes, a few blunts (marijuana cigarettes), or to help persuade someone to do him a favor. And if it wasn't coming from the outside, he'd have to make money on the inside the only way he knew how—selling drugs.

Getting the drugs wasn't the problem. A little money slipped into the hands of the right correctional staffers convinced them to look the other way when certain visitors arrived. The problem was how to move the smuggled drugs from point A to point B inside the jail. The units were small, and the various units didn't often get to mix. Always the entrepreneur, however, John was interested in selling to the broadest number of customers.

"Hey, Gee-Gee," said a jailmate one day, "you hear about the Friday night youth service? Some dudes from Youth for Christ or some outfit like that put it on. They come every Friday, and anyone can go if they want."

Annoyed, John gave the talker a bored look.

The young man shrugged. "Hey, at least it's a chance to see some of the guys from the other units," he said.

John's eyes came open. "Guys from the other units, you said?" A slow smile spread across his face. "Hey, I think I'll go with you this Friday."

The plan worked perfectly. When our staff came to John's unit to call out any guys interested in attending the service, the young New Breed lined up with the others for the orderly march to the makeshift chapel. He sat in the back on the gym-type bleachers and listened politely to the middle-aged white dude preach a nice message from the Bible about the fact that God hates sin but loves the sinner. Afterward, several young inmates milled around, talking to Mr. G, as they called the white dude, and some of the other YFC staff. Bibles came out to look up a text or search for an answer; a few heads bent together in prayer.

Meanwhile, in the back row, a few guys gathered casually around Gee-Gee Johnson and transacted a little business before being herded back to their units.

John was a regular at the Friday night service for the next couple of weeks, and business was going good. When Chaplain Ron DeRose came by the unit and announced a Tuesday night Bible study, John thought, *Why not? That'll just double my delivery options.*

That night, John joined the circle of guys gathered around Ron, but he sat toward the back so he wouldn't call attention to himself. He listened politely to the man, biding his time until he could make his deliveries.

As he listened, however, the Bible study leader seemed to be talking about him, as if he knew John from the inside out. " . . . So maybe you feel life has handed you a raw deal," Ron said. "People you trusted have let you down, or maybe someone you loved got taken out of your life and left you feeling all alone. So, you're thinking, why not stick it to the system? Why not go gangbangin' and get yours any ol' way you can?"

Heads were nodding, accompanied by heartfelt murmurs of "That's right, man" and "You got it." John felt the man had hit the nail right on the head. He'd lost two of the people he loved most in the world—his stepdad and his brother. He'd tried to make it in school, but he'd been expelled for a fight he hadn't started. He'd even tried to work with the system by starting an auto repair business, but his competitors had made sure he couldn't win. Why not be down for the gang and do whatever it took to get what he wanted?

"But have you ever stopped long enough to ask where you're going?" DeRose asked. "Look around you. If you're honest, you'll admit that most gangbangers end up dead or in jail. Your own situation, sitting here in Cook County, should give you a clue where you're headed. If you beat your rap and go back out on the street, what's going to keep you from ending up here again . . . or in a casket?"

The young men were silent.

"And if you're really honest with yourself," Ron went on, "you'll admit that the loneliness you feel inside hasn't gone away, even in the gang. Everyone says they're down for the gang—but in reality, everyone's really down for himself."

John nearly gasped in recognition. Man, that was true. He was out to get *his*, and no one had better get in his way. He was using the gang—just as it was using him.

"But I'm here to tell you about a Friend who will stick closer to you than a brother," said DeRose, opening his Bible. "His name is Jesus. He created you, He knows you, and He's never going to leave you, whether you're out on the streets or in a prison cell. If you want respect, He'll give you the kind of respect where you can look in the mirror and respect the person you see there. And man, has He got a future for you!"

John was listening hard. It was as if the man had been following him around or something. Did God really care about him? It sure didn't seem like it when his stepdad and brother both got shot. But something—Someone—was trying to change him. And suddenly John realized he'd been wanting to change for a long time. It was a new feeling for him, a feeling that there was something *more* he'd been missing. What did he want? Had he ever thought beyond the next day or the next week? Maybe a long time ago he had, when he was a little kid and had dreams about what he wanted to be and do when he grew up. But now he was just trying to get by and do it in style. Where was he going? Nowhere.

Ron DeRose was now explaining how Jesus had given up His own life to save ours. *Maybe,* John thought, *I ought to do some investigatin' on God.*

He was back in his cell before he realized he hadn't delivered the drugs he'd taken to the Bible study. He looked at the plastic bags in his hand and suddenly didn't care. In fact, he realized he didn't care if he ever sold drugs again. With a shrug of his shoulders, he flushed them all down the toilet.

That night in his bunk, he thought about all Ron DeRose had said. In the dark, he slid out of his bunk, dropped down on his knees, and cried out in his heart, "God, if You'll have me, I want to be one of Your boys. I give my heart to You and ask You to be my Savior and Lord."

As John rolled back under his blanket, something felt different. The old thrill of being chief of a gang just didn't seem exciting anymore. A new hope, the possibility of a new life, seemed much more exciting. He knew he was walking into an unknown future, but now he had the Lord walking with him.

❖ ❖ ❖

"LISTEN UP, GUYS," I CALLED AS I WALKED INTO THE SCHOOL WING OF THE county jail one evening and noticed that most of the 250 young men were watching a movie on TV about Al Capone. "You can stay here and learn how to be like Al Capone—but be sure to note how his life ended—or you can come to youth chapel and learn to be more like Jesus Christ. Capone or Jesus, take your choice!"

We had one of our largest turnouts that night.

Our chapel services face stiff competition: movies or sporting events on TV, phone calls home, cleaning clothes for visiting day, and card games, to name a few. But most challenging are the informal gang meetings. They're supposedly banned, but as long as the residents outnumber the guards nearly 80 to 1, underground meetings continue.

The Vice Lords consider us direct competition for the loyalty of their boys, which, indeed, we are. So they schedule their cell-block gatherings for the same time as our youth service. And they subtly—and sometimes pointedly—pressure their guys not to attend chapel.

The Vice Lord leader on the wing at that time was a suburban youth named Derrick Stafford. We quickly knew where each other stood: We both wanted the guys, only I couldn't and wouldn't control them the way he did. He kept a number of guys from coming, making me very unhappy. He made it clear he had no more use for me than I had for him.

What I had no way of knowing was the internal pressure Derrick was under. His court case wasn't going well, and he was facing a possible 60 years for the shooting (though not killing) of a young man who had testified against Derrick's older brother in a murder case.

One day when things seemed to be going particularly badly for him, Derrick called a meeting of all his boys and stunned them by asking, "Where's all this gangbangin' gotten us? Some of you will never see the streets again. You're facin' murder charges and all sorts of things. Me, I'm lookin' at 60 years. Can any of you name one good thing the 'organization' has done for you?"

Nobody responded. The directness of Derrick's challenge left them speechless. When no one spoke up, he continued, "That's what I thought. Well, I'm quittin'. This is it. Tonight I'm out."

The guys couldn't believe what they were hearing. Comments peppered him: "You can't do that. We need you." "Hey, what do we do without a leader?" and, interestingly, "What are you gonna do now?"

"Do?" he answered with a shrug. "Guess I'll go down to the chapel service. There may be somethin' in it I've missed."

So Derrick walked into the middle of our youth service, unexpected and not entirely welcome. I didn't know if he'd come to argue, break up the meeting, or check out who was there for later reprisals. The last thing I considered was that he might have come to really listen. The other boys were as amazed to see him as I was and no doubt had the same questions.

He sat quietly on the side through the service and came up afterward to greet me in our first friendly conversation. Many more would follow.

Derrick told me he had lived in the western suburbs, those supposedly safe retreats from city violence. One day while walking to high school with a friend, a passing car stopped. The driver got out and, without a word, killed Derrick's friend with a bullet to his head.

That tragic incident so alarmed Derrick's family that they arranged for him to go and stay with relatives in Phoenix, Arizona. He did well there but found it boring. "There I was out in the corn fields with the cattle," he said with a laugh, "while my buddies back home were collectin' big money, drivin' fancy cars, and makin' it with the young ladies. They kept sending me letters and pictures. That did it—danger or not, I was goin' home."

Back in the Chicago area, Derrick quickly fit into the fast-paced lifestyle. A few weeks later, events took a sudden turn when his older brother, a powerful leader on the streets, was arrested for murder and then sentenced to 44 years in prison.

The leadership role in the organization fell to Derrick, and he worked hard to earn the respect of his brother's soldiers. First, there was unfinished business. A guy named Kenyon had testified against Derrick's brother, and that had be avenged. It didn't matter that the boy who died in the case was Kenyon's brother—Kenyon had taken on the Staffords, and that could not be tolerated.

Derrick went gunning for Kenyon, found him standing with some friends inside a convenience store, and blew the windows out of the store. Derrick was soon in jail.

As we got to know each other, I recognized Derrick's innate intelligence and leadership abilities. I wanted desperately to see his gifts used for positive goals, not gang leadership, and he started moving in that direction while he was in the jail and when, to the surprise of some and the dismay of Kenyon, he got out. With him opening the doors for us, my staff and I soon met every street youth in his area. They respected him, so they accepted us.

He took other positive steps, too—enrolling in community college, helping in our ministry, and participating in several neighborhood programs. He even changed his mind about Kenyon. One day he learned that Kenyon was being attacked for some reason by members of his own gang, so Derrick rescued him and saw that Kenyon got treated at a hospital emergency room. Later, when Kenyon was ready to go home and his family was away, Derrick took Kenyon to his own home and called me to come over. Kenyon was about the last person I ever expected to find at the Staffords', but there he was—bandaged, recovering, and extremely grateful.

The road wasn't easy for Derrick, however. One day he was arrested for having a gun in a store—an accusation even the store manager denied. Another youth admitted he had been the one who stashed the gun in the store. But the police lost the young man's confession, and the judge chose not to believe the store manager, even though he insisted Derrick was nowhere near where police found the weapon.

Derrick returned to prison, discouraged and troubled. A year later, he was finally released. On his third day home—driving to church, at my encouragement—he was stopped by police and held 18 hours "for investigation." He was released without charges, but for Derrick, it was the last straw. He concluded that the whole world was against him and God didn't care.

We communicate well to this day, but we're not on the same path. Derrick's bitterness led him back to the gang, with its lure of easy money, power, and fancy cars.

We still have a warm friendship and an ongoing ministry with a whole array of his friends, however, so some good has come from the tragedy. I know God is longsuffering and patient, and I pray earnestly for my friend and his younger brother, who is, sadly, following in his footsteps. The enemy of our souls knows how effective Derrick would be if he really turned to the Lord. But Derrick reminds me that every inch of this planet and every person on it are battlegrounds between the Lord and the power of evil. I think I have some understanding of what Jesus must have felt when the rich young ruler came face to face with the truth and then walked away. There's no record that the young ruler ever came back to Jesus, but I pray that Derrick will.

Nine

❖ ❖ ❖

THE ADULT PRISON IN JOLIET TO WHICH XAVIER was transferred was a different world, one dominated by violent power struggles between rival gangs. There, Xavier felt a new kind of fear; he couldn't trust anyone. In Joliet, disputes weren't settled with fistfights but with shanks (homemade knives). To survive, Xavier believed he couldn't show any weakness, not even for a moment. He developed an attitude of cold indifference, though deep inside that wasn't how he wanted to act any longer. He made a seven-inch-long shank in his cell and carried it whenever he felt tension in the yard.

As the Bible says, however, "'There is no peace . . . for the wicked'" (Isaiah 57:21), and the route of surviving by being tougher than the next guy always has its price.

One day a guard tried to handcuff a Latin King member because he had talked to a "brother" in segregation. Xavier quickly organized several other Kings into a "security line" to keep the guard away. The guard wisely backed down, but once everyone was back in his cell, the guards came around and took each man involved in the incident to the "hole." When Xavier had been segregated from the general population in the youth prison, he'd at least had a cellmate. But here, the hole was true solitary confinement.

. Alone with nothing to do for hours and days on end, Xavier had to face himself. He didn't like what he discovered. In fact, he hated what he had become. The long, lonely hours burned that emptiness more and more into his mind. But his self-loathing did not yet bear the fruit of genuine repentance. When Xavier came out of the hole four months later, he was much more sober and disciplined but not changed in heart. His resentment toward the system that was "oppressing" him had galvanized into a deeper dedication to the gang.

The Latin Kings' leadership noticed this, and Xavier was given more responsibilities. He began to move up in command, and in just a short time he had become the third-highest-ranking gang member in that prison.

The Joliet penitentiary is like most American prisons: Gangs have considerable power. The prison administrators know this but can't change it. Instead, they've reached an accommodation with gang leaders to generally keep things running smoothly. The staff want peace and order; the gangs want power and drugs. Both sides get their desires. Only when the balance of power is disrupted is a prison in danger of blowing up.

Under this regime, gang leaders handle day-to-day discipline. One day a guy named Jamie was transferred into Joliet. He was a Latin King, but his story had arrived by grapevine even before he did: In his previous prison, he had "burned" some of his Latin King brothers on a drug deal. Now he had come to Joliet to get away from potential retaliation. The Kings in Joliet pretended ignorance, made him feel welcome, got him commissary supplies, and set him at ease.

Then one day one of them said, "Hey, Jamie, we understand you've been a hit man for the Nation in other joints."

"Yeah, man, you heard right," he responded.

"Well, we was wonderin' if you'd do somethin' for us. Bein' new here, no one would suspect you, and you could get away with it real easy."

Jamie shrugged.

"See, there's this guy named Cuba . . ."

The next day, Jamie met Cuba on the stairs and laid his head open with a pipe, then escaped before the guards arrived. Cuba required 27 stitches in the hospital.

Jamie eluded the guards, but once he'd done their dirty work for them, the gang got him later that same day, on the same stairs, with the same pipe. He ended up in the prison hospital with injuries much worse than Cuba's.

The gang rules, especially in jail. And whenever Xavier thought about the need to change his life, to get off the destructive path he was on, events like the one between Jamie and Cuba reminded him that the gang was not to be crossed.

In the fall, a series of events triggered tensions between the Latin Kings and the Gangster Disciples. With the balance of power unsettled, the gangs went on red alert. Security was intensified, and no gang member walked anywhere alone. Wherever Xavier or any of the other leaders went, three members with shanks walked in front and three followed behind. No one talked in line, and if anyone came close to their line in the chow hall or elsewhere, he was stopped. Even guards were kept away from the leadership.

One day when the Kings were going down the steps as they left the chow hall, a GD tried to walk up. When he was pushed back, he made some cocky remark disrespecting the Kings. Instantly, several Kings moved on him.

Guards closed in, and a full-scale melee was quickly under way. Xavier jumped into the fray, grabbing a guard. Without thinking about what he was doing, he began beating the guard, trying to hurt him seriously. Xavier connected with a solid right, and blood shot from the guard's nose. The blood seemed to bring on a fury, and Xavier's hatred for the system focused on this man in full force. If he had had a shank, he would have stabbed the guard.

Suddenly he was grabbed from behind in a choke hold that caused him to nearly black out. This second guard held on until Xavier was cuffed and the fight ended.

Immediately, Xavier was thrown into the hole. When he came up for official discipline, he was sentenced to a year across the board: a year in the hole and a year of good time lost. He was also given a negative transfer to the Pontiac prison—one of the toughest penitentiaries in Illinois.

❖ ❖ ❖

WHILE BOYCE ALLEN GRIEVED OVER THE DEATH OF TWO OF HIS NEWFOUND brothers in Christ, his stepbrother Walter Davis was also making a new life for himself. He was home one night when he tuned in to the late news and flopped on the couch to relax a bit before bed. Then he sat bolt upright. A cop had been killed on the west side checking out a burglary right across the street from the police station. Three guys were charged, and one of them was critically wounded and might not survive.

When the details came out, Walter was stunned. The group of guys had been his crowd. He had hung with them. If the shooting had happened a few months earlier, he would have been right there with them—and if not dead, possibly wounded and certainly charged with murder. He broke out in a cold sweat. *If I hadn't met the Lord . . .,* he thought.

The critically wounded gangster was Clyde Cowley, age 16, and he'd taken seven bullets. He had been Walter's friend. When a shaken Walter called me, he asked if I'd visit Clyde. "I don't know if he'll make it," Walter said, "but if you see him, tell him I sent you. He needs the Lord."

A few days later, I sat in a hospital room talking with a badly wounded, scared, emotional teenager. He was thin as a rail, and all sorts of emergency equipment stood around the bed, with tubes running in and out of his body. I could hardly see him for the bandages everywhere, and I wasn't sure he would live out the day. But he was conscious, and to my surprise, he could hear and even talk a little.

"I'm Gordon McLean," I told him. "I work with Youth for Christ's Juvenile Justice Ministry, and your friend Walter Davis sent me to see you."

I was flabbergasted at his response. "Thank you," he whispered, "*thank you* for coming to see me. Walter sent you? Man, that means a lot!"

I handed him a Bible, praying silently that he'd recover enough to read it. I told him briefly that the Lord loved him and was eager to forgive him. "Can I pray with you?" I asked. With what little strength he had, he grasped my hand. Tears flowing, I asked the Lord to heal him and strengthen him. I always believe you're supposed to pray in faith, but . . . I didn't have any that day. I never expected to see him alive again.

I had to leave on a trip right after that, but a week later, I went back to see Clyde—this time in the medical ward at the JDC. I couldn't believe the improvement. He still had tubes stuck in him and was in pain, but he was greatly improved physically and in spirit. The doctors, nurses, and attendants at the center were giving him excellent care.

Clyde was glad to see me. He carefully eased himself into a sitting position and directed me to a chair by the bed. Contrary to the advice of his court-appointed lawyer to not talk with anyone about his case, he wanted to fill me in. He hadn't wanted to be with his two older partners that fateful night, he said. They came to his home and picked him up, pressing him to go. As with so many tragedies, this one unfolded more and more as the evening went on, finally ending at the house where the officer was killed.

"I didn't even have a gun," Clyde said. "These wounds are from my friends shootin' wildly. I thought we were just goin' in to see a guy and pick up some money he owed one of the boys. Then all hell broke loose. The cops were there in an instant from across the street, and bullets were flyin' everywhere. Suddenly, a cop was down and I'm shot to bits."

I knew that the seriousness of the case—a policeman killed—gave him little leeway in the courts. In Illinois, as in most states, if you're *with* someone who commits a crime, you're usually found equally guilty, even though the law requires more than mere presence. Only two ways out seem to work: Did you try to stop the crime, or did you call the police right away? Without those elements, the charge stands, and it will usually stick in court.

Clyde had been with the two older men, and he couldn't have stopped the crime or called the police when he was nearly dead on the floor beside the fatally wounded officer. Nevertheless, he was charged with first-degree murder. His only break: In Illinois, 16-year-olds are not eligible for the death penalty.

Week by week, Clyde's wounds healed. Miraculously, none of the seven bullets he took hit a critical area. As time went on, some caring family and church friends visited him, wrote to him, and prayed for him. As a young boy, he had gone to church and given his life to the Lord, and he knew what that commitment meant. But I sensed some hesitation to recommit his life to Jesus.

One day, I faced him with his reluctance.

"I want to recommit my life to the Lord," he said, "but what if people say I'm just doin' it because I almost died or have a big court case? What if they think I just want God to get me out of something?"

"Well, do you?"

"No, I don't. He saved my life, and now I'm healthier inside than I've been in years. The court case is something I have to go through. I'm sure God will be with me, but I don't plan on gettin' out of anything. I just want to do what's right."

"Clyde, never do or not do something based on what people might say," I counseled. "God is the One you need to please, not the cynics and critics. Listen to them and you'll never do anything."

A few minutes later, Clyde prayed and I got to listen in. A hurting, broken young man told God the truth and asked for forgiveness and strength. The prayer was earnest and sincere. I felt I was being let in on a deeply genuine, sacred encounter between the Lord and one of His repentant children.

As the weeks went by, Clyde continued to heal and to grow and mature spiritually. He simply was not the same young man who, a few months earlier, had been a mixed-up dope dealer and gunslinger.

Once he had physically recovered and turned 17, Clyde was moved to a maximum-security cell in the county jail. As his trial approached, his lawyer sought to make a deal: Plead guilty to murder, testify against the other two men, and he could serve 35 years.

Clyde was not enthusiastic about any deal. Without immunity from prosecution and relocation in a witness protection program with a new identity, he could soon be dead for snitching.

Another deal was proposed by his attorney: Just plead guilty in return for a 55-year sentence. Again, Clyde was not eager to have it pursued, though his lawyer tried to interest the state. No such deal would be struck, however.

Clyde was guilty under the accountability law.

No one said he had fired the gun that fateful night. In fact, he had been severely wounded by his partners. But he had been at the scene of the crime, so the jury was told he was legally responsible for all that happened. They found him guilty, and he was sentenced to life in prison without parole.

The gunman received a death sentence.

❖ ❖ ❖

"HEY, SILVIU," CHOLO SAID. "YOU HEAR ABOUT THAT BOOT CAMP THING called Lincoln Challenge? It's run by the National Guard—kinda like the military, except it's for kids like us who need a second chance. At the end of six months, you got your G.E.D. and some money toward college."

"No kiddin'?" said Silviu. *A program I could get into even after bein' kicked out of school?* he thought. *A chance to get my high-school diploma?* The military thing sounded kind of cool, too—uniforms, camaraderie, tough guys . . . that was right down his alley. Gangbangers were tough—they had to be to survive. No problem there.

"For real," Cholo said. "I'm thinkin' about goin'. Krazy J and George, too. Even Shyster's thinkin' about it." Shyster was their chief. "All five of us could go together, have a good time. They got girls there, too."

This was sounding better all the time.

The five Two-Six Boys, including Silviu, registered for Lincoln Challenge and were assured that if they stuck with the program, they'd earn their G.E.D. By the time they boarded the National

Guard bus in Chicago and headed for Rantoul downstate, their spirits were high.

This is great! Silviu thought, looking around the bus at the cadets—several of them from rival gangs—all talking loudly and laughing together, having a good time. A big African-American sergeant in uniform sat in the front, ignoring what was going on behind him.

When the bus pulled into a parking lot and lurched to a stop, however, the sergeant rose, turned around, and bellowed at the top of his lungs, "Shut up and listen, punks!" A tirade of swear words, insults, and threats peppered his instructions. "Get out of this bus!" "Get that luggage!" "Wipe that grin off your face! You think this is funny?" "Don't speak unless you're spoken to!" "All you street rats— attention!" "Parade rest!" "You! I don't like your attitude! Drop and give me 25!" "One at a time, spread-eagle against the bus! Anybody who has drugs or a weapon is history!"

Anger and shock surged hotly through Silviu's mind. On the streets, he and the boys never took disrespect from anyone, much less let themselves be ordered around. Now here was this over-stuffed Smoky Bear throwing insults left and right and ordering them around as if they were five-year-olds. If this bag of wind thought they were going to stand here and take this—

The sergeant seemed to read his mind. Glaring right at Silviu, he barked, "This is the way it's going to be! You'll do what I say, when I say it, and not before. This ain't no nursery school. This is a *military* school. That means I own you—mind, body, and soul— for the next six months. You'll eat when I say, go to the bathroom when I say, exercise when I say, sleep when I say. If any of you street rats don't like it, you can turn around and get right back on that bus goin' to Chicago. *Now!*"

A low murmur ran through the disgruntled recruits, and feet shuffled. Then a handful of guys let loose with a barrage of expletives and got back on the bus.

Silviu's mind was racing. Forget the good-time party he and Cholo had imagined. Maybe he should get out while the getting was good. But something in his gut rebelled against letting this mean-faced sergeant win. The man had thrown down a challenge. Silviu wasn't one to run from that.

He glanced over at Cholo. Cholo, the chief, and the other Two-Six Boys didn't look too sure. But Silviu straightened his back and hardened his eyes. He would stick with the program if it killed him.

The challenge began with a tough schedule: Get up early, do chores, work all morning, go to school all afternoon, do marching drills, and clean up the living quarters. A guy didn't have even a minute to call his own during the day—no TV, no phone, no snacks. For Silviu, just coming off the streets, where he had pretty much done what he wanted, this came close to his idea of hell.

The staff kept everybody off balance, too. The cadets would be all ready to fall into bed, and here would come the team leaders, yelling for everyone to get outside for exercise. While they were outside, officials would search the lockers for contraband and bring in dogs to sniff for drugs.

What really bothered Silviu, however, was the way they messed with his mind. He'd be going down a hallway, see a team leader in uniform, and jump into parade rest as he'd been instructed. But the sergeant would get right in his face and bark, "Did I say you could look at me? Drop and give me 20!"

Silviu would groan inside as he dropped to the floor and did 20 pushups. He had quickly learned he had to ask permission for every move. "Corpsman Spiridon would like permission to recover," he'd say.

"Permission to recover granted."

Gratefully, Silviu would get to his feet and resume parade rest. "Where are you heading, corpsman?" the sergeant would demand.

Silviu would look down and say something like, "Kitchen duty, sir!"

Again the sergeant would get in his face and shout, "Why don't you look at me when I ask you a question? Drop and give me 20!" There was no way to get it right—ever.

At night, he lay in his bunk and wondered how long he could take it. Cholo, Shyster, and the chief had lasted only a few weeks, then packed up and went home. Tough street guys were breaking down every day.

I asked You for a second chance, he ranted angrily at God. *Why'd You put me here?*

One night he dug out the Bible his mother had packed in his suitcase and started to read. Night after night thereafter, he read. It was something familiar to cling to, and suddenly the words he'd heard at home and in church as a child sounded brand-new. Things Mr. G had said to him seemed to fit. "Without me [God] you can do nothing." "If you want to save your life, you must lose it." "I [Jesus] am the Way, the Truth, and the Life."

One night after reading his Bible, Silviu fell down beside his bed in the darkened bunk room and prayed in desperation, "Lord, You know I'm really messed up. I've gone a long way from where You want me. I've done a lot of crazy, terrible things. The only place I'm headin' is prison. I need You in my life or I won't make it—here or anywhere else. Forgive me! Save me!"

Finally, Silviu stood up and was startled by the lightness he felt. The load of oppression that had been weighing him down had disappeared. All that shame . . . all that guilt . . . they were gone! He felt like shouting and praising the Lord. But he waited until he got permission to make a phone call, and then he called his parents. "Mom . . . Dad," he said, his voice choking, "I want to tell you something. I gave my heart to Jesus the other night. . . . No, no, I'm not foolin' with you! I'm sorry, Mom and Dad—sorry for everything. But I'm a new person now—just like the Bible says. No, don't call Mr. G. I want to tell him myself."

During a visit home, Silviu told his friend Cholo that he was down for Jesus now.

Cholo received this news with some uneasiness. "What's this mean for the Two-Six, man?" he asked.

"I don't know," Silviu said. "Don't say nothin' to nobody yet. I gotta do some thinkin' about that."

"What about the Rev?" Cholo asked. "You told him yet?"

Silviu grinned. "Yeah, talked to him last night. He got so excited, I thought he was goin' to turn into a Pentecostal on the spot!"

Back at Lincoln Challenge, Silviu kept reading the Bible. Soon a couple of other guys wanted to know what he was doing, and he said, "Checking out what this Jesus dude had to say." They asked if they could sit in. Before long, the impromptu Bible study had moved into the lounge, and 40 guys—girls, too—were showing up.

The staff didn't know how to react. At first they suspected an illegal gang meeting was going on. But that couldn't be it because known rivals from different gangs were reading the Bible, talking about its message, and even praying together. The officers were still scratching their heads when graduation day arrived.

That day was a high point for the Spiridon family. They applauded wildly when the one-star general, head of the Illinois National Guard, handed Silviu his certificate of graduation and a $2,200 scholarship toward a college education. And when Silviu stepped off the bus in Chicago, he not only had his G.E.D., but also a strong determination to go to college and train for a career. Even that didn't guarantee he would make it, of course. Boot-camp graduates can end up back on the streets if they don't receive follow-up or mentoring. But Silviu came home with something else as well—a personal relationship with Jesus Christ.

❖ ❖ ❖

ON A CHICAGO-STYLE SPRING AFTERNOON—SUNNY AND CLEAR, WITH A stiff breeze blowing off Lake Michigan—I made my way to see Ernestine Hardaway, the mother of Derrick and Cragg. The day after Derrick's sentencing, jury selection had begun for Cragg's second trial. Now the elder brother's verdict was in: guilty of first-degree murder.

Two sons, both still teenagers. Both convicted of murder. Both facing long prison sentences. How in the world does a mother cope with that?

As I drove into the Roseland neighborhood, I was impressed again by the neat, brick bungalows and clean, tree-shaded streets. This was no slum or seedy ghetto. Rosedale is a blue-collar neighborhood, mostly African American, of hard-working families who own their homes. Ernestine is a public-school teacher, and her daughter, Katrice, the boys' older sister, was working on her master's degree in TV and radio at Columbia College.

Yet even in this pleasant neighborhood, the lure of drug money and gang power sucks young people from decent homes into its grip.

I was a little early for my appointment, so I drove around the community until I found Dauphin Avenue, a quiet street running north and south, parallel to the Illinois Central Railroad tracks that lay atop a grassy embankment. I glanced at the signs of the streets deadending at Dauphin: 106th . . . 107th . . . 108th. And there it was, the pedestrian tunnel at 108th and Dauphin that went under the train tracks—the place where Yummy Sandifer was killed by members of his own gang. Bright lights lit the tunnel even in the daylight—a new addition since the tragedy.

A few minutes later, I called at the Hardaway home. Mr. Hardaway was working on his car in the driveway. He had always been cordial with me, but never eager to talk. Mrs. Hardaway was just getting home from work, but she and Katrice graciously agreed to catch supper at the local fast-food restaurant while we visited.

We had the place nearly to ourselves. I was relieved. It would have been difficult to talk about "murder one" with the usual burger crowd hanging over our shoulders.

Ernestine and Katrice Hardaway are both petite, attractive women. I teased them that their tall, lanky boys had stolen all the height in the family. But our talk turned quickly to more-serious matters: How was their family coping with having two young sons locked up in prison?

The mother's answer startled me. "I'm counting my blessings," she said simply. "I'm sorry it took a tragedy like this to make me realize how much God has done for me and my family. I was taking a lot for granted. But now I try to thank Him every day for His goodness."

Here was a mother who saw her sons only once a week—on Sunday, visiting day at the jails. She had sat through scores of hearings, the three trials, and Derrick's sentencing. Cragg would be sentenced in a few days. This mother loved her children, was married to their father, and had raised her kids as best she could. Their adolescence was rocky, but wasn't that to be expected? Then came the suspicions, finally the knowledge, that her sons were involved with the Black Disciples.

At last came that terrible day when the police picked up both her teenage sons, charged them with murder, and took them away— not for a week or two but for long, agonizing months that had now stretched into years. Even under the best possible circumstances, Derrick would be 36 before he became eligible for parole, and Cragg might be locked up even longer.

And she was counting her *blessings?*

"God is the One in charge," she said softly. "If the boys have to spend years in prison, then that's where God wants them. I may not understand why, but He has a plan."

"I love my brothers; I always will," said Katrice, a captivating person with a wealth of talent and ambition. "I'll always be there for them. That doesn't mean I condone anything they've done wrong, but I pray for them and know they can and will come out of this as better men. I'm already glad to see the good changes in their lives."

Mrs. Hardaway admitted that it hurt every time she picked up a newspaper or turned on the TV and saw another story describing her sons as cold-blooded killers. "I could never have gotten through all this if I didn't know the Lord was with me," she said. "I pity any person who tries to go through a deep crisis alone, without God. That can turn disaster into despair."

No despair weakened her strong voice, though. Her faith was solid in spite of—maybe even because of—the horrible, ongoing ordeal. I had the feeling that I wasn't there to encourage her so much as I was to learn how she could encourage others.

"What would you tell other parents who are concerned about their children possibly being involved in a gang?" I asked.

She thought for a moment before answering, "To be alert to things that just don't fit, that don't make sense—and then follow through. Cragg was driving friends' cars. I should have insisted on knowing which friends, and why, and made sure he had a driver's license. Then the boys had money, but when I asked where they got it, they said it came from doing yard work in the neighborhood. I should have asked, 'Whose yard? What address?'—and then followed through.

"But, like many parents, I wanted to believe my boys, so I just took their word for it. They took advantage of my trust. Oh, sure, they'd come in at night when I asked them to. But once I was asleep, they snuck out the back door to hang with their friends on the street. If I'd followed through on the little things that didn't fit, I would have learned much earlier that their newfound affluence and access to cars were coming from gang activity, not a job."

I nodded. "That's much like kids who get caught up using drugs," I said. "Parents are hesitant to react to the changes in appearance, lifestyle, friends, and attitude that practically shout that something is seriously wrong with their children."

"We were kind of lulled into thinking little could go wrong," Katrice added. "Our family had its problems, but no more so than many others. We live in a nice neighborhood, with good schools. We didn't think the boys would turn to gangs and drug sales—not where we live."

Mrs. Hardaway sounded another important note: "Parents really have to keep the lines of communication open."

"You've got that right!" Katrice agreed, nodding vigorously.

"Parents should talk to their kids," her mother continued, "and also listen. Let them know they can tell you anything, discuss any hurt or problem or failure and you won't interrupt. Let them know that you won't accept wrong behavior, but you *will* always accept them. Hold to a firm line of expected good behavior, even if you're the only parent in the neighborhood doing it. But also let your children know that you love them no matter what."

I've said similar things to parent groups. It sounds easy. But from what I've observed, finding time to just be with and talk with your kids, being consistent in your discipline, *and* showing unconditional love are some of the biggest challenges in parenting teens.

"Looking back on it now, I see things I wish I could change," Mrs. Hardaway admitted. "I would have gotten the boys involved regularly in church at a young age. That should have been a bigger priority in our home, but we were all busy with different work schedules and activities. Somehow, reading the Bible together was one of those things we were going to get around to eventually, but we never did."

Her honest admission didn't mean she was wallowing in guilt, however. "I'm a schoolteacher, and I enjoy so much inspiring young people to learn and make right choices. What happened to my boys can't be hidden from my students—not when it's a major story day after day. But I can use their experience to talk to my pupils about their life and future, and I believe many of them listen seriously."

Katrice nodded again. "It's scary raising kids today," she added. "Things have changed even since I was little and growing up. But I hope what has happened to my brothers will help another boy or girl or another family find a better way."

"I believe God is using this to strengthen our own home," her mother continued. "I hope and pray that all we've been through will bring their father to a place of faith in the Lord for his life." Then she smiled a smile that radiated peace and hope. "Our family will stick together through this. We always have and always will. I believe my sons will be out of prison in God's time, but not before God finishes molding and maturing them. They are in His hands. They know it and I know it, and that's an excellent place for them to be."

Yes, I agreed silently, *it is an excellent place for Cragg and Derrick to be—in God's hands.* I drew a letter from my pocket and handed it to Ernestine Hardaway. "I got this letter from Cragg a few days ago," I said. "It's written to other kids out on the street, but I thought you might like to read it."

I sat back in the molded-plastic seat while mother and daughter read Cragg's letter.

I'm 18, and . . . I've been found guilty of first-degree murder. The reason I write to you all is because Gordon is a very close friend of mine, and so all of you don't turn on the road I'm headed down.

Those who are gang affiliated and those who are thinking of joining—it's a nowhere destiny. Your fellow gang brothers claim it's much love and say they will die for you. But just think: When you come to the mob, the question is, what can you do for them, not what you believe the mob can do for you.

Many guys are confused and misled by gangs, and before they become aware of the true situation, it's too late. Then they end up in the situation where I am at now. They don't tell you what happens. After so long, the guys who you claim to belong to fade out, and the girls, too. Then you're left with your family, if you have any, and God.

The system is not designed to help you but to lock you down and keep you in. And once you are in, it is hard to get out.

Without God there is no help. He has to come first, everything else second. A lot of things happen for a reason. My incarceration saved me from death and has given me a new direction with the Lord. Most important, I now have a peace that whether I'm in jail or out can't be taken away from me.

I thought gangbanging, making it with girls, and selling drugs would make me happy and give me peace. Instead, I found myself looking over my shoulder and running from the cops, the stickup man, and from myself. My destiny was hell. But now that I have God in my life and know the Lord, it's not like that anymore. I've learned more about God with Gordon in two years, now going on three, than I knew before in my whole life.

If you're reading this, would you be willing to pray with me? Like this: "God, I have sinned, and I want to put You now at the head of my life. Forgive my sins, and I accept Jesus as my personal Savior. Please mold me into a better person, and give me a new mind, heart, wisdom, and strength to face each day. I want to be acceptable in Your presence. In Jesus' name I pray, amen."

I prayed like that in the detention center, and so did my brother, Derrick, quite on his own. I was nowhere around him at the time. It was the start of a new life for both of us. Perfect? Far from it. We both have a long way to grow, but we've started.

Maybe you're thinking: Why should I give my life to God? Just answer one question: Where will you be when you get where you're going? If you don't like your honest answer, let the Lord change it. Derrick and I know God can and will do that.

Your friend,
Cragg Hardaway

Cragg's mother looked up from the letter, her eyes moist. "Thank you," she said softly.

A few weeks later, I was at Cragg's sentencing: 60 years in the penitentiary. The judge said, "If it deters just one person from doing what you did and it saves one life, then I've served my purpose."

I watched the sheriff's deputies take Cragg away. *Would* this sentence deter anyone, I wondered, or would it simply snuff out the potential of a young man who had already started turning his life around? I had the sinking feeling that, once again, the system was shutting down the hope of tomorrow on a promising young man in exchange for revenge and retribution.

❖ ❖ ❖

I HEARD ABOUT JOHN JOHNSON'S AMAZING DECISION TO BECOME A Christian from others on our staff, and I was eager to talk to him about it. I'd seen him several times at the Friday night youth service, sitting in the back. Although he'd seemed quiet and not too eager to talk, we had become acquainted. His reputation from the streets was impressive: a bright, young leader with command over a lot of territory and much respect on the bricks. With all that "going" for him, what had opened his heart and mind to the Lord?

I went a few minutes early to his unit the next Friday, hoping to speak with him before the call for the service went out. "'Evening, Reverend McLean," the attendant on duty said pleasantly.

I looked around the "day room" where the guys gather when they aren't in lockup. I spotted John Johnson all right—right in the middle of a group of guys I recognized as New Breed gang members. To the casual observer, it looked for all the world like a prayer meeting. The guys' heads were bowed, and one person was repeating the "prayer to the nation"—a gang prayer.

Frustrated, I could do nothing but wait. I reminded myself that guys in prison sometimes get the equivalent of "foxhole religion." I'd need to be careful here, but I was still determined to talk to the young man they called Gee-Gee.

When the gang meeting broke up, it was already past time to put out the call for the Friday-night service. But after the service, I got together with John face to face and didn't pull any punches. "What's going on?" I demanded. "I heard you had accepted Jesus as your Lord and Savior. My staff's been telling me you're serious about turning your life around. Now tonight I see you running a gang meeting."

A slow smile spread over his face. "Easy, Mr. G," he said. "It's cool. What you saw was me retirin' from the gang and passin' my rank on to someone else."

I looked at him dubiously. "Just like that?" I demanded. But I was curious. "What was their reaction?"

"Well," he admitted, "some of them were upset and asked me why. So I told them—I intend to serve the Lord from now on and don't think I can be on both sides of the street. The rest didn't know what to think. I mean, I'm one of the top leaders here. But in the end, the brothers gave me their blessin' and said we'd still be friends." He shook his head in obvious relief. "Actually, I was surprised it went so well. The few guys I know who've chosen to leave the gang went through a lot of pain to do what I did tonight."

I was impressed. Now some of the things I'd heard about this young man came into focus. He was bright and intelligent, and whatever he set his mind to do, he did 100 percent.

John and I became good friends while he waited for his court date. If found guilty on both counts (drug "possession," which had been updated to "delivery," and unlawful use of a firearm), he faced 17 years in prison. But after the sentencing, he had good news for me. "Hey, Mr. G," he said, "the judge sentenced me to three years in prison *or* four months in boot camp followed by three months of house arrest. Man! You better believe I took boot camp. Sure don't want to do any more prison time."

I smiled. It was good news. Adult prisons can make a juvenile delinquent into a hardened criminal, which is especially tragic for someone like John who was determined to turn his life around. Still, from what I knew of the "boot camps" run by the correctional system, John was in for some surprises. Nothing could be further from life on the streets.

❖ ❖ ❖

WHEN I PRESENT THE WORK OF OUR JUVENILE JUSTICE MINISTRY TO ADULTS, I often find that they assume the young people we work with are losers. Maybe they're remembering their own youth, when the kids involved in drugs, fighting, and other crimes were on the fringe of society. But as I pointed out earlier, in many parts of the U. S. today, that's no longer the case. We've developed such a broad and calcified underclass—often concentrated in our cities—that a new subculture has developed. Here the winners—and therefore the role models and heroes—are not the doctors, lawyers, teachers, farmers, and industrialists who inspired Americans for generations. Those people escaped the ghetto long ago and have been replaced by a new breed of businessmen. These brightest and most entrepreneurial young men rise in the ranks of gang leadership and oversee a vast financial market: drug dealing. It's the only route to "success" where the steps are readily available—if the person will hustle and work hard.

Keith was one such young man on Chicago's south side. His business was crack cocaine, with some heroin and marijuana thrown in on the side. His clients were mostly yuppies who drove into his neighborhood for their supplies. He made good money until the police busted him and locked him up.

That's where I met him, in the county jail. He was on the same wing with Derrick Stafford, who introduced him to me.

Keith's bail was set at several thousand dollars, which shouldn't have been a problem because he had the cash. But getting to it proved a challenge. He was afraid to tell his boys where the bucks were stashed, as they might help themselves and forget to post his bond. That's a real hazard in the drug business—you just can't trust your partners. Keith's closest relative was his grandmother, but he didn't want her to know about all the money, either. She might decide he was far worse than she already suspected.

Fortunately, Grandma took pity on him and agreed to bail Keith out herself. *Great!* he figured. But she insisted on some conditions: Keith would have to accompany her to church every week *and* attend the Christian high school her church operated in the neighborhood. Keith wasn't too sure about that, but it was better than jail, so he agreed.

The next time I saw Keith on the streets, I asked how things were going.

"Well, I can handle the church service on Sunday," Keith explained. "There's some great music from a good choir. They can really get down with the sounds. And the school isn't too bad— only a couple of hundred students. The teachers are kind of nice. They don't lay on the homework too heavy. They hold chapel several times a week, and the pastor calls down fire and brimstone on all kinds of youthful evils, from makeup to dope peddlin'. I don't know what he would say if he actually knew he had a dope peddler enrolled in his school and sittin' in the audience."

"Has it made any difference in your life?" I asked casually.

He grinned. "Don't know if I should tell you this but . . . one day the principal told us the school was in financial trouble, so serious that if they didn't get $17,000 in the next two weeks, the school would have to close its doors. He called for special prayer from the students, and they really cried to out to the Lord over the need." He shrugged. "That kind of touched me. In the midst of all those prayers, it occurred to me that I could solve their problem. That night, I took $17,000 from my drug money, went to several currency exchanges, and bought a supply of money orders for that amount. I signed various phony names on them and put them in an envelope mailed to the school. I didn't want to let the school know who sent the money orders. Too many questions might be asked, but they were perfectly good money orders."

I'm sure I was raising an eyebrow or two at this point in his story. But Keith plunged on.

"You should have seen chapel two days later. The principal came in walking about two feet off the ground. 'Praise the Lord!' he shouted. 'He has heard our prayers and sent down the exact amount we need from donors I don't even know! Let's just stop now and thank the Lord.' So all the students got excited and started praising the Lord, and I joined in with the rest of 'em."

Keith grinned at me. "The principal kept saying, 'God surely works in mysterious ways.' I guess that's so. Besides, I figured the devil had had that money long enough, so the Lord and the school got it. It's not every day you get to save a whole school!"

I just shook my head. Keith was a remarkably generous entrepreneur in a high-risk business. But there's a good deal about right and wrong he has yet to understand. For openers: *It's never right to do wrong to get a chance to do right.* (It provides perspective, however, to note that this problem isn't much different from what some otherwise "good" people face in other businesses, using the ends to justify the means.)

Keith's friend Jimmy was so enthusiastic about big evangelistic meetings that he used the same dubious method to be involved. When I met him in the jail, he told me he had enjoyed taking his mother and grandmother to a Billy Graham team crusade in Hawaii.

"Oh?" I asked. "How did you manage that?"

"Hey, no problem. I just took some of the profits from my business, bought the tickets, and went. Mom and Gram were thrilled."

I didn't need to guess what the "business" was.

Jimmy said he was hoping to get out on bail so he could take the two ladies to another Graham rally in Cleveland.

"Hmm. Just one question," I said. "Do you ever listen to the messages at the crusade rallies?"

"Well, yes, I do. Sometimes they hit home. I know what you're gettin' at." He held up his hand defensively and turned his face away. "I gotta get out of the business, and I intend to . . . soon."

But he didn't quit soon enough. Jimmy was gunned down on the street by rivals shortly after his release on bond. When I visited his grandmother, the grieving woman showed me the last gift her grandson had bought her: airline tickets to Cleveland and paid hotel reservations. She would get to use them. He wouldn't.

Ten

❖ ❖ ❖

I HADN'T HEARD FROM XAVIER FOR SOME TIME. I thought he was still in the Joliet prison, but we don't have enough staff to maintain close contact with young men in the adult system, even if we've known them previously. So I was surprised one day when I received a thick envelope from him with a return address indicating he was in the Pontiac penitentiary. *Oh, no,* I thought. *What has he done to get himself sent there?*

I opened the letter and learned the answer. Xavier had written his life story (which I've adapted for the pages of this book, with the names of other individuals changed). I read to the point where Xavier had been sent to Pontiac after being charged with gang activity, inciting a riot, dangerous disturbance, and finally assaulting an officer.

Shaking my head, I murmured a prayer for him and then read on as follows:

Gordy, the more I was involved in these activities, the less I wanted to be. But it took a major crackdown and a long time alone before I truly turned to the Lord like you told me.

Now I realize how stupid I've been all my life. God was speaking to me, opening my eyes to truth I didn't want to face. After a couple of weeks of reading the Bible,

187

prayer, and weighing everything, I knew I had to put my trust in Him.

At that point, I didn't trust anybody—the gang, the officers, my old partners, even myself. God forced me to face both my pride and my fear. I was 18 years old, and ever since childhood, I had considered the gang my family. I couldn't imagine life apart from the organization. My heart, like my chest, was branded with the symbol of my gang, and I actually cried when God forced me to realize how deceived I had been all along. I had been blinded by illusions, and Satan attacked me in my weakest spot—my heart's need for love.

Trying to find love, I had settled for lying, stealing, defying my mother, hurting people, idolizing my gang, participating in a murder, hating my neighbors, and letting Satan use me as a vessel of destruction. The only thing God had at the end of all that was my broken spirit.

But I remembered what you told me: Jesus died to forgive my sins, and He said, "It is not the healthy who need a doctor, but the sick. I have not come to call the righteous, but sinners to repentance." I even found that verse in Luke 5:31-32 like you showed me.

And then I prayed: "God, I know my wicked ways have separated me from You. But please give me a new life. Can You possibly forgive me for everything in my past, including murder? I don't want to live an evil life anymore." Anyway, I prayed like you told me, and I know God answered.

I even decided to leave the gang, a very serious decision many of my brothers advised me against. I thought I might face a heavy violation when I sent word from my solitary cell that I was leaving the organization—many guys have.

But I really had no choice. A rule book far more powerful than that of our organization told me: "Therefore come out from them and be separate, says the Lord. Touch no unclean thing, and I will receive you. I will be a Father to you, and you will be my sons and daughters, says the Lord Almighty" (2 Corinthians 6:17-18).

Surely God is more powerful than any gang on earth. I received an early release from the hole. And when I went to my gang partners to express my reasons for wanting out, I was given a discharge on good terms. Once God sets you free, you are free indeed.

Soon, I'll be sent to a medium-security prison, a much better place than the maximum-security lockups. There I look forward to taking some college studies and preparing to lead a productive life when I get out.

I have the hope of the gospel. I look up at the sky and see beauty in it I never realized before. Through my awesome God and Savior Jesus Christ, I've found a love that is real in its purest form. I know a love that teaches me it's wrong to lie, steal, defy parents, idolize anything in this world, kill, and hate people.

I don't have to live with regrets anymore. I'm forgiven, free, and blessed. And if I ever look back into my past, as I do from time to time, it is only to glorify God—first, for who He is, and then for what He has done.

I'll be out before too long, and I look forward to serving the Lord who never gave up on me during my long, torturous trip from street madness to the only freedom there really is—in Jesus Christ.

Your friend,
Xavier

Letters like this make all the heartbreak and disappointment I face out on the bricks and in the detention centers worthwhile. The fact that the other Latin Kings allowed Xavier to walk away unharmed spoke volumes in itself. Leaving a gang can be highly dangerous—even fatal. But the one way out that generally gains respect from all the gangs, including the Kings, is to make what the group accepts as a genuine commitment to the Lord in Christian conversion. Backsliders and phonies, however, are dealt with quickly and firmly. (One part of the Bible gang leaders understand is Acts

chapter 5, where God struck down Ananias and Sapphira for trying to deceive the church.)

Xavier knows life won't be easy once he's released. But he's been
preparing himself physically, mentally, and spiritually as best he
can. By the time he comes up for parole, he will have his B.A. degree
from Roosevelt University's special extension program for prisoners.
He especially enjoys creative writing and is developing computer
skills. He has also gotten involved in sports competitions within
the correctional system, winning several boxing trophies and plac-
ing second in the state in the 5K run.

On a personal level, Xavier has some serious goals as well. In
a phone conversation he told me, "I have to get reacquainted with
my family, Mr. G. So much has changed since we were last
together. I'm going to get into church, and I want to help the
young brothers out on the street who are charging so hard down
the wrong road." Then he chuckled, and I could almost see the shy
grin tugging at his face. "And who knows, in church I just might
meet the right young lady. Then we could get married and have a
family. Now, Mr. G, wouldn't that be somethin'? A real gift from
God! With my college degree and if I can keep up on my skills,
I could support my family and serve the Lord, too. What could be
better than that?"

Indeed, what could be better than that? But like all the young
men who are trying to turn their lives around with the Lord's help,
Xavier will need people praying for him, standing with him, and
willing to get involved in his life. That's where the church and God's
people come in—if they're willing.

❖ ❖ ❖

BUILDING A NEW LIFE AS CHRISTIANS WASN'T EASY FOR THE DYNAMIC
Duo of Boyce Allen and Walter Davis. But both were determined to
keep going on a positive track.

Boyce left the street life and drugs behind and married his
lady, Tiffany, by whom he already had two children, with another
on the way. He got a good job and was active in our Youth for

Christ ministry. Since he was still known on the streets, he had immediate respect when he talked to younger gang members.

His stepbrother, Walter, also continued to work hard. He earned a certificate in medical care and went to work at a senior-care center. He loved his work, the management spoke highly of him, and the elderly patients and their families adored him. He not only did his hospital duty, but he also took time to visit with the patients, read Scripture with them, and even pray with them.

Things seemed to be going well as he changed jobs to another care center with more responsibility and higher pay. Few young men were more fulfilled in their work and sense of calling.

Then a new law forced all hospital employees with a criminal record out of their jobs unless the state issued a waiver. Walter told his employers about his background, and they reluctantly let him go, saying they would help with the waiver process in any way they could. "If it comes through," he was told, "we can assure you that your job will be waiting."

As Walter's minister friend, I wrote him a reference letter and told him not to worry, a waiver should be issued quickly. I was wrong. The red tape became a nightmare. He kept calling the government agency and was repeatedly told, "Any day now." This went on for several months, and he finally learned they couldn't find any record of his conviction on the state computer, so they couldn't issue him a waiver. He found whatever jobs he could while waiting for the confusion to be resolved. He's still waiting.

God came through when the state did not, however, opening another door. Walter was able to get his health-services license in another state and is now working in his field again.

In the meantime, Boyce was having his own problems. Married life wasn't easy. He had to overcome substance-abuse problems and struggle step by step to make his marriage and family work. Without the caring counsel and support of Rock Church and Circle Urban Ministries, he would never have made it. But he is succeeding because of the compassion and practical help from this church family.

Then one day on his way to work, the police stopped Boyce

and announced that he was under arrest—as it turned out, for an old drug charge. Supposedly, Boyce had been arrested and released five years earlier pending trial. When he hadn't shown up in court, a warrant had been issued. Only now had the police gotten around to tracking him down. But given Boyce's record, a conviction would put him in prison for a long time, just when his family needed him the most. And no consideration would be given for how his current life demonstrated genuine transformation.

The truth was, however, that Boyce *hadn't* missed any court date for an old drug charge. Somehow the police had the wrong guy.

"Yeah, yeah, of course you didn't do it. That's what they all say," the arresting officer said as he cuffed Boyce and hauled him off to Cook County Jail.

When Boyce first appeared in court, his public defender noted that the name the court had was Allen Boyce, not Boyce Allen. "Your Honor," said the attorney, "there's been a mistake here. This warrant is for a Mr. Boyce, not Mr. Allen. You have the wrong man."

But the assistant state's attorney argued vigorously that it was a simple clerical error and that releasing Boyce would be letting a dangerous criminal loose.

"Well, then," said Boyce's public defender, "can we see the mug shots and fingerprints recorded when the man in question was originally arrested five years ago? They will certainly show that my client wasn't Mr. Boyce."

The prosecutor said those records were not immediately available and would have to be dug up out of the police archives.

The case was continued, and Boyce went back to jail. While he waited behind bars, Tiffany was not doing well. She had no source of income, could not manage the children, and was feeling tempted to take refuge in drugs.

In a few weeks, Boyce returned to court. Again there were no mug shots or fingerprints. The prosecutor begged for more time, saying that the clerks had been overwhelmed lately and the records had not yet come in. Back to jail went Boyce while other people were too busy to respond to his attorney's request.

A third and fourth court date came and went, and finally Boyce pleaded with me when I visited him. "Mr. G, I need someone else to represent me," he said. "The public defender's nice but can't follow up on my case."

I asked John DeLeon, an outstanding criminal lawyer, to help Boyce.

At the next court hearing, there were still no records, but DeLeon had subpoenaed the police officers who had supposedly arrested Boyce five years earlier. Ultimately, all three of them admitted they couldn't remember who they had arrested that long ago or what he looked like. By then, even the judge was getting frustrated with the prosecutor for not delivering the records that could easily prove whether Boyce was the person the state wanted.

At home, things were falling apart. Tiffany was out of control, and the Department of Children and Family Services had removed the children. How would Boyce ever get the family back together when he got out of jail?

Finally, at the eighth hearing, after Boyce had sat in jail for four months, the assistant state's attorney admitted that mug shots and fingerprints of Allen Boyce—supposedly arrested five years earlier—simply did not exist.

"What makes you sure this is the man, then?" demanded DeLeon.

"Nothing," the assistant state's attorney said and shrugged.

"What do you mean, *nothing?*"

"I mean, I guess we have no *proof* that this is the man. But . . ."

"And you even have his name wrong," interrupted DeLeon.

Finally, the judge stepped in, addressing the assistant state's attorney. "Is that all?" he demanded.

"Yes, Your Honor."

"Then I find Mr. Allen not guilty!"

After spending four months in jail for something he hadn't done, Boyce was released with no earthly compensation for the time the state had taken from him.

But, as frustrating as the experience had been, the time had not been wasted as far as Boyce was concerned. He had spent his days and nights on the deck witnessing for the Lord. Dozens of guys took part in regular Bible studies he organized, and many came to know Jesus as Savior. He never allowed bitterness to take control and kept faith that the Lord was in charge in much the same way He had sustained Joseph when he had been falsely accused and imprisoned in Egypt.

Now, Boyce would have to put his life back together. His wife and children had suffered during this time as well, but the Lord would be with him in that, too.

❖ ❖ ❖

Silviu Spiridon's old gang partners hardly recognized him with his military haircut, new confidence, and change in vocabulary. But they were most disconcerted when he showed no desire to return to street life. "I got new plans," he announced. "I'm goin' on to college."

He kept in touch with many of his boys, like Cholo, and made it clear he was still a friend. "Hey, come to church with the Rev and me," he'd say. Some of his old gang liked that and respected him for it, but others didn't. Silviu left it up to them. He figured that if they dropped him for trying to do something good with his life, what kind of friends were they?

As Silviu's friend and spiritual mentor, I had high hopes for him. Here was a bright, natural leader who knew what he wanted and went after it zealously. All the commitment and energy that had been poured into being down for the Two-Six Nation was now chafing at the bit to be down for Jesus. I asked if he would consider helping us at the Juvenile Justice Ministry by working with kids in his neighborhood, and he gave me an enthusiastic, "You got it, Mr. G!" Before long, he became secretary general of our United Nations meetings and was going with me to speak to youth groups and churches. The kid who came from Romania and could once barely speak English soon became a fluent and popular public speaker.

I was pleased when both Silviu and his brother, Tib, got involved again in their parents' church and made plans to attend

DeVry Institute of Technology in Chicago. A foundation that had expressed interest in our ministry was impressed with the brothers and offered to help underwrite their college costs.

But, as always when gang kids make the transition to a new life, there's a period of time when technically they're still in the gang, even though internally they've turned in a new direction. Dual membership in a street gang and "God's gang" can't last long. As the Bible says, a Christian can't serve two masters; one or the other will win out. This was true for Silviu as well. But I didn't push him on the issue. I knew what he would say: "Hey, Mr. G, you're not the one whose bones are goin' to get crushed, so spare me the preachin'. This is a decision I gotta make."

One night the phone rang. It was Silviu. "Two-Six got an SOS out on me, Mr. G," he said.

I took a deep breath. An SOS meant "shoot on sight." "What happened?" I asked.

"Nothin'," he said. "What I mean is, the Two-Six had a party, and I didn't show up. I didn't feel right partyin'—not with all the booze and girls. Sometimes the guys get real crazy . . . things happen. But they felt offended that I didn't come around and decided I'd gone soft on the gang."

"What are you going to do?"

"It's time to get out," he said simply.

The next day, Silviu called his chief and said he wanted to say something to a meeting of the gang. The night before the meeting, Silviu went with me to speak at a service at Berwyn Bible Church. After giving his testimony, he told the congregation, "I've decided now that I have to make a clean break from my old gang. But that involves a violation, and I'll have to take whatever punishment they dish out. Please remember me in prayer tomorrow as I go to the gang meeting and get out."

The congregation didn't wait until tomorrow but prayed right then and there that God would go with this young man as he "faced the lions."

All the next day, I waited anxiously for my pager to beep and let me know it was Silviu. I knew Cholo had agreed to go with him and speak on his behalf. But there were no guarantees it would sway the verdict. I kept praying.

Finally, the call came. Was I glad to hear Silviu's voice! "Hey, Mr. G," he said with his characteristic good humor, "it was a piece of cake."

"What do you mean, 'piece of cake'?" I asked dryly.

"Okay, I went to the gang meeting and spoke first to the main guy and told him I've become a Christian. Told him I wanted to go to college and I wasn't plannin' on comin' back to the gang. 'So,' I said, 'do what you gotta do.' Cholo put in a good word for me, said I wasn't makin' this up, that I'd really got religion. So . . . they ordered a one-minute head to toe."

I almost breathed a sigh of relief. There were worse things than a one-minute beating, but still . . . "Tell me about it," I said.

"Well, we went out into the alley, they put me up against a garage, and five guys lit into me all at once. One guy picked up a bottle to break over my head, but Cholo caught his arm and said, 'No way!' One minute and it was all over. We shook hands, I walked away, and that was it!" His voice was jubilant.

Silviu was probably bruised and sore, but he was free. Berwyn Bible Church's prayers had been answered. Not only that, but he had also kept the respect of most of his boys by being up-front with them and taking his violation "like a man." This left the door open for him to reach out to them in the name of Jesus.

I often asked Silviu to help with some of the younger guys I'd made contact with in the JDC—kids like Andre, a 14-year-old Gangster Disciple. Andre's major talent was auto theft. He already had been picked up by the police 47 times. He was a bright, likable kid who, according to his teachers, was "capable of doing better work, but not a bad student." He had a bad habit, however—he stole a different car each day to get to school.

I met him during his longest detention, after he'd already been attending some Bible study sessions. He had often gone with his mother to church but had never made the connection between what he heard on Sunday morning and what he did the rest of the week. In our ongoing conversations, however, he indicated his desire to open his heart to the Lord.

I asked Silviu to go with me to Andre's juvenile-court hearing. "What's goin' to happen?" Silviu asked outside the courtroom.

"When the probation officer brings out her file, look at the size of it," I suggested. "If it weighs under one pound, he's going home; if it's over that, he's probably headed for Charleytown"—the Illinois Youth Center at St. Charles.

"They go by the weight of the file?" Silviu asked, flabbergasted.

"Not really," I said with a shrug, "but it's as good a gauge as any of the result."

When we saw the file, it was thick and heavy. "Oh, boy," Silviu noted, "he's in trouble."

The state's attorney wanted Andre locked up for as long as possible—they always do. The public defender wanted him to be given another chance—they always do. The probation officer was somewhere in the middle—meaning, to me at least, the file was right at about one pound.

I gave the court a review of YFC's Juvenile Justice Ministry and told of our contact with Andre in detention, his positive response, and our desire to continue working with him back in the community. Silviu indicated he would be our staff volunteer helping Andre.

The judge was a young, black man, up from the streets, who had overcome his own rough upbringing to become a lawyer and now a judge. He got down to basic issues in a hurry, and youngsters in his court quickly learned he couldn't be conned. He was interested in only two things: He wanted a young person to take responsibility for his past and have clearly defined plans to change his future.

"Why should I even consider letting you go home?" the judge demanded, looking straight at Andre.

To our surprise, the judge paid close attention when Andre told about the changes he'd made in his life and his desire to be a bone specialist ("because my mother suffers from a severe bone disease, and I'd like to help people like her"). Andre then showed him the new, laminated ID card he carried in his wallet—a card we give kids who drop their gang flags. It read: "Retired Gang Member."

The courtroom was silent for a minute. "All right," the judge finally said, "I'll give you the chance you're asking for—but if I see you in my court again, your next hearing will be a very short one. Do we understand each other?"

Andre nodded.

Silviu gave him a ride home and took Andre under his wing. As the months went by, he reported that Andre was staying in school, had dropped his old gang friends, and was attending church every week. He liked coming along with us to church and community meetings, and Silviu and I both agreed that we had an outstanding young man on our hands.

Not that his path was smooth. The first day he took the city bus to school instead of stealing a car, he was recognized by rival gang members and beaten up so badly that he had to be taken to the emergency room. And a few weeks later, Silviu called me late one night to report, "The cops picked up Andre. Car theft."

Instantly I was wide awake. And I was steaming when I confronted Andre at the JDC.

"Don't blow your top, Mr. G, it ain't what you think," he quickly responded.

"All right, tell me what happened," I growled, "and this had better be good."

It was a good story, all right. According to Andre, four of his friends were driving around in a stolen ride when the cops stopped them. "The guys said *they* hadn't stole the car, that I took it," he reported. "The first thing I know, the cops came to my house, woke me up, arrested me for car theft, and took me to the station! Then they let the other boys they found in the car go, no charges on them."

I looked at him skeptically. I learned long ago not to take at face value whatever a kid tells me about the charges against him. And a story as crazy as this made no sense. "Police don't arrest a guy at home for car theft and let the guys in the car go," I told Andre. "No way."

But I was wrong. When we talked with the probation officer who had the police reports, we learned that was exactly what had happened.

Silviu and I knew the case would wash out once it got to court, and I asked Silviu to show up with Andre, as I had to be in another courtroom. When Silviu got there, he couldn't find either the probation officer or the public defender, just a new judge presiding and a prosecutor urging continued detention. So Silviu spoke up and asked the judge to review the police reports in front of him. He then gave an account of Andre's progress in school and involvement in our ministry, and he asked for his release. The judge agreed, shaking his head in disbelief at the police reports, and ordered Andre discharged.

Hearing about it later, I realized half the people in court that day thought Silviu was Andre's attorney, and the rest thought he was the probation officer! I smiled to myself. No, Silviu was an ex-gang-banger from the street, now a fluent, neatly dressed college student arguing to help a friend. And he had won.

Silviu has proved himself a good friend in other ways as well. He and Cholo would often talk. They were still friends from the streets, even though they've traveled very different paths.

"I wish I could trade places with you," Cholo said one day to his old partner. "You'll be getting your college degree, you've got a good job, a nice ride, and you're helping a lot of the shorties, too."

"We don't need to trade places," Silviu countered. "You just need to get your life going in the right direction. You've got all the ability any guy needs, and as far as what I'm doing in the Lord's work and church, well, you're the guy that introduced me to Mr. G in the first place. But you're still out there, hangin' with the boys, always sayin' tomorrow you're goin' to get it together. Come on, man, no time like today."

"I wish I could, Silviu, I really do. But this is my life now, and I'm not sure it will change."

"Nothing will change until you decide it should."

"I guess you're right, but I'm just not ready, not right now."

The conversation ended, and a few days later, Cholo was shot on the street. It was a leg wound, not too serious. He made a quick recovery. Sadly, however, he eventually took his own life.

The day Silviu graduated from college was a proud day for the entire family, and he was soon offered a good job in an innovative, cutting-edge industrial company, with a church youth leadership role on the side. It's a long way from the gangs on the street to the halls of respectability in the academic, business, and church worlds. Or is it? Silviu sometimes wonders.

"I don't get it," he complained to me at lunch one day, frustration written on his face. "Out on the streets, I was used to rivals coming after me, out to rip me off and do me in. But those street guys could take lessons from the business world. Man! At my job, they do it with real finesse and lots of smiles while they go behind your back to mess you over. Gang leaders order hits; company chiefs downsize with outplacement. Maybe it's less messy, but it's the same ballgame: Get rid of somebody who's in the way."

"I see you've discovered all is not sweetness and light in the business world," I replied. "Greed and selfishness can come in a three-piece suit as well a gang jacket. But what about the church?"

Silviu rolled his eyes. "The other day, I was asked to drive a packed vanload of kids on a church activity. Man, Mr. G! I've been chased on the streets, attacked, and shot at—but this was one of the scariest experiences I've ever had. Those kids were like a war party, screamin', fightin', hollerin', even pullin' at me while I was tryin' to drive. I was shakin' all over. Give me a load of down gang members anytime—just keep me away from those spoiled, bratty, junior-high church kids!"

I couldn't help laughing. "Come on, Sil," I said with a grin. "Kids will always be kids. They probably had a blast, thought you were a great guy, and want you to drive them to all their future events."

He looked genuinely horror-stricken. "No way, Mr. G!" he protested. "Believe me, I'm outta there!"

But I know he'll be back.

❖ ❖ ❖

I SAT WITH A GROUP OF COMMUNITY LEADERS AND BUSINESS PEOPLE IN A south-side suburb, discussing the problems of young people. The TV news and press headlines had just reported Cragg Hardaway's sentence for his part in the slaying of Yummy Sandifer.

"Maybe 60 years in the slammer will show those young gun-slingers on the street they just can't get away with this madness any longer," said a professional woman.

"If you ask me," snorted a small-store owner, "that isn't long enough. People like those Hardaway brothers should rot in their cells. They've got no feelings, no values, no morals—they're just punks. You know, real psychopaths."

I said nothing. These people were typical of many whose only knowledge of kids in trouble consists of sensational headlines. I wanted to hear what they were thinking.

"The gang leaders who put these kids up to crimes like this—they're the ones who ought to get jailed," a banker pointed out. "You know, it's really sad. Those gang leaders have to be pretty smart to get to the top of a gang at a young age. They've got brains and skills; too bad it's going nowhere."

"But our society has tried a lot of things to reach these kids, and nothing seems to work," a college teacher offered. "Affirmative action, welfare, the war on poverty, more cops, midnight basketball, more prisons—but the violence is still out there."

"Huh. Kids today just aren't raised like we were," a barber said, shaking his head. "No family life. Either they're being raised by single parents or both parents are working, whether they really have to or not. No one's raising the kids; they're raising themselves. They have their own rules. Man, it's dangerous out there!"

"Yeah, kids have this attitude, 'I want everything now, and I don't care how I get it,'" said the teacher.

"If anybody wonders what divorce, neglect, abuse, and raising our children in child-care centers do to kids, just look around. It's costing us more in ruined lives than we want to admit." The banker again.

"Unfortunately, the system isn't good at drawing lines between the hard-core incorrigibles and the gullible ones who just got dragged along," said a family counselor who was on to something important. "They throw the book at all of them."

"Forget that," interrupted the store owner. "They're all alike. Those Hardaway brothers don't have a decent bone in their bodies. The longer they spend in prison, the better."

I figured it was finally my turn. "Do any of you know the Hardaway brothers?" I asked innocently.

"Are you kidding?" snorted the barber.

"Don't you have pretty strong opinions about two kids you know nothing about except from the headlines?" I asked.

Some in the group shrugged off the question as if the media reports are all we need to be told to form our opinions.

"Well, I do know them," I said. "I've spent hours with both brothers. And I'm out on the streets every day with gang members in their hoods, in their homes, and with their groups."

The group shuffled uncomfortably until an insurance agent cracked, "Remind me not to sell you life insurance!" The laughter eased the tension and brought smiles to the group.

"Don't worry," I said with a smile, "I've never felt threatened or in danger with those kids. On the contrary, they treat me and my ministry staff with great respect and concern."

Several in the group looked skeptical. "Isn't that a little out of character for street punks?" one ventured.

"Not really. We get respect mainly because we treat *them* with respect. And probably because most don't want to be what they are. I don't have to tell many gang kids that what they're doing is illegal and morally wrong. Most are painfully aware of that, even when they're making money and putting up a tough, indifferent front. They're backed into a miserable corner, and they know it. They just don't know any way out. Too often we just want to slam them down harder. Why don't we show them the way to change?"

"But how can you help these kids and treat them with respect, knowing they're guilty of hideous crimes?" demanded the store operator, who added that he had more experience than he cared to recall with belligerent teens.

I don't doubt the problems he faces. Too many kids are not only *in* trouble but also *are* trouble. I wondered aloud, however, "Do you ever ask that question of a doctor in a hospital emergency room? Of course you don't. If a shooting victim is brought in, the medical team doesn't ask whether he deserved it or if he has a police record. They just do what they can to get him better."

Several in the group looked at each other. They'd never really thought of that before.

"I work on the front line, trying to recover moral basket cases," I continued. "It's not an easy job. There's a saying—'Some people serve the Lord 'neath a steeple and bell; I run a rescue shop within a yard of hell.' The same is true of a good lawyer—it's the lawyer's job to represent his or her clients, not judge them. We need to remember that if the worst among us don't have their legal rights protected, the rest of us really have no rights either."

"But that attitude in the courtroom could mean a guilty criminal goes free," objected the store owner. "I'm really sick of these do-gooder defense attorneys."

It was time for a little education. "Our legal system isn't perfect," I admitted. "But if a guilty person gets off, it's for one of two reasons: Either there wasn't adequate evidence of guilt to convince a judge or jury, or the evidence wasn't well presented by the prosecutor. Neither shortcoming is the fault of the defense attorney. Unfortunately," I added, "the weight of the legal system today is leaning more and more toward revenge and punishment rather than toward giving a young person who has really changed a chance at rehabilitation."

Murmurs swept the room. People have a lot of feelings about crime and young criminals. It was good to get them out on the table.

"But how does a judge tell which kids have truly turned around and deserve some leniency in spite of having committed a terrible crime," the college teacher persisted, "and which kids really haven't changed or are even faking it in the hope of getting leniency?"

"Right," the barber piped up. "After all, if the judge opts for leniency and his assessment of the kid is wrong, doesn't he put the public at risk by releasing a dangerous criminal from prison sooner than would otherwise be the case?"

"Those are legitimate questions," I answered. "A judge needs to consider the seriousness of the offense, the threat to the community from a possible repeat violent act, and the impact the tragedy has had on victims. That's certainly as it should be. Unfortunately, however, the process usually stops there."

"What do you mean?" The banker leaned forward and seemed genuinely interested.

"With youthful offenders, especially, there's more to consider. What has this particular boy learned from his arrest and confinement? Has this girl realized the wrong she did and made reasonable efforts—where possible—to right that wrong? Does the offender have the potential to be a useful and contributing citizen in the community? Are resources available from churches, social service agencies, and schools to help him or her succeed if put back in the community?

"These are questions my staff and I ask about the teenagers we work with. If the answers are positive and corroborated by experienced correctional staff, I don't hesitate to testify on their behalf, urging a lower bail pending trial, probation instead of confinement if convicted, or as short a sentence as possible. In the process, all the sentencing options should be considered: intensive probation, home monitoring, restitution, community service, reconciliation with victims, boot and wilderness camps with careful follow-up, diversion from court processing with referral to counseling groups, and an opportunity to later have the conviction cleared from the record. Both schooling and employment obligations should be part of the package, too."

"But both the public and politicians want to do away with those options and try these youthful offenders as adults with stiffer, mandatory sentencing laws," the banker pointed out.

"Exactly. Too often, the law severely limits these options and denies them to youths who could genuinely benefit."

"Seems like a lot of money and effort to waste on kids who aren't worth much to society," said the barber, shaking his head.

"Actually, the opposite is true," I said. "When considering young offenders, revenge and punishment as the only goals are a waste of lives and taxpayer dollars. A youthful offender with potential for rehabilitation could be sent to the most-expensive college in the country for less than it costs to keep him locked up. I've met few young people in my years of work who were 'worth' the half-million-plus dollars it costs to lock each one up for the duration of a long sentence. Our hurting society and its troubled kids need better than expensive warehouses. I want to keep urging the alternatives for suitable candidates."

I could see the perplexed struggle some in the group were going through, even those who tended to be sympathetic toward troubled kids.

"But even if an offender is remorseful, has become a Christian, and has the potential to become an upstanding citizen, doesn't he still have to pay his debt to society for his crime?" asked the teacher.

"Absolutely. Kids who have committed crimes and offenses must be held accountable for their actions. But again we have to ask: What kinds of sentences will actually help a young offender 'learn his lesson'? If he doesn't or won't, then by all means, lock him up to protect society. But punishment simply for punishment's sake without redemptive value . . . well, that's not the way I see God working with you and me."

A few heads nodded.

"But don't you often get disappointment with these kids?" the teacher returned. "Surely not all of them respond the way you might hope."

"Yes," I admitted. "There's been a lot of hurt and heartbreak along the way from kids we put effort into who just didn't make it. Maybe we should have tried harder, or perhaps they just made a deliberate wrong choice. But the kids we see in big trouble whose lives do get turned around—there are a lot more of them."

"But aren't the really entrenched gang kids impossible to reach?" the professional woman wanted to know.

"Most people think the hard-core gang members won't change. But they're often our best prospects, especially when we get to them in the Juvenile Detention Center or county jail while they're awaiting trial—our 'captive audience,' so to speak." There were chuckles all around. "The guys with the most-serious charges are most often our best success stories. They've been pulled up short by what they did, and they know what they're facing, and when their lives turn around, it's a wonderful thing. These are some of the most-zealous, caring, dependable, intelligent young people I know, and I'm not about to write them off."

A sober silence followed, broken when the teacher asked, "Do you consider these Hardaway boys like that?"

We were back to where we had started. "Yes, I do. Both Derrick and Cragg have shown a long-term, positive turnaround while awaiting trial for 30 months. That's a long time in a kid's life. They're not perfect, and they've had some ups and downs, but still the brothers are on a very positive track. My greatest fear is that putting them into the adult prison system will destroy the progress they've made."

"But," the teacher persisted, "won't that deter some other kids from going the same way?"

I shook my head. "I doubt it. Slamming Bobby hoping to scare Billy doesn't make much sense. Bobby gets angry, and Billy just feels lucky it wasn't him who got caught."

As the discussion broke up, I knew some in the group agreed with me, but others didn't. And it's that second group, bent on revenge and punishment, who are the most vocal in our society. They make it hard for a judge to dismiss a weak case or give a kid in trouble another chance. Those decisions take courage. An angry citizenry will criticize judges if they do what they think is right in an individual case. Newspaper editorials will blast them for being "soft on crime"—a designation far worse in politics today than sexual indiscretion or having your hand in the till. Prosecutors will attack them and then run against them in elections as law-and-order candidates.

Most judges yield to the pressure and go along with the hard-liners. The price of courage is more than they choose to pay.

❖ ❖ ❖

NO ONE WAS HAPPIER THAN ME TO SEE JOHN JOHNSON GRADUATE FROM the boot-camp program. "You made it, man!" I cheered when I dropped by his sister's apartment to see him. "There were times when I wondered."

John grinned. He knew I was referring to the collect phone

calls he'd made telling me *this* time he really was going to quit. "I kept prayin' to the Lord to get me out of that place," he admitted. "But I think He answered my prayer by gettin' me *through* it instead."

"Pretty bit of jewelry you're wearing there," I noted, nodding at the ankle monitor he was wearing for his three months of house arrest and supervision. "But your probation officer told me that if we call him and tell him you're going to be with me, we can get you over to the United Nations meetings, things like that. Why don't you come to church with me on Sunday?"

"That's cool," John said. Both he and I knew he needed to make some new connections now that he was back home. "Say, Mr. G, I had some visitors yesterday."

"Ah, I'm not surprised," I said quietly. He had already told me about a call he'd had from his chief the day he got back. The man had been friendly enough; he'd heard some good things about John settling down and trying to get his life straight. But he had come right to the point: "Gee-Gee, some of the brothers think you're chillin' out on us because you're plannin' to start your own mob in opposition to the New Breed. Is that true?"

John chuckled. "They just don't get it. I assured him that I wasn't leavin' to start my own thing. If that was my plan, I would have done that a long time ago. I said, 'Actually, I am into somethin' else, though. I'm in Jesus' crew, and that's where I'm stayin'.'"

He thought the conversation might end there, but it didn't. The gang leader asked him to explain, and John did. After a few minutes, John's caller admitted soberly, "Man, guess I can tell you I'm gettin' tired of this life, too. It's a war zone out here at times, and I gotta think about my future, too—you know, my family and settlin' down. I'd like to get away from the whole thing."

Surprised at the direction the call was going, John invited the chief to come talk to him. When he did, John gave him a Bible and again related his own testimony. He wasn't surprised to hear later that the young man had left town to get away from the pressures and do some serious thinking.

I knew not all the gang members would respond to Gee-Gee's

defection with the same grace, however. "So tell me about your visitors yesterday," I encouraged.

"Well, see, four cars pulled up in front of the apartment, and about 15 of my boys got out." He shook his head. "I didn't know what to expect, but I knew whatever was goin' to go down, I didn't want to risk anyone in the apartment gettin' hurt, so I went outside to meet 'em.

"'We heard you quit the organization,' they said. 'You know you joined for life and nobody leaves. The only way out is death.'"

I knew that, and John knew it, too. That's why I respect a young man's sense of the right time to make his move out of the gang.

"Funny thing, though," John continued, "but the way they said it wasn't really threatenin'. I was nervous, all right—after all, I'd taught most of these boys the ways of the gang and how to use a gun—but I just said outright, 'So you've all come here to kill me?'

"They looked at each other, and then one of the boys said, 'Well, no, not exactly. We really want to keep you in the gang. You've been a good leader, and we want to give you a higher-rankin' position.' And to sweeten the offer, Mr. G, they said they'd throw in a nice ride."

This story is certainly going in an interesting direction, I thought. But I just let John tell it without interrupting him.

"So I said, 'Okay, I'm goin' to accept your offer. I'm goin' to be you-all's chief.'

"'All right!' they said, and they opened the trunk of a car, brought out the beer, and said, 'Hey, let's party! We got our chief back!'

"But then I said, 'Okay, but if I'm goin' to be your chief, we're goin' to do things my way.' They looked at me kinda funny and said, 'What way is that?' 'Well,' I said, 'from now on we're not goin' to do any more gangbangin'. We're not goin' to sell drugs; we're not goin' to try to take someone else's turf.' Now they were *really* lookin' at me funny.

"'If we not gonna be gangbangin', then what we gonna do?' they wanted to know.

"So I laid it on the line. 'From now on, we're goin' to go to school, we're goin' to get jobs, and we're goin' to go to church and study the Bible.'

"'Hey, man, you can't do that!' they protested. 'That wouldn't be right.'

"'Well, too bad,' I said. 'If I'm chief, that's the way it's gonna be. Maybe you better think over just how badly you want me back.'

"They milled around for a few minutes, talkin' to themselves, then one of 'em said, 'We'll take it up with the big man in the joint and let you know what he says.'"

John shrugged. "What they don't know is that the big man in the joint already knows about my decision, and he blessed me out. Guess that's the last I'll be seein' of those boys." He grinned. "And I thought they wanted me to be their chief!"

We laughed. But deep in my heart, I knew that the Lord had a serious soldier in His kingdom ranks.

I never cease to be surprised by some of the things happening with and around John. One day he brought another young man to see me, and they told me one of the most amazing stories I have ever heard on the streets.

One day—before he got busted on the drug charge and landed in jail when he was 17—John and some of his boys were hanging out near one of their spots in the hood. A boy named Anthony Mason, age 16, showed up; immediately the tension rose. Ant was a rival Unknown Vice Lord, and his crew was competing with John's for the same drug spots and customers. It was not a friendly rivalry.

The two boys exchanged sharp words as Ant went into a store. When he came out, John was waiting for him, alone, armed with a 9-mm handgun, and he fired four bullets at close range. Ant was hit in the leg, the arm, and twice in the back. There were no witnesses. But the gunfire attracted attention, and some people came out of the store and saw Ant lying on the ground. He was rushed to the hospital, where he slipped in and out of consciousness for several days.

The pain was excruciating. Ant lay in a hospital emergency room fighting for every breath. He might not live. If he did, he might be paralyzed. At best he faced a long recovery.

As soon as he could talk, police officers came in and asked if he could identify the shooter. Anthony slowly moved his head from side to side, indicating no.

But Ant knew very well who had shot him. He wanted to get a gun himself, go after the guy he knew as Gee-Gee, and take care of his own business. *I want him,* Ant vowed to himself. *I'm not gonna let the cops take him away first. My boys better not go after him, either. This guy is all mine, and I want him dead!*

Ant was under medical care for six months. To the doctors' amazement, he suffered no permanent damage and healed nicely, though slowly. His anger and desire for revenge, however, continued to fester.

Ant's uncle, a pastor who knew the streets, came to see him. "Ant," said his uncle, "I think you know who shot you, and I also think you would rather get revenge yourself than give the gunman up to the law. Am I right?"

Ant clamped his jaw and just looked away.

"Revenge isn't yours to take," his uncle cautioned. "That's God's business, and the law's."

Ant didn't want to hear it.

Then his mother's pastor also came to see him. Their talks got serious as Ant recuperated. "Ant, hatred and revenge are poisons that can do more harm to you than even your physical wounds," the lady said. "Long before you get even with your assailant, hate will destroy you."

"How would you handle it then?" Ant asked bitterly.

"Give it over to the Lord, son. He will repay those who deserve it. Ask forgiveness for what you did wrong, and start a new life!"

The pastor's message took a while to sink in, but Ant knew it was right. The desire for revenge was eating him up. He could think of nothing else. So he made a simple but life-changing decision: He opened his life to Jesus and decided not to go back to the streets. Church, school, and work gradually replaced his former activities.

One day, one of Ant's sisters said, "Hey, Ant. You gonna be home this evenin'? I wanna bring this guy I've been datin' by to meet you."

As the only boy in the family, Ant looked out for his four sisters and liked to be sure the boys they went out with were okay. "Sure," he said, "bring him over."

That evening, his sister came home with her new boyfriend. Ant leaped to his feet, stunned. Standing there in his own living room was Gee-Gee Johnson! His sister looked confused. She didn't know this was the guy who had shot her brother. And John hadn't realized whose sister he was dating. For a few moments, it looked as if the whole thing would blow up.

Ant glared at John. "You oughta be grateful I don't have a piece handy or I'd take you out right now!" he shouted.

"No, *you* oughta be glad I'm not packin' or I'd finish what I started out on the street!" John snapped back. But suddenly John backed off and calmed down. "Actually . . ." He cleared his throat. "I don't carry a gun anymore. That's not what I'm about."

"What *are* you about?" Ant demanded.

"Well, see, I'm a Christian now, tryin' to help young guys get away from the street and do somethin' good with their lives."

"A Christian! . . . So am I," said Ant. It was hard to tell who was more surprised, John or Anthony. Ant's poor sister looked from one to the other, crying because she was sure a shootout was about to happen right there in the living room.

"Sit down, Gee-Gee," Ant said, regaining his composure. "Tell me about it."

For a long time, the boys talked, comparing notes on their separate roads to meet the Savior. Gradually it dawned on both of them that not only might they become friends, but they were actually brothers in the faith!

"Gee-Gee, do you think I could help you in the work you're doin'?" Ant finally asked. And that's how I met Anthony. John brought him to see me, and both youths told me one of the most amazing stories I'd ever heard.

After that, John and Ant were often together at churches, on the streets, or in a youth counseling session. Then one day John had an idea. "Ya know, Mr. G, I think it would be a neat idea for Anthony and me to tell a United Nations meetin' about how we met and what the Lord did for two guys who used to hate each other. Really learnin' to respect each other—isn't that what it's all about?"

With a big grin on my face, I said, "Yes, John, it is. Let's do it!"

Now that John has been released from his ankle monitor and house arrest, we've invited him to come on staff with the Youth for Christ Juvenile Justice Ministry. And we're working him hard. We've got him out in the community on the west side of Chicago—known as "K Town" because all the street names start with the letter K— reaching out to the young kids on the fringes of the gangs. "They're still reachable around 12, 13, 14," he says. "But once they turn 15 or 16—then it's trouble." Using his love of basketball, he's putting together a neighborhood basketball team. He also hangs out with the street guys, pulls out his Bible, and gets them involved in a spontaneous Bible study. He's not working alone; his cousin Marvin has also accepted the Lord, and the two young men make a good team on the bricks.

I take John with me, too, when I make presentations about our work at various churches around the city. He gives his testimony, then invites questions from the audience. Adults who aren't from the inner city are curious about the gang mentality; John helps bridge the gap between what they read or see in the media and the real people and real stories behind the headlines.

Recently someone asked John, "How do you like working for Youth for Christ? Are they keeping you busy?"

With a nod and a chuckle, John replied, "Well, to tell you the truth, I did less work and made more money when I was workin' for the devil! But I've come too far to turn back now."

❖ ❖ ❖

A CHANGED LIFE JUST MAKES MY DAY. AND FRANK ROBINSON IS A GREAT example. Physically strong and alert, this 17-year-old African-American youth was a leader in a Latino gang, the Spanish Cobras. He had enormous power among the detainees on the youth wing of the county jail, and he also earned the respect of the correctional staff. That was no small accomplishment.

His nickname, Sweet Pea, was given to him as a baby by his mother, and it stuck. He not only accepts it but likes it.

Frank and his older brother face murder charges in the death of a friend of their mother. The boys say the victim was drunk and abusive, and they killed him and disposed of the body in a garbage bag to protect her. She was also charged with assisting in the cover-up.

Oddly, the charges against his mother led to more trouble for Frank. "When we got out on bail," he told me, "I was so concerned about the charges against my mom that I did somethin' really dumb. She needed money for a good lawyer, so I robbed a store. That put me back in jail."

Frank has a church background, so he could easily relate to the message of the gospel, and it soon led him to be truly transformed. He not only had a changed attitude and a desire to use his considerable influence to bring boys to our meetings—all that could be dismissed as jailhouse religion—but he also displayed a willingness to put himself on the line for his faith.

One day, a kid named Charlie came on the jail deck. He was a neutron (not gang related), had no friends to show him the ropes of survival, and clearly had never been confined before. His naiveté and lack of "protection" led him to make some unwise mistakes.

At his first lunch, Charlie sat at one of the tables reserved by members of a certain gang. He was bluntly told to move, finally finding a vacant chair at another table. Then he had the misfortune to spill some milk on a gang leader—not deliberately, but still considered an act of disrespect.

After lunch, the guys who were plugged into the gang met, Frank among them. "This kid's gotta learn respect," said the boy with the milk stains on his pants.

"Forget it," Frank argued. "He didn't mean any harm. He's new and too scared to challenge anybody on the deck. It was just an accident."

Frank's appeal fell on deaf ears. "He's gotta get a violation," the other leaders decided. "And Frank, 'cause you're the one frontin' for him, you gotta give it to him."

"No way," Frank said.

"Yeah, man, you will or you get it yourself," they threatened.

To their surprise, Frank said, "If that's the way it's gotta be, give it your best shot."

The other gang members were only too happy to oblige. They jumped on him, kicking, punching, and hitting until he could barely stagger to his cell.

The next morning, Frank felt too sick to attend school classes. But when a friend told him the boys were taking bets on how long he'd be unable to get up, Frank mumbled, "Oh, they are, are they? That settles it. Uhnnn . . . help me get dressed. I hope they lose their commissary money!"

That's when I saw him in the jail hallway, limping along, obviously hurt. "What happened?" I asked.

"Oh, nothin'," he mumbled, "just a little accident. I'll be okay."

Not until much later did I learn from several detainees what had happened. But that wasn't the end of Frank's trials. Shortly thereafter, Juan, a Latino gang youth, came on the deck. He had been charged with murdering a partner of several of the other boys on the deck. That put him at considerable risk.

Then things got worse for Juan. Legal papers aren't checked coming into the jail, so when a packet arrived from his attorney, no one on staff noticed that several gruesome pictures of the deceased victim, lying in a pool of blood, had accidentally been left in the folder. Juan didn't flash them around, but somehow some of the boys learned about them and, when Juan was away, went into his cell, found them, and passed them around the wing. The place almost went up in a riot, and several guys decided to pull a hit right on the deck.

In the quickly called gang leaders' meeting, a storm raged. But when it was Frank's turn to speak, he took a decidedly different tack. "Look," he said, "who among us doesn't have a serious case? I face murder charges, so do most of you, and only God knows how many more things we've done that we never got caught for—all of us. So who are we to take out Juan? We're not much better than he is."

"No! No!" came the fiery retort. "He dies, and that's that!"

"There's one more reason I can't go along," Frank said. "You didn't hear me out. Juan is my brother."

"Your brother?" one of the Cobras said incredulously. "He's not your brother! He's a rival, a creep, a rat, that's what he is. What do you mean, your brother?"

"I'll tell you, if you want to know." Frank looked around at the hard faces glaring at him suspiciously. But he went on. "God is his Father, and God is my Father. Two guys with the same Father are brothers." He was indicating that Juan had come to know the Lord there in jail, and that he and Frank had, indeed, crossed gang rivalry lines to respect each other.

But it was no sale on the deck. "We're goin' to get him!" was the determined response. "That boy dies."

The group was sitting around a table. Frank stood up. "No, he doesn't," he insisted. "Because if you're going to get him, you're going to have to take me out first. Am I clear?"

The other boys couldn't believe what they were hearing. Frank was firmly but calmly saying he would give his own life to protect a rival gang member. The line was drawn. Already the gang leaders had demonstrated that they wouldn't tolerate anyone standing up to their authority. And Frank had shown that he wouldn't back down before their intimidation.

The guys looked at each other. No one knew what to say. The meeting broke up in confusion when the bell rang to summon them back to their school classes.

Juan was never touched, and Frank never bragged to him about how he'd stood up for him. But after Juan was convicted and sentenced to 20 years for his crime, I took him aside and told him how Frank had saved his life by offering to die in his place. Juan was overcome.

When Juan later tried to thank Frank, Frank waved it aside. "Just doin' my duty," he said simply.

Now, that's a man who's been changed by Jesus.

Frank's murder case took so long to come to trial that he pled guilty to the robbery charge, served the time, and was back out on parole before the murder trial even began.

Life on the bricks wasn't easy for Frank, though it was certainly better than being in jail. It's hard to build relationships and make plans knowing you're facing a murder trial and could well go to prison again.

Nonetheless, he met and became close friends with a nice young lady named Connie, and the two tried to think ahead to what their life could be together. "I really want to get married," Frank told me, "but I can't. It just wouldn't be fair to Connie if I'm going to be sent away. Everything has to stay on hold even though we really love each other."

But the waiting was difficult. "It's been six years since Frank was arrested," Connie fumed, expressing her own frustration. "The trial keeps being postponed as both sides appeal different issues. When this happened, Frank was a young 16-year-old. Now he's 22—a much different, mature man." She shook her head tearfully. "It's so unreal that now they might snatch him away to serve a long prison sentence when he's done so well and made so much progress. It just doesn't seem right!"

It was true; Frank had made a new life on the outside. He often helped me at the seminars I lead for law-enforcement and community groups, discussing how to understand and cope with gangs. He brought in a rich experience, impressive firsthand knowledge of the streets, and a great ability to talk to crowds.

He also got a job in the retail auto parts business. When the store manager learned that Frank was awaiting trial on a murder case, he was reluctant to hire him. But after he met Frank and talked with him, he decided to give him a chance. Frank became one of his most-reliable workers and even a personal friend to the family, going bowling and out to dinner with them.

When the trial finally took place, Frank and his older brother were convicted. On sentencing day, his boss and I and several others testified on Frank's behalf, trying to show that he had already proved to be an excellent candidate for rehabilitation. Nevertheless, the judge sentenced him to 20 years and his brother to 22. (Later, their mother received two years of unsupervised probation on a reduced charge.)

Frank remained calm, expecting the result. His mother was

naturally distressed, but the most deeply hurt person in the courtroom seemed to be his store manager. He felt he was losing an excellent employee, a fine all-around person, and a close friend. He asked
me to explain the rationale for the sentence after a six-year delay and
the change Frank had already demonstrated in his life. I couldn't.

Frank now keeps in contact with me from prison. He's earning
half of his time off for good behavior because the crime was committed before the truth-in-sentencing law. Had it happened today,
he would have had to serve the whole sentence, and he sadly reports
meeting many kids behind bars in exactly that predicament. His
family plans to start a limousine service operating in the suburbs
when he comes home.

"But don't forget, Mr. G," he often reminds me, "I'll be helping
your team with the young brothers when I get out. There's no way
I want any of them to go through what I've experienced."

A changed life just *makes my day!*

Epilogue

I T'S SUMMER NOW, WHEN THERE'S USUALLY A lot of action on the streets. But on this warm, breezy day with not a cloud in the sky, our United Nations members drive from all across the Chicago area to the western suburbs, to Mark Beedle's home. Mark is a businessman and longtime friend of our ministry. He hosts our warm-weather sessions in his spacious yard with its swimming pool, volleyball, and basketball court.

Between activities on these Saturday afternoons, we enjoy plenty of broiled burgers and spend time relaxing and catching up on the happenings from the streets back in the city.

At these U.N. meetings, you're apt to meet any of the young men mentioned in this book, plus people like Killer Boy, Krazy J, A-Train, Rabbit, Tiger, Night Crawler, Bam Bam, Spook, Vicious, Phantom, Slimy, Little Loco, Silly, Shyster, Menace, Stash, Maniac, Trouble, Player, Slick, Forty-five (his favorite weapon), Mad Dog, Ponce, Baby Juice, and Psycho—not the nicknames of kids found in the typical church youth group.

On this particular day, Gee-Gee, Marzell, and Night Crawler ride together as they often do when they go to church and other events. Yet back on the streets, they're from three organizations that are bitter, deadly enemies. What's unusual today is Night Crawler's broken arm. Several of the guys ask him about the cast, and he grins and says, "I'll tell you later, when the whole group gets here." Now everybody's really curious.

Jorge Roque arrives from Little Village with a large contingent of Two-Six Boys from his hood, and they greet Heavy B from their antagonists, the Latin Brothers. Some Latin Kings from the north side pull in and greet everyone. Jim Leslie brings several Latino brothers from the Pilsen district, and Cheryl Larsen, a veteran volunteer, drives in with some Black Disciples from the Washington Park Housing Project on the southeast side.

Silviu comes with Vino and Andre. Then Papito, Michael Secreto, Michael Smith, and Daring Dexter roll in—groupings impossible to imagine a few miles away. If members from their organizations met on the bricks, the best to expect would be cold stares, hard looks, and snarled insults. The worst would be an instant shoot-out.

But not with these young men—not here, and not today. The hatred and barriers are gone, and in their place is a sense of genuine brotherhood and mutual respect.

Private defense attorneys John DeLeon and Clarence Burch are on hand to update the kids on changes in the law and advise them on what to do if arrested, a frequent occurrence even for kids who have left the gang life behind.

There's talk about job openings, and Gerald Burk, an executive with White Hen Pantry Stores, tells the kids how to apply for a job, fill out an application, dress, and follow up on an interview.

After a good time of shooting baskets and swimming, with plenty of food and soft drinks, the guys convene informally on the spacious deck around the pool for some serious talk. Silviu, as secretary general of the U.N., explains to the first-timers how these gatherings came about.

"We used to be at it hard and heavy back in our hoods," he says. "But we woke up. We realized we had futures to plan and lives to live. We don't want to end up dead or in jail, like so many of our friends. That's why I came to the Lord. Then I found that many other guys, even my former enemies, have a similar faith. We're brothers workin' to make the streets a better place and to help the shorties grow up right. I don't know anyone else but the Lord who could bring this group together."

When Silviu is finished, he introduces Chente by saying, "Back in the old days, Chente and I would have let a .38 do our talkin' if we ran into each other on the street. Now I want you to listen to my friend and brother." Silviu emphasizes *friend* and *brother* with great sincerity.

Chente steps to the front of the group. He's obviously highly intelligent, forceful, and fully in command. "On the streets," he begins, "I was a Satan's Disciple, certainly a good name to shock adults. We had no use for satanism, but parents and teachers never knew that, so they viewed us with a certain fear, and we liked it that way.

"It was my older brother pickin' up a murder case that led to my change. When he got out on bail, he brought the Rev by the house to meet me. They were acquainted from the youth services my brother attended at the jail.

"I am a Mexican and proud of it, and I was down for my boys, so I had no use for preachers. Since my brother was on his way to prison, I figured he'd need Jesus and the Bible, but not me.

"But things happen that can change your mind." Chente rolls up his sleeve to reveal a badly scarred arm. "Not long after I met the Rev, I was hit at close range by a shotgun blast that nearly tore my arm off. The doctors did tests, then told me the arm had to go. For the first time, I was really frightened. There was nothin' I could do, nothin' my boys could do.

"So there I was on my bed, tears in my eyes, talkin' to the only Person there at the time—the Lord. I told Him I wanted my arm back, and He could have my life. I know you don't bargain with God; I knew that much even then, but I just didn't know any other way to say how I wanted to serve Him as a whole man.

"Well, the arm stayed, as you can see. It's scarred, but it works fine. There were plenty of painful bone and skin grafts, includin' some that didn't take and had to be redone. I went through times of such intense pain that I almost wished the arm was gone. I thought I was goin' through this hellish ordeal all alone. But lyin' in that bed, I heard God in very clear words: 'I'm here, I'm with you, and we'll do this together.'

"And we did. Seein' me with my arm shootin' baskets a while ago or swimmin' or workin'—you think that's a great miracle. Okay, it is. But I've got a bigger one. It's not my arm restored, it's my heart and my life healed. Now, there's the miracle! A rough, street-brawlin', young gangbanger helpin' people instead of hurtin' them, showin' them the right way instead of the wrong—that's some change!"

As Chente sits down, a new guy shoots his hand up and says, "But what about your enemies, those dudes who shot you?"

I would have let Chente answer, but he looks over to me, so I stand up. "If you'd like to get God's idea, let's go the Rule Book and see," I suggest. Then, when I've turned to Romans 12, I read about how we're to bless our enemies instead of cursing them, feeding them when they're hungry and giving them a drink when they're thirsty, overcoming evil with good.

"Does that mean I gotta take one of those creeps to McDonald's and buy him a Big Mac and a Coke?" one hearer bursts out, and the crowd laughs.

"When you seek revenge," I explain after the laughter dies down, "you're not only breaking the law, but you're doing God's business. You're saying He can't take care of it. On the other hand, if you want to get the best of evil, do good, not more evil."

I realized even as I was talking that that's revolutionary stuff for guys whose rules on the street are, "We don't get mad, we get even," "What goes around comes around," and "It's payback time!"

"No one said it would be easy to be a friend of Jesus, but it's worth it," I remind the boys. "And the death benefits of serving Him are out of this world!"

Finally, the meeting closes with a time of prayer, and the requests turn into a session unlike any you'd find almost any-where else:

"Pray for Juan from our gang. He's been shot. Right now he's in Mount Sinai Hospital and may not make it." The group prays for Juan.

Then, "Pray for José from our organization. He's in the county jail, charged with shooting Juan."

And we don't forget the brothers who aren't with us, either. We pray for Xavier in prison and the Hardaway brothers, Sweet Pea, and Cat Daddy. Antwaun Cubie and Jeremy Bruder's family are lifted before the Lord. And we pray for Derrick Stafford and other young men who have heard the gospel but are still struggling to find faith.

Finally, I close the prayer time and dismiss the meeting.

"Wait a minute!" shouts Papito. "We haven't heard how Night Crawler broke his arm."

"Forget it," says Night Crawler, waving his hand at Papito. "It's all too crazy."

"No, no!" hoot the boys. "Tell us. We want to hear."

So Night Crawler, who's a Four Corner Hustler, stands up, looking a little embarrassed. "Well, here goes," he says. "The younger brother of our chief was beat up and killed by rivals. Mr. G and I went to the wake to see the family. Later that day, the family went out for dinner, and the same group that killed the boy barged into the restaurant and broke up the family gatherin'. Feelin's that were already bad just blew up.

"The next evenin', I was at night school. Many of the rivals attend that same school, but they've never bothered me there. We just do our studies. But suddenly, a whole group of boys from my organization charged into the classrooms and tore the place apart. No guns, but plenty of bats and table legs—man, you can bet everybody was scared. The place went up. It was total devastation.

"Followin' the rumble, 10 of us went to the hospital with various injuries. I was one of the luckier ones with only a broken arm."

Everyone sits in awkward silence. I send up a quick prayer, realizing we walk some fine lines here. What does this mean for our U.N. gathering? Some of the guys present are from organizations that are rivals to Night Crawler's Four Corner Hustlers.

Sensing the tension, Night Crawler puts up his hands. "I ain't lookin' for nothin'," he offers. "In fact, that's the end of street brawls for me! I've got more-important things on my mind. I still care about the younger brothers. If I have to, I'll give up my rank. If I'm goin' to be down for anything, it's gonna be for the Lord."

"Phew," I sigh under my breath. "Thank You, Jesus."

Appendix A

Keeping Your Child Out of Trouble

Come with me to a meeting of concerned parents. It might be a men's conference, a women's group, a Rotary Club, a church seminar, or a media interview. But regardless of the setting, one question always stands out: "How can I keep my child from getting into the kind of trouble you deal with every day?"

That question might not have come up just a few years ago. Gangs, violence, and youth crime were mainly confined to the inner cities of our large urban areas. It was easy to turn our backs on the problem; after all, that was someone else's kid in a ghetto far, far away. No longer. Now almost every suburb, small town, and rural area confronts issues with kids we could hardly have imagined a short while back.

It's also an international problem. Whenever I meet with my ministry colleagues from Youth for Christ around the world, I quickly learn they're concerned about teens in trouble in Europe, Africa, Asia, and South America as well.

Heartbreak knows no economic or cultural boundary, grief no racial lines. But the concern does point out a positive reality: Many fine parents and other caring adults out there want to do the best they can in guiding children down the right path.

Although I've told the stories of several kids in serious trouble throughout this book, I have no wish to label a whole generation as delinquent. Most young people—across all races and social and economic groups—are enthusiastic, eager to be successful and find a right path. We must not let the activities of a minority, even a growing one, label all young people as "criminally inclined" or "problem kids."

225

The fact remains, however, that kids don't turn out either good or bad by accident. Many complex factors, *usually produced by the adults around them,* determine which way a youth will go. But even here, I don't want to recklessly label all these problems as "the parents' fault." Many heartbroken moms and dads have said to me, "We did the best we could, and we don't know why our child went wrong. Where did we fail?" The parents or grandparents may not have failed at all; it may be the child who failed. Some young people—even from the finest backgrounds—make choices that lead to dire consequences. All parents can do is the best they know how.

The Bible tells of a prodigal son who left home and messed up big-time (see Luke 15). The story illustrates the best father imaginable—God—whose child still went astray. The dad was without fault, yet the son bombed for a long time—which can and does happen today. (The good news is that the son finally realized "father knew best," came home, and was reconciled. The love and time the father had given his son over the years finally bore fruit.)

Excellent materials are available today to help parents guide their children on the right path. Some are mentioned in Appendix C. And that's only a start. Focus on the Family and Dr. James Dobson, along with many other Christian agencies and publishers, constantly produce programs, magazines, videos, and books to deal with the ever-changing youth culture. But since we've raised a lot of the serious issues kids face today in this book, let's review some of the basics concerned parents need to know.

How Can You Tell If Your Child Is Involved with a Gang?

Youthful gang involvement is like an addiction and has many of the same symptoms.

A negative change in attitude toward school, work, and home responsibilities should alert you to a frustrated, unhappy, or angry child who may find solace associating with others of like mind. Everything from the nicknames he chooses to the language he uses can be clues to a developing antisocial attitude. Defiance toward parents and other authority figures, excessive truancy, and alcohol and chemical abuse all give further indication a child may be involved in a gang.

Keep a careful eye on who your child picks for friends. Be alert to the role models she's choosing to copy. Never accept her excuse to you, "I'm not in that group. I just hang around with them." Experienced police officers will tell you, "If it looks, dresses, talks, and acts like a duck, it's a duck." The same is true of gang association.

Watch for gang signs, symbols, or initials on a notebook cover or phone pad. Such artwork is rarely incidental and may indicate more than a passing interest in the gang. Watch for a five- or six-pointed star, walking cane, champagne glass, devil's pitchforks, Playboy bunny; for names such as Bloods, Crips, Kings, Royals, or Two-Six; for initials such as MM (Mexican Mafia), GD (Gangster Disciples), VL (Vice Lords), LKN (Latin Kings), AP (Almighty Popes), or 2-6 (Two-Six). Keep in touch with school and parent groups so you know what gangs are in your area and what their signs are.

Not every gang is what it appears to be on the surface. Consider Straight Edge, a group that started in New York as a quiet rebellion against chemical abuse and indifference. The New York and California branches continue on that path. But Straight Edge in Utah has taken a decidedly different turn with the white, more straitlaced kids to whom it appeals.

The gang has grown from a handful to more than a thousand in the center of Mormon country, using computer web sites to present itself as a group of courageous, sober soldiers in a dangerously corrupt and polluted society. And the members enforce their mantra, "True Till Death," with brass knuckles, baseball bats, knives, and Molotov cocktails. Utah law-enforcement authorities have traced at least 40 cases of vandalism, arson, and serious assault to Straight Edgers. Several high schools have become gathering places for the group, prompting officials to ban students from scrawling phrases such as "Drug Free" and "Stay Sober" on their backpacks.

Watch out for unexplained sources of money. Where does your son get spending money? How is your daughter able to purchase expensive clothing? An unknown source could well be money from drug sales, thefts, or extortion.

Be alert to unexplained absences from home, especially late at night, and to your child's driving "a friend's car" when the ownership can't be verified.

Signs of kids' involvement in gangs can be subtle. A parent may see some apparently meaningless numbers printed on a notepad. What Mom and Dad don't realize is that each letter of the alphabet is numbered in order by gangs, and some numbers represent phrases.

For example, 1-9-15 means *All is One,* an identification with "the Folks," one of the two big gang federations out of Chicago. "The Folks" are the various brands of Disciples and their allies, while "the People" are the Vice Lords, Latin Kings, and their cohorts. 2-7-4-14 refers to the Black Gangster Disciple Nation. A Los Angeles teen might write 4-20-1-2, indicating "death to all Bloods," the main rivals of the Crips.

Sportswear can also indicate much more than loyalty to a particular team. Gangs adopt team colors and styles to show affiliation to their gang. The Chicago Bulls' red and black, for example, appeal to the Vice Lords, Mickey Cobras, Black P Stones, Bloods, and Spanish Lords. The Maniac Latin Disciples like the horns on the Bulls' logo.

UNLV, the University of Nevada at Las Vegas initials, when turned around become Vice Lord Nations United, while the Phoenix Suns' letters P and S appeal to the Black Pea Stones.

The Orlando Magic apparel in blue and black appeals to "the Folks" gangs. They can X out the five-point star on the Magic logo as a put-down to "Peoples" organizations and their five-star symbol. Meanwhile, the Spanish Cobras are quick to pick up a Boston Celtics hat or shirt because of the green and black colors.

Local police departments and gang intervention programs can often provide additional and up-to-date information on gang graffiti, clothing styles, and other indications to watch for gang affiliation.

Of course, parents and teens don't always agree on clothing styles, music tastes, choice of friends, and use of money and time, but that's a normal part of adolescent life. And keep in mind that some kinds of peer group participation—athletics, music or drama, Scouts, or youth group—bring kids together in positive ways. The key is to distinguish between the normal pattern of adolescents seeking to show their independence and errant behaviors and attitudes.

Don't be afraid to pursue answers when you have reason to be seriously suspicious that things are amiss with your child. Not every suspicion will be justified; be willing to be wrong. But jails are filled with kids whose parents rarely bothered to find out what their children were doing or to take steps to stop their offspring from going down a wrong path.

Don't jump to conclusions, however, if your child is having behavior problems at school or in the community. Begin by having vision, hearing, dental, and medical exams done. Sometimes deficiencies in these physical areas can be at the root of learning problems, which often lead to subsequent concerns about behavior. Also, if a child has a mental illness, that needs to be treated by a competent medical professional.

Most behavior problems are not due to mental illness or physical deficiences, though; they're the result of choosing to act irresponsibly. It's important to treat illness, but character disorders call for discipline and accountability, not excuses. Be careful about defending your child with, "He just got in with the wrong crowd." The chances are overwhelming that he *chose* that crowd. If you're tempted to say, "He was just in the wrong place at the wrong time," be brave and wise enough to finish the sentence with the rest of the facts: ". . . with the wrong crowd he chose, doing the wrong thing."

Kids can outgrow many of these problems if they receive good, firm guidance from caring parents and other adults. Remember, a "good citizen" is often one who, as a child, did something wrong, was not arrested, was redirected into positive behavior, and went on to become a productive member of the community. A "criminal," on the other hand, might be one who broke the same law, was put through our legal and penal system, and as a result is now well on his way to a life of crime.

CHARACTERISTICS OF KIDS IN TROUBLE

Too many families are in crisis, and we're losing too many of our youth to drugs, gangs, and violence. To do something about it, we need to understand the factors that often characterize kids in trouble.

1. *Lack of a positive, male role model.* Countless kids today have no father in their lives. Or if there is a dad in the home, he's too busy, has too many problems of his own, is inadequate, or is otherwise unwilling or unable to take responsibility for raising his children.

This puts a tremendous burden on the mother, who may be doing the best she can under difficult circumstances. It's not my place to criticize these moms, God bless them, and some are succeeding against all odds. But many troubled family situations would look quite different if a committed, caring male were available to his wife and children.

In the inner city, kids often look up to the drug dealer, with his fancy ride and gold chains, as the image of male "success." Many concerned, hardworking fathers have already moved their families to the suburbs, and they have no desire to go back, even to help in their old community—unfortunately leaving the city void of male role models such as doctors, lawyers, teachers, construction workers, bus drivers, and small *legitimate* businessmen.

The gangs, then, fill the void by providing acceptance, social life, respect, a way to make money, excitement, and even discipline—an appealing package to a frustrated youth. That's why gangs have to do so little recruiting; kids are eager to join. (Of course, if they get in trouble with parents, teachers, or the police, they cry, "The gang forced me to join!" Don't believe it—at least not at first cry.) Unfortunately, no one tells them the excitement ends when they die too soon or go to jail for too long. By then it's too late.

2. *Lack of a supportive family and community.* Families headed by only one parent—usually the mother—are more likely to experience the devastating effects of poverty. But even two-parent families face difficulties, often being stretched between two jobs, either by choice or necessity, and leaving no one home to be with the kids. The children end up being bounced around between

day care, school, other relatives, and empty homes—sometimes
with little coordination or communication between caregivers.
For some families, this is simply survival: The parents are doing
the best they can to provide for the kids and hold the family
together. For others, the parents themselves have been sucked
deeply into drug or alcohol abuse, gang life, prison, or simply the
despair of poverty.

Whatever the reason, too many kids are left to raise themselves
on the streets. Even those parents who are able to keep their children out of trouble through elementary school feel that they end up
losing the battle as the kids move into junior high and high school.
The lure of the streets is just too strong, and many teens feel it's the
only "realistic" and "available" lifestyle for them.

The parents who move to the suburbs to escape often learn to
their dismay that the problem is already there—or worse, that they
brought it with them. Their child is the problem and wants to brag
about his exploits in the city. That's one way gangs spread.

Unfortunately, no one is immune. Even families who have
enjoyed relative safety and peace of mind to this point are coming
to realize that the culture of violence is pouring into their homes and
influencing their children via television, music, movies, videos, and
what's considered "cool" and fashionable. It's hard to swim against
that tide without a strong extended family, church, school, or local
community that upholds a different set of values—and invests the
necessary time, money, and personal relationships to protect and
guide its youth.

3. *Lack of a moral and spiritual foundation.* No society can survive indefinitely in a moral vacuum, though ours continues to try.
We have succumbed to a smorgasbord of values (with the highest
value being "It's your choice!"). We've removed any semblance of
religion and its moral values from the public square. "Tolerance" (a
positive value if we're talking about respect for people different from
ourselves) is commonly interpreted as "Anything goes"—and if
you're offended by my gross or uncivil behavior, that's your problem.

Kids on the street have learned their values from our amoral
society and so believe nothing is wrong if they aren't caught, and

that it's not fair for some people to have more money or things than they do. Therefore, it's perfectly all right to forcibly take what they want to balance the scales. If someone is their enemy, they "take him out of the box" (kill him). Against the law? Sure, so watch out for the cops. But wrong? It's just someone else's "cultural standard," which is forcing biblical morality on them. There are no absolutes; everything is up for grabs; they can live as they choose. And if their friends say it's all right to steal and do drive-by shootings, that's what they do.

Further, the television and music industries tell them that even the crudest and vilest habits are okay. Authority figures such as parents, teachers, and police are vilified. Sex is a game, money and what it buys are the goals, and getting high on drugs is a way of escape. When gangsters sell or use drugs, or use violence to get what they want, they're only doing what many voices in our society have glamorized and encouraged.

Then we arrest them and lock them up.

It's little wonder our young people are confused, looking for something in which to believe.

"Let's face it," writes Dr. Laura Schlessinger, noted radio counselor and author, in volume 2 of *Go Take on the Day,* "when a society degrades stay-at-home moms and dads, reveres parents who have busy schedules with complicated careers, canonizes full time, institutionalized day care, disrespects religious institutions and religiously observant individuals, equates morality with tyranny, revels in pop-psychology which elevates personal feelings above honor and obligation, and makes heroes out of oddballs, you have a generation with no notion as to how best to live and find meaning in life."

4. Lack of a vision and hope for the future. Many families in our inner cities have little hope of breaking out of the cycle of poverty and despair. Businesses and factories that once employed "the working poor" have moved out to industrial parks in the far suburbs— or have replaced human workers with advanced computer technology. "Get a job?" these folks would say. "Get real!" In addition, racism continues to subtly keep ethnic groups and minorities "in their place"—a place too often accompanied by schools with inadequate funding, few job opportunities, and a dependency on welfare. Members of this generation are some of the first in the history of our nation who have little expectation of doing better than their parents did.

When all these factors are added together, many kids come to the conclusion that the key to life is to "get by any way you can." Why should a kid stay in school and get his high-school diploma so that he can work for minimum wage in a fast-food joint—when he can make a thousand dollars in a weekend selling dope? If this kid's not thinking about the future, it may be because he's not sure he *has* a future. A high percentage of the men he knows are dead or in prison. For a child who lives in gang turf, the best way to survive and get a little respect is to join the gang that "owns" his hood. He doesn't think about what "society" (parents, school, the government, or the police) expects of him; he's only concerned about his "rep" with his immediate peer group—the gang. To him, no one "out there" (and this includes the church) really cares about him.

FAMILIES AND CRIME

I wish I didn't have to write this section, but it has become increasingly important for parents to talk with their children about confronting crime on the school campus or in the neighborhood, and about what to do if they should witness a crime.

The police have a vital job to do, and they can do it only with the cooperation of citizens, including young people, who give them information. The officers not only have a responsibility by law, but also a divine assignment outlined in the Bible (see Romans 13). When they do their job right, they're carrying out God's work in protecting the community and apprehending the offender. As such, law-enforcers must be treated with respect.

So children should be encouraged to cooperate with the police when they witness a crime. Unfortunately, there's a thin line between being a witness and becoming a suspect, and the advice on how to respond in the two situations is quite different.

You know that line has been crossed when an officer advises someone being questioned that he has a right to remain silent and consult an attorney, and that anything he says can be used against him in a court of law. At that point there's only one safe, logical course of action: *Say nothing until you talk to a lawyer.* And just as a child needs to know the name of a doctor to call in an emergency, increasingly children also need to know the name of a lawyer. I realize how bizarre this sounds to many people, but we're living in a time when crime is rampant—even in once-safe places—and the pressure to clear a case makes some officers less than precise about whom they pick up. I wish this weren't the case, but I've seen far too many tragedies result when a youth just tries to be helpful and honest in a police station—and ends up accused under the technicalities of the accountability law, which now exists in almost every state.

No good parent will encourage a child to do wrong, condone illegal behavior, or cover it up. The *seemingly* logical thing to do when you're called to the police station where your child is being held (once the initial shock wears off) is to ask the child to tell you and the officer the truth about what happened, and to do it right now. *Unfortunately, that's rarely wise.* The nice, friendly officer's task is to gather information in order to file and prove a charge; he's *not* on your side. While I can't stress too much the importance of a youth taking responsibility for his or her behavior, I still insist that admitting you've done something wrong to an overly aggressive police officer can be unwise. However, it's essential that young people be taught to respect the police and to not "wise off" or give them any physical resistance. (For more on the positive and negative aspects of our justice system, see Appendix B.)

My best advice if your child is arrested is: Call your lawyer and have him or her meet you at the police station. Then go directly to the station and insist on seeing your child, and let no questioning go on without your attorney present. Even if you're not allowed to see your child until the questioning is finished, you may have opened a legal route to protect him by later saying in court that you were there to see the youth. However, while police must promptly notify a parent if his or her juvenile is in custody, the law does not prohibit police questioning when no parent is present.

To take such steps to protect your child's legal rights is not in any way excusing or approving of wrongdoing. Your conversations alone with your child at the station or later at home should get that message across in no uncertain terms. You want your child straightened out, and you desire the best help to make that happen. But realize that the legal system is increasingly focused on conviction and punishment, not on correction. You may find an individual police officer, probation officer, school counselor, or other official eager to help you—there are many good people in those fields; be grateful for them and accept their services—but take care not to legally endanger your child.

What Can Parents Do?

Many parents feel overwhelmed by the riptide of changing societal values, a media-driven culture, and the seemingly vicious cycle of dysfunctional families, which can create feelings of isolation and despair. But caring parents can help stem that tide with the right kind of love. "Love?" you ask. "What's love got to do with it? Of course I love my kids!" Most parents love their children. But the kind of love that guides a child into responsible adulthood involves a sacrificial commitment to family, making time with your kids a priority, unconditional acceptance, effective communication, the courage to provide discipline, being an example of integrity, providing positive role models, and moral and spiritual training.

Let's break that down and look at each element more closely.

1. Be committed to your marriage. Obviously, not every family has an intact marriage at the core. But for married couples who are concerned about their children, remember this: The most-important thing a father can do for his children is to love their mother. Far too many children—and this is certainly not confined to urban delinquents—do not see mutual love and caring between the two most-important people in their lives. That's why

I'm so grateful for the impact of Promise Keepers and its stadium rallies, where men commit themselves to caring for their wives and kids. But even parents who are divorced or not living together can speak and act respectfully toward the child's other parent and support the other parent's active involvement in the child's life. Do it for your child's sake.

2. *Make time with your kids a high priority.* Today, time may be the hardest commodity of all to find. Many a father gives his child a few bucks and says, "Don't bother me." Or he's simply too busy or tired to be available. This is as true of a CEO as it is of someone who's unemployed or working two blue-collar jobs. One industrial tycoon I know said, "I can't understand how my daughter got into trouble. I told her she could make an appointment to see me at my office any time she wanted."

The people you love should never be a bother. No job is more important than that of raising your children. Don't try to fit them into an already overcrowded schedule; make spending time with them a top priority. If you don't spend time with your kids, the TV, radio, videos, or even hanging out on the street with "nothin' to do" will fill the gap. In our society, TV has become a cheap baby-sitter for the overly extended parent—usually to the child's detriment. And a kid raising himself on the street is a sure recipe for trouble.

A businessman friend of mine was offered a major promotion with plenty of perks and a good pay increase, but he was warned he would have to work long hours as well as travel frequently, leaving little time for family. He told his boss, "That's too big a price to pay. I've already made my choice, and my family comes first." He saw the handwriting on the wall and knew he had to leave the company. Good positions in his field don't come easily, and he went through some difficult times before he got a good position with adequate pay in another company. It wasn't the exalted post he turned down, but it met his needs, and he was able to meet his family's needs.

A while back, I asked another businessman friend to come to an important meeting on a particular evening. I needed him there.

"Sorry to disappoint you, Gordy, but there's no way I can make it," he replied.

"Will you be out of town?"

"No, I'll be here. But that night my daughter's basketball team plays for the league championship, and I told her I would be there. And I will."

At first I was disappointed by his choice, but the more I thought about it, the more I saw he was right. You make time for your first priority.

Having time for your kids also involves making the effort to know where they are and with whom they associate. Many kids manage to live two different lives: one at home and school, another out on the street. Don't settle for "Out" when you ask where a youth is going. "Out" is too big a place, and coming in "When I get here" is much too late. Invite your children's friends to your home so you know who they are; try to meet their parents as well. And make your house a place where kids can hang out safely.

3. *Give kids unconditional acceptance.* Many of us are quick to tell a child when she's wrong, but how readily do we say, "I love you! I'm so glad you're my daughter"? Children need to know that Mom and Dad care for them. Of course, love can be shown in many ways, but it's wonderful to say it—often—as well!

Acceptance also means learning to know and encourage your child as an individual—her hopes and dreams, his unique strengths and weaknesses. All siblings are not alike and don't want to be treated that way. Comparing one sibling to another doesn't encourage; it discourages. And many parents try to live out their own dreams through their kids—usually with disastrous results. Parents need to accept each of their children for the person he or she is—not set up unrealistic expectations that only lead to feelings of failure. ("Why should I try to please Mom and Dad? I can never get it right.")

4. *Learn how to communicate effectively.* I once saw a report on the three things college students most remembered their fathers saying to them as they were growing up. They were:

"Don't bother me, I'm tired."

"No, we can't afford it."

"Go ask your mother."

Some communication!

The average teen watches five hours of television a day but spends only a few minutes talking to his parents. Many parents are actually afraid of talking to their kids or don't know how. Here are a few suggestions:

- *Never show shock at what a teenager tells you.* A teen's approach is to tell you a little of the story, see how that goes over, and then decide whether to divulge the rest. If you blow up at the first hint of trouble, you may never get the whole story. Stay calm.
- *Avoid adult clichés.* Stay away from such time-worn phrases as "How could you do this to us after all we've done for you?" and the ever-popular "Back when I was your age . . ." Frankly, you never were the age of today's teens. You had your problems, no doubt, but you probably didn't go to a school where it was easier to get coke (the drug) than Coke (the soft drink), or to a school where you had to dodge shoot-outs on the way home. Also, skip the part about trudging through snow to the one-room schoolhouse—all you do is date yourself. Today's kids can't imagine a world without TV, computers, and the Internet.
- *Be a good listener.* As adults, we consider ourselves "answer people." We often think we have the solution before the kid has even thought up the question. But go slow in offering answers.

    One day, a young lady came to our Youth for Christ office and wanted to talk about a problem she had. I invited her to sit down, and she started in on her story. It didn't take me long to grasp the essentials, though she insisted on a detailed "I said . . . then they said" account. I was getting frustrated, wishing she would stop talking so I could dispense some of my excellent advice.

    No such luck. She just kept talking at about 100 miles an hour, with gusts up to 150. Finally she started to wind down, and I thought I was going to get my chance. Instead, however, she decided to review with a series of "Did I tell you . . . ?"

At last she stopped. But just as I was getting ready to respond, she got up and declared, "You are the greatest counselor I have ever talked with! Thank you for your time. You'll never know how much you helped me!" And she left.

That young lady is going through life without my good advice. (I don't know how she'll make it!) But she forced me to do something I had no inclination to do: be a listener. She didn't need any advice; she needed to talk through her concerns with someone who would listen, and I was drafted for the job. Many young people need that listening post, but instead they hear, "Let me tell you, young lady . . ." or "If I were in your shoes . . ."

- *Never treat lightly a problem that a child considers serious.* You may be tempted to brush off the broken-up junior-high romance with, "Remember, dear, teenagers go steady for better or for worse, but not for long." But at the time, this is a painful experience for the child. Listen carefully, treat the problem seriously, and then, when your child is facing something really important you should know about—sexual temptation, peer pressure, lure of drugs, and so on—he will come and tell you.

- *Be trustworthy.* Trust, once broken, is not easily restored. *Say what you mean and do what you say.* Many times I have heard a kid say something like, "My dad was going to take us to the fireworks, but he didn't show up." And just as damaging is the parent who makes exaggerated threats ("If you don't pipe down, I'm going to cut your allowance for a year!") that the child knows perfectly well can be ignored.

  Being trustworthy also means keeping a child's secrets. Hold sacred what the child tells you in confidence, not even sharing the details with others "so they can pray more intelligently."

  On the other hand, don't let a foolish promise keep you from acting when you must. A young person might say, "I'll tell you something if you promise not to tell anyone else." I reject that condition, and so must you. Here's my answer: "If you trust me enough to tell me whatever it is you're going to say, trust me enough to do what's right with the information you give. If not, don't tell me." I've never had a kid reject that arrangement—though, admittedly, there still could be a first time. It's a delicate balance. Don't go blabbing, but if a young person tells you of impending criminal activity, sexual abuse, or any other serious problem, you must take action, and that could mean getting outside help. To avoid doing so under the guise of "protecting a confidence" is a terrible disservice to the young person and, in some circumstances, could even be against the law.

- *Always be available.* Turn off the TV when your child talks to you. Leave your phone number in your kid's pocket when you travel. Even technical advances can help parents keep in contact with their children. Pagers can help the parent or child reach each other quickly, as can cellular phones. These helpful devices should not be considered by families and schools as just the tools of the drug dealer; they can be useful in a caring family as well, especially in emergencies.

5. *Provide consistent discipline.* This is another important way parents love their children. But remember that discipline is not the same as punishment. Rather, it comes from the biblical word meaning "to disciple"—to set a direction and encourage a follower.

Despite their frequent protests to the contrary, young people need and want discipline as long as it's fair, reasonable, and consistent. Set the limits based on a child's age, maturity, and responsibility. Any parent knows two siblings can be entirely different, and that needs to be understood and accommodated. Age obviously makes a difference as well. An older youth should have more freedoms and the opportunity to make more of his or her choices. But the freedom and privileges kids want and expect as they grow older should be given based on how they handle responsibility at home and school.

Perhaps it's hard to accept, but the role of parenting is to work yourself out of a job, not to keep an older youth tied forever to the parents' rules and restrictions. How wonderful it is when, as two adults, parent and child are good friends!

Time spent doing homework, watching TV, and talking on the phone; how many nights they're allowed out; what time to come in; and responsibilities around the house—these major requirements need to be in place and the expectations clearly understood by a child growing up in the home. An unwary parent may find herself intimidated by the intangible "They"—as in, "They all let their kids stay out late" or "They all let their kids go." But don't be taken in. I suggest this response to your child: "You have my deepest sympathy. Without a doubt, you have the meanest parents in the whole world. But we're not responsible for what other kids do; we're only responsible for you, and the answer is *no.*"

Then stick with it. Our juvenile jails are filled with young people whose parents never bothered to check on them, to learn who they were with or where they were, or to monitor the times they came in. You may also want to acquaint your child with another rule from the streets: *Nothing good happens after midnight.*

Parents may disagree at times over the discipline in the home, but don't allow the child to play one parent against the other. Discuss your disagreements in private. In front of the kids, support each other in a united front. Kids must know four things: who's the boss, what the rules are, who's going to enforce them, and what the consequences are for breaking them.

Finally, keep your priorities in order. Every issue is not a crisis. To my knowledge, no kid ever died from "dirty room," "messy bed," or "uncut lawn," but many have been destroyed by drugs, alcohol, gang companions, and sexual promiscuity. Major on the majors. Give issues a priority rating, and deal with them accordingly.

An important component of self-discipline and responsibility comes in teaching a child the value of work and earning money. Jobs aren't easy for kids to find, especially those under age 18, though with a little creativity some openings can develop. Yard work, community summer job programs, and part-time work experience at various businesses all provide a starting point. The most-common form of work for young teens is at fast-food restaurants, and these can offer a positive experience for kids seeking to enter the workplace.

But be alert; problems can arise. Some employers want to pay kids in regular jobs with cash (no taxes or Social Security withheld); that's illegal. Some fast-food managers exploit kids by working them more hours than the law permits, not taking into account their obligations at church, school, and in sports. At that point, the work experience may be more detrimental than it's worth. Know where your child is working, know the employer, and see that the workload is balanced with other responsibilities appropriate to your child's age.

6. Be an example of integrity to your child. Too often, adults seem to be saying, "Don't do as I do; do as I say." What folly! The adult with a cigarette in his hand, blowing in the breeze from too much liquor and yet telling a kid about the evils of smoking and alcohol abuse, is only playing the fool.

But there are less-obvious and more-subtle areas adults need to consider as well. How safely do you drive your car? How often do you tell a child, "Answer the phone, and tell whoever it is I'm not home"? What kind of business ethics does your child see you practice? And then there's the common attitude, "Son, I think you should go to Sunday school. Church is important, you know." Of course, the kid wants to know why Dad doesn't go if it's so important.

Are you modeling the kind of home you want your child to have when he or she leaves the nest? Are you demonstrating the kind of parent and marriage partner you want your child to be? Husbands and wives shed one another much more easily than children cut ties to their father or mother. Not only is the breakup of parents emotionally wrenching for the children, but it also offers kids little in the way of a good example in establishing their own future homes.

Live-in arrangements or temporary liaisons where people become mother and father without becoming husband and wife are common today. But these unstable homes tend to perpetuate poverty, delinquency, and a whole range of personal and social problems, with the children most often paying the heaviest price. Not growing up with a father, or perhaps not even knowing the man, is a devastating burden to place on any child. Remember: There are no illegitimate children, only illegitimate parents.

Take care in what you model in your sexual activity as well. Abortion is often the way out when sex is separated from the readiness to parent a child (i.e., marriage), and what starts as a serious mistake in becoming pregnant becomes a guilt-ridden tragedy in taking the life of the unborn. The opposite of life is not "choice" or "rights"; it's death. What are we adults modeling to our children about the value of *all* human life? If a life can be destroyed for no other reason than inconvenience, why can't another person be robbed or abused for profit or pleasure? Children are great imitators. Their attitudes and actions are most often "caught," not "taught."

Kids don't expect their parents to be perfect. In fact, they're usually very forgiving when an adult admits he or she made a mistake. But kids reject hypocrisy. They see too much of it at school and in politics and business, the sports world, entertainment, and even at church. Don't practice phoniness in your home.

7. *Provide positive role models for your children.* If there's no father in the home, perhaps another caring adult can fill some of that role: for example, a grandfather, uncle, Sunday school teacher, coach, church youth leader, Big Brother, YFC Campus Life leader, Fellowship of Christian Athletes huddle leader, or Scoutmaster. Even children from two-parent families often need outside mentors when they hit the tumultuous teen years. I can't stress enough how important *adults who care* can be to our teens. That's why this book is not only for parents, but also for church and community leaders.

8. *Offer moral and spiritual guidance.* Most parents want their children to grow up with some sense of moral limits, but we live in a morally ambiguous world where consensus between school, church, and home is strained at best. That often makes it difficult for parents, neighbors, police, teachers, coaches, and youth ministers to work together.

A good school program will emphasize self-discipline, respect for others, and regard for the well-being of the community as necessary moral skills. But too often, the popular educational approach emphasizes personal self-esteem and developing one's own potential in a context of relativistic values—an inadequate combination to produce a mature, principled young person. Kids are taught to "be themselves" instead of "behave themselves."

We can't expect the school to accomplish what isn't happening at home, however. What kids need is for Mom and Dad to be *authoritative*— meaning, firm about reasonable expectations and standards, all in a family context that's warm and accepting as well as supportive of the child's individuality—an approach that's neither too permissive nor too autocratic and controlling.

Contemporary society, including the schools, avoids telling children that there are absolutes of right and wrong. But there has to be a higher standard of conduct than public opinion. In his book *In the Grip of Grace,* Max Lucado says, "The hedonist world of no moral absolutes works fine on paper and sounds great in a college philosophy course, but in life? Ask the father of three children whose wife abandoned him, saying, 'Divorce may be wrong for you, but it's OK for me.' Or get the opinion of the teenage girl, pregnant and frightened, who was told by her boyfriend, 'If you go ahead and have the baby, it's your responsibility.'

"A godly view of the world, on the other hand . . . challenges those with cricket brains to answer to a higher standard than personal opinion: 'You may think it's right. Society may think it's OK. But the God who made you said, "You shall not steal"—and He wasn't kidding'" (p. 28).

The God who made all of us gave some specific rules, and He didn't refer them to a committee for a consensus agreement. The Ten Commandments are still relevant. The Bible is not what Jesus would say to us *if* He were here; it's what He's saying because He *is* here. Yet the message of our country's spiritual heritage is kept from nearly all our public schoolchildren. Rarely are they told that "we are God's workmanship, created in Christ Jesus to do good works, which God prepared in advance for us to do" (Ephesians 2:10).

What kind of spiritual foundation are you providing for your kids? "That's their job down at the church," some would say. But, in fact, that task must be the number-one assignment at home, with help and support from the church.

And it's a father's job. Take a look at Deuteronomy 6:20: "In the future, when your son asks you, 'What is the meaning of the stipulations, decrees and laws the LORD our God has commanded you?' tell him . . . *go ask your mother.*" No, it doesn't say that! It says the father should give a thorough, reasonable answer for why we must follow God's laws, as well as point out that He will be with us when we do.

The church then becomes a natural extension of what the home stands for. Admittedly, too many church services start at 11:00 sharp and end at 12:00 dull. Jim Rayburn founded and built a youth movement on the premise that "It's a sin to bore kids with the truth," and his successors in Young Life, along with similar evangelistic youth programs—Word of Life, Youth with a Mission, and the Campus Life Clubs of Youth for Christ—have done a phenomenal job of challenging teens with the truth about God.

To their credit, many churches have developed special youth ministries, work closely with the parachurch groups mentioned above, and together have had an enormous impact on young people. The youth ministry volunteers and staff members I meet in churches of all denominations are an exciting, dedicated, and talented group of people with much to offer. Do everything you can to be sure your kids know them.

But even a generous plate of religious involvement is not the answer by itself. Many kids who have been around church have enough religion to be comfortable there, but not enough to affect their conduct on a date or with their peers on the streets. (Some of the gang kids have a song about that. Part of it goes: "You can't go to heaven in a stolen car, the darn thing won't go that far.")

Many are seeking to get by with God on a family member's faith. But if being raised in the church would make those kids Christians, then being raised in the garage would make them Chevrolets! God has plenty of children but no grandchildren.

Somewhere along the way, a child's faith must be personalized into his or her own relationship with the Lord. Then the youth is ready for the exciting adventure of knowing and living for Jesus.

Kids need to know the salvation of God is not something to *achieve* but rather to *receive*. It's not based on something we do but on what God has already *done*.

The issue is pointedly put in the Bible: "For all have sinned and fall short of the glory of God, and are justified freely by his grace through the redemption that came by Christ Jesus. God presented him as a sacrifice of atonement, through faith in his blood. He did this to demonstrate his justice, because in his forbearance he had left the sins committed beforehand unpunished—he did it to demonstrate his justice at the present time, so as to be just and the one who justifies those who have faith in Jesus" (Romans 3:23-26).

A young person who understands that relationship with the Lord, has experienced it, and is growing in it in company with a good church will be a poor prospect for the gangs.

Yes, the spiritual training at home is crucial. Consider this strong challenge from one of the earliest biblical books: "Only be careful, and watch yourselves closely so that you do not forget the things your eyes have seen or let them slip from your heart as long as you live. Teach them to your children and to their children after them" (Deuteronomy 4:9).

This challenge also comes with God's promise: "Train a child in the way he should go, and when he is old he will not turn from it" (Proverbs 22:6).

FIVE THINGS KIDS IN TROUBLE NEED

In my experience, kids in trouble need five things in place if they're really going to make a turnaround:

1. *A realistic, meaningful faith in Jesus Christ, along with . . .*
2. *An education*
3. *Some type of career opportunity*
4. *A positive family structure, either in the parental home (for younger kids) or in marriage (for older youth)*

5. *Supportive mentoring from the church, a parachurch ministry, an adult Christian friend, or even a concerned staff member of a community agency—which is especially critical if number 4 isn't possible*

Sound like a big order? It is. Many Christian parents today have all they can do to provide this kind of foundation and guidance for their own children. But what about the thousands of youth on the streets or in our correctional institutions? Who will come alongside them, introduce them to Jesus Christ, and mentor them? We here at the Juvenile Justice Ministry of Youth for Christ can't do it alone. We need men and women in every city who are concerned about kids to invest some of their time in leading a Bible study or mentoring a particular young man or woman.

We can't reach everyone, but we can reach some.

Will your church hear the call?

Will you?

Appendix B

"A Mighty Flood of Justice . . ."

Come with me to a school play. It's similar to a production you might see at your local high school—but with some distinct differences.

The production is excellent, with good staging, sound, and lighting. The actors and actresses are well chosen for their roles and play them with strong characterizations and enthusiasm. The musical numbers are effectively staged, and an added bonus at the end is greeted enthusiastically by the audience—a demonstration of tumbling skills that would do Chicago's famed Jesse White Tumbling Team proud.

The play, *Temporary Lockdown*, has been scripted and produced by the kids. Certainly they had good help from teachers, counselors, and expert technicians, but this is their project, and they do an outstanding job.

I'm busy the night I meet with the play's actors and stage crew. I really can't stay to see it, but they insist, and since I know so many of them I can't resist. They assure me I'll see an outstanding production, and they don't disappoint. The story and music are a poignant, powerful, sometimes humorous look at youth life in the urban ghetto, and there's even a note of faith that includes a moving rendition of "Amazing Grace" at the funeral of a child.

Who are these young people? All of them are in the Cook County Temporary Juvenile Detention Center in Chicago, awaiting disposition of court cases, some of them on very serious charges.

The lead actress faces two armed-robbery cases. The friendly greeter at the door, impressively dressed in a nice suit for the occasion, is 15 and faces two murder counts. A college instructor is there; her son is in the play. So is an off-duty police officer, for the same reason.

When the play is done, the cast is encouraged by a prolonged standing ovation from the capacity crowd. A beautiful buffet is spread for the cast and visitors in the lobby, as this is the last night of the play's run.

One young lady introduces me to her mother, who has tears in her eyes. "I didn't know my daughter had talent like this," the mom says. "It was a great evening! These are such talented kids, with a great future." The crowd certainly agrees with her analysis. The sad thing, however, is that her opinion would not be the view of the community at large.

The public, often egged on by the media, can't see much beyond a serious criminal charge that will mark a young person for life. No thought is given to the idea that the offender could learn a lesson from her mistakes, that she could mature and grow out of a delinquent pattern. She committed a serious crime. That's it. Never mind how she got that way or the potential for change. File the most-serious charges, move her case from juvenile to adult court, convict her, give her the longest possible sentence, and complain that it can't be more. Then tell the media, "You'd better believe we're hard on crime and young punks in this town! Zero tolerance, that's the name of the game."

I'm not surprised when a cynical and angry citizenry expresses these ideas. If you believe young offenders can never change, then trying them in adult court and warehousing them in expensive misery makes sense. That view also makes building prisons one of the fastest-growing industries in America as we lock up more people than any other nation except Russia.

There, in a few sentences, you have the model for the way many people want to fight youth crime.

What's the opposite approach—be soft on crime? No thank you! But how about being realistic? Kids won't learn to live in responsible freedom while locked in a cage.

Actually, it's not only reasonable to look at the overall picture of justice, but it's an obligation for anyone who takes the Bible seriously. True justice is a special challenge to the family of faith. The Old

Testament prophet Amos laid the concern right on the line: He condemned those who "trample on the heads of the poor as upon the dust of the ground and deny justice to the oppressed" (Amos 2:7).

The Lord will devour like a fire when we "turn justice into bitterness and cast righteousness to the ground" (Amos 5:7). "But you have turned justice into poison and the fruit of righteousness into bitterness" (Amos 6:12). "Hate evil, love good; maintain justice in the courts" (Amos 5:15). "But let justice roll on like a river, righteousness like a never-failing stream!" (Amos 5:24).

And King David proclaimed, "For the LORD is righteous, he loves justice" (Psalm 11:7).

The biblical word for *justice* also translates as "righteousness," so what you have is a call for personal *and* community righteousness. The biblical mandate is not one to the exclusion of the other. God's message is to pursue both. Indeed, they're inseparable—changed people will most assuredly affect the world around them when they are living out their faith. If any believe a person can change, the Lord's people should, and if they do believe it, that premise must be at the base of their views on criminal justice.

Excuse wrongdoers? Make light of serious crime? Hold people less than accountable for their conduct? No, and anyone who does so makes a mockery of the righteousness the Bible demands from cover to cover.

But the question is: *Can we serve the interests of justice for young offenders in a way that offers redemptive potential, not just destruction?* And the answer is that yes, we can.

A REALISTIC APPROACH TO JUSTICE

Whose needs should be considered in a realistic approach to justice? What are the strengths and weaknesses of our present system? Are the changes in the wind of public opinion for good or for ill?

Justice for the Public

Our first consideration must be for the safety of the public. A child molester or someone with a history of violent, dangerous acts must be confined to protect the community. So must a sociopath who can't and won't learn from experience, though that label needs to be applied by a competent professional after careful tests and evaluation, not glibly by lawyers and the media.

Fortunately, those definitions apply only to a few criminals. Many young inmates *can* change for the better. Prevention programs should be aimed at younger children, where the most good can be accomplished. But intervention efforts to turn a youthful offender away from criminal activity often work best not with younger teens, who rarely realize the seriousness of their wrongful lifestyle, but with older teens and those facing major charges—they're much more ready to be disillusioned by their folly. I know that conclusion flies in the face of conventional wisdom, but our staff and many other youth workers have found it to be true.

Justice for Victims

Next, we must be concerned about victims' rights. While criminal trials are designed to deal with offenses against the state and civil suits are meant to settle wrongs between individuals, we increasingly see victims turning to the criminal courts for satisfaction.

Victims are kept informed of trial dates, progress on the case, parole hearings to consider early release, and so on. A "Victim Impact Statement" is often included in the legal process. Many courts have a victim-witness assistance program and assign staff to work closely with those who have been hurt and want to come to court—an excellent plan. (Unfortunately, in Cook County, Illinois, the victim-witness program is run by the state's attorney's office, so its fine service is not available to witnesses for the defense, who also need information and guidance. Transferring the function to the court clerk or another judicial office would allow everyone to be served.)

Bringing the victims' concerns into the court process, however, can be dangerous. Understandably, victims often seek revenge and hope to see the offender punished in the severest and longest form. And because that's a popular view, it can distort the fairness that needs to guide the system. What court would not feel an overwhelming sympathy for those who have been grievously hurt? But we've moved much too far in the direction of an eye-for-an-eye system of justice. Carried to its ultimate conclusion, this will leave far too many people blind in our world. That's why Jesus told us to change it (see Matthew 5:38-45).

Civil court is the place, wherever possible and appropriate, for grievances between individuals to be settled, including those of victim and offender. Mediation and out-of-system settlements often accommodate the need for damages to be repaid—certainly a much better route than looking to punitive sentencing in criminal court.

A number of states have funds to reimburse victims of violent crimes. These services need to be expanded and more generously funded. As well, victims need to know they can take advantage of such help.

Victims coming together can be supportive to each other and enhance community involvement in crime issues. Families and Friends of Murder Victims is one such organization; it's a dedicated, helpful, and caring group.

The court process needs to be speeded up, too. Justice delayed is justice denied for everyone, especially the victims. Justice that's swift and sure also cuts down violence rates, as Boston, New Orleans, and other cities have learned.

Justice for the Police

Good law enforcement begins with a carefully screened, well-trained police department that's held accountable to the community. I know the dedication of many police youth officers, and they do an outstanding job. In recent years, *community policing* has gotten officers in close contact with the people they serve and with groups of concerned local citizens. The next trend may well be *area task forces,* especially where there's a cluster of small communities with not enough personnel, experience, or resources to deal with sophisticated criminal activity that crosses jurisdictional lines.

One of the most innovative forms of community policing is a three-man Chicago team called The Slick Boys. Three African-American youth officers formed the group as a way to get a positive message to an audience of young gang kids. They also wanted to counter the negative images of rap artists, as well as wean kids away from drugs, gangs, and guns. The Slick Boys have a network TV program, make more than 200 appearances a year in schools (they sing for 20 minutes and talk for an hour), sponsor a baseball league, and have a book out listing the things they've done as police officers.

We also need to be on the alert, however, for those officers who abuse their position, making careful and thorough investigation of citizen complaints. The fact is, communities get the kind of policing they want and expect, and if they encourage officers to stretch the law and be brutal to the people the community doesn't like, that's exactly what will happen. Police can't solve the gang problem alone, but the community will never solve it without strong police cooperation.

Justice for the Offender

Truth-in-sentencing is a fairly new concept enjoying wide support. It mandates that all parties to a case will know exactly how long a convict will serve without the confusing modification of time off for good behavior and other qualifiers. However, we need to consider two dangers: First, it has been used to dramatically lengthen sentences where that's not needed. (Certain mandatory sentences were established in the law before truth-in-sentencing took effect, under the old understanding that a convicted felon would serve half the time with good behavior. Now those same mandatory sentences are keeping convicts incarcerated twice as long.) This imposes a wasteful cost on taxpayers. Second, truth-in-sentencing removes the incentive for cooperation and good behavior within the prison population.

Three-strikes-and-you're-out laws—and there are all sorts of variations on the basic premise around the country—mandate that those convicted of three violent felonies will receive a life sentence. Some states cut the number to two, and some include juvenile offenses. The most irresponsible version mandates 25 years to life in prison for *any* third felony, meaning a petty theft by a convict can bring on the harsh sentence, producing skyrocketing prison costs that are hardly justifiable.

The accountability law, which played a part in the stories of several young people in this book, is, in my opinion, one of the most draconian concepts imaginable. Like many such laws, it sounds good, even virtuous, at first reading. It states that the accused is responsible for whatever crime someone he was with committed, providing that he participated in some way. Aimed to crack down on gang activity, on more-careful examination it demeans justice and even simple fairness.

Suppose some in the group had no idea what was happening and did not assist the wrongdoer. In my experience, the system says, "Too bad. You were there; you're guilty." Proponents say the law doesn't say that and cases don't turn out that way, that only active participants are charged and convicted, but they're wrong. In case after case, the unknowing and the unwilling are held equally guilty with the actual perpetrators. Further, prosecutors too often go first after the easy convictions. It's simple to prove someone was at the scene if that's all that's practically required for a guilty verdict. Even though the law requires some direct involvement in the crime, most judges and jurors consider that an unnecessary technicality and ignore it. If you were with the bad guys, you're guilty. Then, when public outrage and media attention have cooled, some other technicality may exempt the real perpetrator from conviction.

Much better is an *accomplice* law that holds an individual responsible for what he or she did, not what someone else did, and with an appropriate lesser punishment than that given the primary perpetrator.

Justice in the Court System

One of the first ways to work toward justice in our court system is to *speed up trials.* Trial by jury is the cornerstone of our justice system. But it's unconscionable that young people can wait in custody for two years or longer to go to trial in serious cases. Everyone involved is inconvenienced by such delays, especially the defendant, who may be found not guilty yet has no way to recoup important time lost in his life. I can show you case after case where the prosecutor knew a conviction wasn't possible, so he or she delayed the trial for more than two years as a way of delivering punishment anyway while the defendant sat in juvenile detention.

One way trials could be sped up is by *eliminating peremptory challenges* to potential jurors, an unnecessary procedure that allows attorneys on both sides to excuse a certain number of jurors without stating any reason. If such challenges are not totally eliminated, they should be limited to a couple on each side. This gives attorneys the opportunity to eliminate someone they consider prejudiced (but can't prove it) without allowing them to reshape the whole jury.

Some students of law have urged the *admission of evidence improperly obtained* by police in violation of constitutional protections—now prohibited under the exclusionary rule—insisting there are other ways to discipline officers who break the rules besides excluding their evidence. Fortunately, the exclusionary rule affects few cases, though it usually attracts media attention when it does come up. But allowing such evidence would be a slippery slope. We dare not play fast and loose with the safeguards of our Bill of Rights, however unpopular that may appear in the occasional high-profile case.

If you've been at many trials, you soon learn to view with a great deal of caution two oft-used pieces of "evidence": eyewitness testimony and the confession of an accused.

Eyewitnesses often see the criminal briefly during a time of great stress and later are subject to manipulative suggestions in viewing a police lineup or looking at a picture book of suspects. The testimony of two witnesses to the same event may conflict, because people often fill in the "facts" with their own presumptions and prejudices. Witnesses can also be manipulative themselves, lying to cover for a fellow gang member or falsely identifying a rival as a perpetrator. Either abuse thwarts the goal of justice. Even worse, some attorneys knowingly present such testimony just to win. When police officers condone false testimony to convict a suspect, they justify it as "the only way to get the bad guys." Of course, not all attorneys or officers stoop to such tactics, but the practices are far more prevalent than most of us realize.

If witnesses are sometimes of dubious value, all is not lost, however. The use of DNA evidence, ballistic reports on weapons, and other advances in forensic science can make court decisions much more accurate and precise.

Confessions by the accused can be equally weak, but they're a lot easier to obtain than the effort required of an officer to find, interview, and record statements of witnesses. Does anyone doubt that a young person in a big-city police interrogation room, held for many hours without outside contact, likely threatened and possibly beaten and subject to all sorts of expert psychological pressures, will end up saying and signing anything? Skeptics about this sadly underestimate the resourcefulness and determination of police questioners. In court, the officers will be nicely dressed, polite to a fault, and insistent that the statement was entirely voluntary and in no way coerced. Don't count on it.

Also, in a trial, *instructions to jurors* should be given when the trial starts so the jurors will have them in mind as the case proceeds, and they should be as simply worded as possible. They might be reviewed by the judge just before the jury deliberates. In some courts, jurors are still not allowed to take notes, but they should be.

Under careful control and supervision, *trials should be open to the media,* including TV. The only way the public at large can learn how our courts operate is through television. Some notable abuses of that coverage dictate the need for the judges to spell out how the coverage will be provided in each case, but they're not an argument for denying all coverage.

The Juvenile Versus the Adult Court System

Increasingly popular in our legislatures are bills that would authorize more juveniles to be tried as adults. Teenagers can't vote, so they make easy targets for ambitious politicans. In a time when gang criminals are getting younger and Americans have been shocked by the viciousness of some young criminals, the outrage and urge to "make society safe from these predators" is understandable. And I agree, some incorrigible youths should be tried as adults and put away for a long time as a matter of public safety.

But, as is often the case, the urge to "do something—now!" often leads to a "solution" based on emotional overreaction and erroneous thinking. This bill is much more popular with the public and with legislators eager for their votes than with people actually involved in the justice system.

In most places, the juvenile court system is getting a bad rap and does a much better job than is generally acknowledged. The first juvenile court in the nation was founded in 1899 in Chicago and Cook County by legendary youth reformer Jane Addams, and it remains one of the largest and best in the country. Some competent, caring judges hear juvenile cases, and the Juvenile Detention Center is a clean, modern facility with a good educational program—the Nancy B. Jefferson School, staffed by capable and understanding faculty. The Cook County Juvenile Detention Center is one of the few facilities of its kind accredited by the American Correctional Association, a recognition of both the facility and the fine staff and many community volunteers who help the more than 700 children housed there.

In a city noted for politics as the key lever in getting government jobs, the juvenile probation department has been remarkably free of that influence and has attracted a well-screened, well-trained, and well-led professional staff of counselors and supervisors. The adult probation department, in contrast, is understaffed and overworked, with probationers getting little attention outside a once-a-month reporting in.

Yet here, in the Chicago area, along with much of the rest of the country, there's been a determined effort to destroy the juvenile court, severely limit the clients it can serve, and transfer juveniles to the unprepared and unwilling arms of the adult system.

Laws have been passed here, as elsewhere, mandating automatic trial in adult court for youngsters who commit serious offenses, with no review by any judge of whether the kid should be transferred. Consequently, most of the time, the juvenile-or-adult-court question is decided not by a judge but by prosecutors, based on the charge they file. In Illinois, 13-year-olds can be sentenced to prison for life. These are kids deemed too immature to get a driver's license, serve on a jury, vote, or even sign a release for their own basic medical care, but in the criminal courts we want to treat them as mature adults.

In the correctional system, the network of juvenile institutions offers far-more-appropriate resources to handle young offenders, but many will still be funneled into the adult penal system with its gang-controlled inmate population, drug proliferation, and sexual abuse.

It's hard enough for a young person who wants to change to go through the court system, so why throw deliberate roadblocks in the way to make the change even more unlikely? If a young person completes his probation or sentence successfully, that arrest and court record should be sealed and expunged, opening doors to various professions, trades, and military services that are now closed to former law violators. And though juvenile court is not a criminal court and is confidential (though it should never be secret, and I've always believed delinquency hearings should be open to both the public and the media; names could be protected while still reporting what happened), its history with a youth often ends up in adult court should that youth later face charges there.

I have two other concerns regarding moving youths from juvenile to adult court. First, the decision to try a child as an adult should never be automatic, based simply on the seriousness of the unproved charge. Instead, the decision should be made by a juvenile court judge hearing *all* the facts and circumstances of the case, along with the background and attitude of the accused.

Second, a youth moved to adult court is supposedly eligible for release on bail pending trial. (In the juvenile system, the accused are either held until trial or released to the custody of their parents, depending on the charge.) However, the amount of bail set is often not designed to guarantee that the accused will appear in court—the legal purpose of bail—but serves to make sure the youth cannot be released because the amount ordered is so high. This is a serious disregard of the young person's rights. If the youth is so dangerous that no bail should be permitted, that should be stated in open court, the reasons explained, and any bail denied. But pricing his right to freedom out of reach is not a reasonable alternative.

I urge parents—when they can afford it—to post bail for a youth charged as an adult. If they question whether the child actually committed the crime, or if they believe his or her attitude is such that they can relate well at home pending trial even if the charge is true, then by all means secure a release. A young person can help prepare for court better in the free world and also has the opportunity to bring a good record of accomplishments to a later court hearing.

Some parents want to leave a child locked up to teach him or her a lesson. In jail, the child may well learn many lessons, but not the ones good parents have in mind. You don't leave a child for long in terrible filth to teach cleanliness. The shock value of even an overnight stay in jail does whatever limited good such exposure will accomplish.

Justice and Drugs

One question about the law many are discussing is, "Should drugs be legalized or decriminalized?" Sadly, drug abuse among kids is on the rise, and the drugs they use are often more powerful than those used by previous generations. The simple summary to our politically promoted war on drugs is: Drugs won. As long as the economies of a number of countries in Asia and Central and South America—including Mexico at our doorstep—are dominated by drug trafficking, that's not likely to change.

We can't even keep drugs out of our jails and prisons, places surrounded by barbed wire, high walls, and armed guards. How are we ever going to keep them out at our borders or off our streets and campuses? We'll win some skirmishes, we'll take the small dope sellers off some corners (while rarely touching the big dealers), the politicians will take the credit at election time, and the battle will continue to be lost unless we look to the root of the problem.

We need to put our emphasis on the market—the people who will buy and use drugs—but that would take an all-out moral and spiritual emphasis to our youth, and we as a nation have neither the will nor the desire to mount such a campaign.

So should we legalize drugs? For whom, children? Are we going to allow junior-high students to go down to the corner store and buy marijuana or crack cocaine? We certainly could never limit the sales to just adults. Though they can't legally make purchases, kids everywhere get tobacco and alcohol. Shall we add cocaine and heroin to that list? It's difficult to imagine how anyone who has seriously thought through the implications of legalizing drugs could support the idea.

Justice for the Future

My staff and I go with many young people through the court process. We don't speak up for every youth, but where we know and have confidence in someone, we will perhaps help secure an attorney, obtain witnesses, testify at a bail bond hearing so he or she can be released, or come to court and give testimony at a trial or sentencing. We're especially interested in encouraging sentences that have rehabilitative or redemptive qualities.

Many good alternatives exist to incarceration. Among the newer alternatives being discussed is *restitution,* though it really isn't new. Check out Exodus 21:22 and 30 and the story of Zacchaeus, who said he would pay back four times whatever he wrongly took (Luke 19:8). This is justice that has positive ramifications for the offender (taking personal responsibility for his or her actions) and for the victims (receiving reparations for the wrong they have suffered).

Highly effective *diversion programs* have also worked well in traffic violations, small drug cases, car thefts, and petty stealing. At her discretion, a judge may direct that a youthful offender must complete a counseling program, a drug education class, or a course in driver's safety. (Of course, such programs are relevant only to those who need them. For instance, some gang kids sent to drug education programs would never use the stuff; they only sell it.) If the program is completed successfully, charges may be dropped. These programs are possible only because of the strong support of the states' attorneys, police, and other law-enforcement agencies. The group counseling sessions have been well received and have benefited the community. The sad thing is that the law limits far too much the offenders who can be referred to them.

And there are other alternatives. *Boot camps* offer a short, intense dose of military-style discipline that can be highly effective *if* there is support and follow-up in the community (from schools, churches, and adult mentors) upon return. *Home confinement* and *electronic monitoring* both allow for close supervision of a youth while perhaps allowing time-out for work or school. *Intensive probation* is a strong program with several probation officers giving round-the-clock supervision and good counseling. *Community service* requires young people to pay back the county through work projects or being assigned to local nonprofit organizations or churches. These all work well where they're used, but unfortunately they're not available to many young people who could benefit from them.

Some kids are beyond our help, however. Their fate is set by the charges, the circumstances, and the required sentence. But we will still speak up for them. Even if they're sentenced to long terms, they will know we believe in them, said so in court, and were willing to be with them, no matter how unpopular our support may be to some. That's the least we can do as the Lord's servants. We need to be a voice for sanity and sense in a system often gone mad.

A stunning fact that many people don't realize is that the kids with the most-serious cases are often the best prospects to respond to help and come out of the legal system as good citizens. Too many kids with lesser charges (and even some of their parents) aren't impressed with what happens, shrugging it off and asking, "What's the big deal?"

If a caring businessperson asks me how to help kids trying to straighten out their lives, I have a simple answer: "Hire them. Give them a chance." Can it be risky? Possibly. But the risk of not helping is far greater. Depriving a young person of real opportunities to turn his life around almost ensures he will return to a life of crime, selling drugs, or being reabsorbed by his old gang.

I recall an instance where a girl with a criminal history was hired into a good position and did well in her work. Many months later, someone tipped off management about her past—no one had asked if she had a record in her employment interview—and she was summarily dismissed. The law usually prohibits private employers from checking into arrest records, but of course it's done all the time, to the detriment of young people trying to rebuild their lives.

One young man worked at a shopping-mall shoe store and was considered an excellent employee. One day, a security guard stopped the boy as he was walking in the mall and remembered him from two years previously, when, as an unruly kid, he had been banned from the mall. The security guard ordered him out of the place, and the mall management refused to allow the store to keep him as an employee. His job was gone. Fortunately, the store manager was able to place the young man in a company shop elsewhere, where he continues to perform well.

I know it's not easy for employers. One told me he had to go through 50 applicants at his firm to find one who could pass a drug test. That's pathetic. But another, who had hired a number of formerly troubled kids, reported their success rate was better than that of the off-the-street hires they made day by day.

Jobs can play a strong role in preventing young people from getting into trouble. Many—though certainly not all—wouldn't be stealing or selling drugs if they could get a decent job, but there are few available in poor neighborhoods, and practically none for those under age 18. Unless the community works together to open up jobs for urban youth of all races in the private sector, we have no grounds to complain that kids are drifting into idleness and crime.

Justice and the Church

A businessman here, a committed volunteer there—these individuals can make a difference. But it's not enough. *The church itself needs to be involved.* Fortunately, some local churches are, though many others are concerned but need direction and a way to intelligently help the hurting urban youth.

A community group was meeting at the prodding of the police department to discuss a unified response to gangs and violence. (Good police departments are wise enough to know the problem will never be solved without them, but also that they will never solve it alone.) The task force came up with some good recommendations for law enforcement, the schools, probation, job training, recreation, family counseling, and other people and groups whose efforts were needed.

So what about the churches? The panel recommended they open their gyms to streets kids, do family counseling, and get members to volunteer with other agencies. That was it. *That was it!* You could give those assignments to a Scout troop, a YMCA, or a Boys and Girls Club. Those are fine ideas—but they're not the unique contribution the church brings to the table. We must not settle for simply being social workers with a Bible under our arms. We have a greater calling. We're to be evangelists who care for the whole person.

People frequently ask in reference to our Youth for Christ Juvenile Justice Ministry, "Aren't you trying to make bad kids good, or emotionally sick kids healthy?" No, the job is far greater than that. Our goal is to bring spiritually dead kids to eternal life! They don't just need to be fixed up; they need to be *raised* up. We tell them of a Savior who "made us alive with Christ even when we were dead in transgressions" (Ephesians 2:5). We introduce them to the One who would rather die for them than live without them.

"Are you one of those born-again Christians?" I'm asked.

I didn't know there was any other kind! Where there is faith in Christ, a turning away from wrong, and a new life, there is a Christian.

We don't have time to waste with those who would offer a buffet of beliefs, with Jesus as one of the options. We tell kids the Bible says what it means and means what it says; that knowing the Lord is one "heaven" of a way to go; and that the lake of fire is neither a myth nor a tourist resort. Besides, as Max Lucado observes in his book *In the Grip of Grace,* "Every other approach to God is a bartering system; if I do this, God will do that. I'm either saved by works (what I do), emotions (what I experience), or knowledge (what I know)." Those approaches just don't cut it. The Lord is the initiator. The apostle Paul put it this way: "For it is by grace you have been saved, through faith—and this not from yourselves, it is the gift of God—not by works, so that no one can boast" (Ephesians 2:8-9).

Johnny Cash summed it up well when he told interviewer

Barbara Walters, "Religion is for those who want to stay out of hell. Jesus is for those who have already been there."

Religionists, inclined to think miraculous changes in people's lives stopped with Saul on the road to Damascus 2,000 years ago, haven't been looking very far or very carefully. God still changes lives, and perhaps that's no more evident than in our jails and prisons. I'm convinced there are more conversions behind bars than there are in our churches, where the self-sufficient think they need nothing.

Many church people, in addition to those outside the church, have trouble believing a person accused or convicted of a serious crime can really change—or should even have the opportunity. In our own thinking, we have locked them away for as long as possible, and good riddance. Then the amazing thing happens: They come to the Lord and are transformed. Far from being thrilled, we're suspicious and standoffish; we think it's a ruse. We believe God smiles on nice people like us and frowns on those horrible people who make headlines. We need to remember God alone is the judge, and He doesn't do it until the end of our days. Who are you and I to write people off sooner, or even at all? Yes, we hate the sin. But let the Lord deal with the sinners. He never called us to hate those people; in fact, He commanded us to love them.

Besides, as Max Lucado observes poignantly in *In the Grip of Grace*, "There is no difference between the ungodly party-goer, the ungodly finger-pointer, and the ungodly pew-sitter. The *Penthouse* gang, the courthouse clan, and the church choir need the same message: Without God, all are lost."

In proclaiming our message, we can use such contemporary tools and resources as sports teams, mentoring, family counseling, job training, and medical and legal services, and many of the most-effective churches do exactly that. In the Chicago area, for example, you will find those services at such fine ministry centers as Rock Church and Circle Urban Ministries, Lawndale Community Church, LaVillita Community Church, LaSalle Street Church, Truth Triumphant, Rock of Ages Baptist Church, Jesus People USA, and many more. Kolbe House serves as a ministry base for concerned

Catholics, providing chaplaincy services, counseling, release follow-up, and an excellent paper prepared by inmates with the record of their faith.

You also will find Christians supporting such vital ministries as Good News Jail and Prison Ministry, Inner City Impact, the Cabrini Friends Youth Center, Olive Branch Mission, Pacific Garden Mission, Prison Fellowship, the Salvation Army, and others.

My own church, Christ Church of Oak Brook, is a white, suburban, wealthy congregation, home to many corporate and professional leaders. But we have a heart for the city and have adopted as part of our worldwide missions program three inner-city churches where we offer volunteers, supplies, and financial assistance. Willow Creek Community Church has similar programs, and many other churches are catching the vision of "across the street" as well as "across the globe."

I often tell church conferences, "God will judge our love for the lost we have never seen overseas by how concerned we are for the lost right at our own doorstep. The words *home* and *foreign* don't belong in a missions program—all the lost are missions."

Take a look at the New York area. David Wilkerson, famed preacher from *The Cross and the Switchblade*, founded and pastors Times Square Church. Or go out to visit Brooklyn Tabernacle, where Jim and Carol Cymbala have not only released recordings of outstanding music from their choir, the Brooklyn Tabernacle Choir, but have also built a multiracial ministry to the hurting in one of the neediest areas of the country.

Bill Wilson founded and pastors Metro Church. Introduced to the nation by Dr. Robert Schuller on *The Hour of Power* telecast, Wilson's staff and volunteers have a growing fleet of buses bringing children from all over the New York area to the nation's largest Sunday schools, with 16,000 in attendance and growing. Each child is personally contacted and visited every week!

Then there's my friend Buster Soaries, pastor of First Baptist Church in Somerset, New Jersey. Saluted as a local hero in *Time* magazine, Soaries intervened to secure the release of 12 junior-high boys jailed for leading a brawl. He founded Brothers Working

Together, which he says aims to "help young people realize that they have options beyond the street corner." The program offers guidance and tutoring for 60 at-risk students. One pastor, one church, and they're making a difference.

In the heart of Philadelphia is Deliverance Evangelistic Church, with seating for 5,000 and a wide variety of services for the African-American community it serves: adult and youth literacy, drug abuse counseling, a prison ministry, and much more. Sister churches have spread from Michigan to Georgia.

Dr. Tony Evans at Oak Cliff Bible Fellowship in Dallas serves his community with a variety of caring ministries, and he serves the nation with the radio program *The Urban Alternative.*

Sports Illustrated paid tribute to a professional football player, Reggie White, who co-pastors Inner City Church in Knoxville, Tennessee. Besides offering worship and Bible teaching, the church has developed an investment bank that gives loans, runs financial and job-skill seminars, and helps small businesses get access to office equipment. The church also has a radio station, WDMF—What the Devil Mostly Fears—and operates a home for unwed mothers.

Across the country in Los Angeles, Dr. E. V. Hill pastors Mount Zion Baptist Church. Busy as he is with the heavy responsibility of a senior pastorate as well as speaking around the nation, Hill still has time for the kids in the church's neighborhood. He knows personally the leaders of the Bloods and Crips gangs and is considered the chaplain to both rival groups. No wonder many gang kids have come to the church, met the Lord, and turned their lives around.

In communities large and small across the country, people have gotten out of their "comfort zone" in the church pew and are reaching out to meet local spiritual and material needs. They aren't in the headlines but are making a vital difference. In many ways, however, these efforts are still a drop in the bucket. We need many more individual Christians and whole churches to catch the vision of reaching out to the mission field at our doorstep: the hurting, troubled youth in our communities.

The mission field is ripe. Many gang-involved young people from the African-American and Latino traditions have a biblical background from which they have turned away, yet they still know many basic truths. They're *immoral*, striving to evade the truth they know. Unfortunately, most Caucasian kids in trouble have no such basic concept of faith—nothing on which to build. They're *amoral*. And then there are the waves of young people on the streets from all over the world, including the gang kids from Asia, many of whom come from a Buddhist tradition.

This greatly concerned my staff and me when we met a number of Cambodian kids with serious cases in juvenile detention. I was even more amazed to find the largest gang in Rochester, Minnesota, of all places, was the Royal Cambodian Bloods. But all the Cambodian youths who had earlier lived in Chicago had been involved in a youth athletic-outreach program at Uptown Baptist Church, where the seed of the gospel was firmly planted. Though some of these kids did get into trouble, we had a base of Christian understanding that surprised us but was beautiful to build on.

A church needs to be sure it is committed to the gospel. Then it must ask: Is our goal to build our church or minister to our community? If it's to reach the community, the church will venture across denominational, racial, economic, and social lines, and spiritual results will follow.

If the church is going to be relevant to issues of justice, we must also speak out and take a firm stand whenever racism rears its ugly head. Overt and obvious forms of prejudice still exist in hiring, housing, and political harangues by what remains of the Ku Klux Klan and other hatemongers. But there are also subtle attitudes of racism that demean people of color, such as when they're instantly considered to be the secretary, not the boss; the delinquent, not the honor student; or the troublemaker, not the hard worker.

Note the difference in the treatment of two carloads of teenagers stopped by police because the driver was speeding. One car is filled with white students, the other with African Americans. Which group will be treated courteously, given their citation, and sent quickly on their way? Which will be hauled out and handcuffed while their car is searched and their identities are checked for outstanding arrest warrants?

Interestingly, the same treatments will probably occur whether the police officers are white or black. Minority kids often say that if they're stopped, they hope it's by a white cop, because they will usually be treated much better than by one of their own. Minority officers, it seems, are often angry at kids who are considered to give all their people a bad name.

Unfortunately, prejudice and racial hatred are often a two-way street. Minority kids need to be as responsible for their behavior as anyone else; to require less is to say they're not equal and perpetuate a cruel form of discrimination. When African-American extremists mouth hatred for whites or Jews, or Asian gangs and Latinos turn on each other, it should be labeled for the vial poison it is.

Will the church meet the challenge? The kids on the street aren't so sure.

I met one day with a youth gang leader from the Chicago suburbs. He was personable and intelligent—he had to be to put together the drug-selling and power structure he led. We were distinctly at odds on many issues, and I made sure he understood that, but we did share—at least partially—one area of concern. He didn't want to see the shorties in his gang in trouble, ruining their lives.

With that in mind, he told me that he had called on a dozen churches, trying to get the leadership to come together to help the kids. "It was the most-frustrating experience I've had in a long time," he said. "I couldn't get these preachers to agree on anything. They were all concerned that the other guy would get more recognition, the other church might gain more converts than he did, whose name would be on the letterhead—I finally just threw up my hands in frustration and decided to forget the whole thing. And I haven't had anything to do with the churches since, until you asked to meet with me now."

What a sad story. I couldn't do what a dozen churches wouldn't, but our ministry could and does reach out to help some of the shorties he knows. And I certainly shared with him the message of the

Lord and assured him of my prayers. I still pray for him.

I also pray for my brothers and sisters in the churches, that we will shed our comfortable cocoons and get out into the streets and jails. George MacLeod summed it up well when he made this poignant statement on the role of the church in Carl Burke's book *God Is for Real, Man:*

> I simply argue that the cross be raised again at the center of the marketplace as well as on the steeple of the church. I am recovering the claim that Jesus was not crucified in a cathedral between two candles, but on a cross between two thieves; on the town garbage heap; at a crossroads so cosmopolitan that they had to write his title in Hebrew and Latin and Greek . . . at the kind of place where cynics talk smut, and thieves curse, and soldiers gamble. Because that is where he died. And that is what he died about. And that is where church men ought to be, and what church men should be about. (p. 5)

Appendix C

Annotated Bibliography

Abrahmson, Leslie. *The Defense Is Ready*. New York: Simon & Schuster, 1997. A brilliant defense attorney reminds readers that what we hear at first in sensational cases is almost always incomplete, misleading, or downright wrong.

Alicia, Gil C. *The Air Down Here*. New York: Chronicle Books, 1995. A teenager describes his life in the urban ghetto.

Anderson, David. *Sensible Justice: Alternatives to Prison*. New York: The New Press, 1997. A report on the political forces that made for the enormous growth of the nation's prisons, and possible alternatives to jailing offenders.

Anson, Robert. *Best Intentions*. New York: Random House, 1993. The well-intentioned efforts to help a ghetto youth get a new life go sadly amiss.

Arterburn, Stephen, and Jim Burns. *Drug Proof Your Kids*. Ventura, Calif.: Regal, 1994.

Ayers, William. *A Kind and Just Parent: The Children of Juvenile Court*. Boston: Beacon Press, 1997. A veteran teacher in the juvenile detention center in Chicago describes his unique students.

Bennett, William J. *The Book of Virtues*. New York: Simon & Schuster, 1993.

————. *The Moral Compass*. New York: Simon & Schuster,1995.

Bing, Leon. *Do or Die*. New York: Harper-Collins, 1991.

Blankenhorn, David. *Fatherless America*. New York: Harper-Collins, 1995.

Bode, Janet, with cartoonist Stan Mack. *Herd Time: A Real Look at Juvenile Crime and Violence*. New York: Bantam, Doubleday, Dell, 1996.

Chicago State University. National Gang Crimes Research Center. *Journal of Gang Research*. Chicago: National Gang Crimes Research Center.

Collins, Marva Nettles. *Values: Lighting the Candle of Excellence.* New York: Dove Press, 1996.

Colson, Charles. *Justice.* Colorado Springs, Colo.: NavPress, 1988.

Colson, Charles, with Daniel Van Ness. *Convicted.* Westchester, Ill.: Crossway, 1988.

Corwin, Miles. *The Killing Season: A Summer Inside an L.A. Police Homicide Division.* New York: Simon & Schuster, 1997.

Cruz, Nicky. *Code Blue: Urgent Care for America's Youth Emergency.* Ann Arbor, Mich.: Vine Books, 1995.

Currie, Elliott. *Crime and Punishment in America.* New York: Metropolitan Books, Henry Holt, 1998. An international authority, Currie gives a well-reasoned explanation, from a secular perspective, for why the solutions to our crime problem haven't worked, and what will.

DeSantis, John. *The New Untouchables.* Chicago: Noble Press, 1994. A disturbing look at some unfortunate but all-too-prevalent trends in law enforcement.

DeSisto, Michael. *Decoding Your Teenager.* New York: William Morrow, 1991. The director of a Massachusetts school for troubled teens gives a secular perspective on relating to youth.

Dineen, Tana. *Manufacturing Victims.* Montreal: Robert Davis Publishing, 1996. While showing deep compassion for real victims of violence, Dineen takes the psychology industry to task for creating false victims and reaping a financial windfall treating them. Available through General Distribution Services. U.S.: 800-805-1083. Canada: 800-481-2440.

Dobson, James. *Parenting Isn't for Cowards.* Dallas: Word, 1987.

———. *Love Must Be Tough.* Dallas: Word, 1983.

———. *The New Dare to Discipline.* Wheaton, Ill.: Tyndale House, 1992.

———. *Preparing for Adolescence.* Ventura, Calif.: Regal, 1989.

Drowns, Robert W., with Karen M. Hess. *Juvenile Justice.* St. Paul, Minn.: West Publishing Company, 1995.

Dunston, Leonard G. *Report of the Task Force on Juvenile Gangs.* Albany, N.Y.: New York State Division for Youth, 1990.

Elikann, Peter T. *The Tough-on-Crime Myth.* New York: Insight Books, 1996. A unique report detailing what's wrong with our "lock 'em up" strategy for criminals. Includes some constructive alternatives.

English, T. J. *Born to Kill.* New York: Avon Books, 1995. An insightful history of the rise and fall of a bloody, young Asian gang.

Ewing, Charles Patrick. *Kids Who Kill.* Lexington, Mass.: Lexington Books, 1990.

Fletcher, Connie. *What Cops Know.* New York: Pocket Books, 1990.

Fox, Robert W., and Mark E. Amador. *Gangs on the Move: A Descriptive Catalogue of Over 1,500 Active Gangs in America.* Placerville, Calif.: Copperhouse Publishing, 1993.

Gardiner, Muriel. *The Deadly Innocents: Children Who Kill.* New York: Basic Books, 1976.

Glasser, William. *Choice Theory.* New York: Harper-Collins, 1998.

Hubner, John, and Jill Wolfson. *Somebody Else's Children.* New York: Crown Publishers, 1996. A report on the juvenile court in San Jose, California, presided over by my friend Judge Leonard Edwards, honored as best judge in the country in a court of special jurisdiction by the American Bar Association.

Humes, Edward. *No Matter How Loud I Shout: A Year in the Life of Juvenile Court.* New York: Simon & Schuster, 1996.

Jankowski, Martin Sanchez. *Islands in the Street.* Berkeley, Calif.: University of California Press, 1991.

Jones, LeAlan, and Lloyd Newman. *Our America: Life and Death on the South Side of Chicago.* New York: Scribner's, 1997. Two teens tell about their growing up in the ghetto.

Katz, Burton S. *Justice Overruled.* New York: Warner Books, 1977. A former California prosecutor and judge provides a candid look at the justice system.

Knox, George W., Edward D. Tromanhauser, and Thomas P. McCurrie. *Schools Under Siege.* Dubuque, Iowa: Kendall-Hunt Publishing, 1992.

————. *An Introductiion to Gangs*. Bristol, Ind.: Wyndham Hall Press, 1994.

Korem, Dan. *Suburban Gangs*. Richardson, Tex.: International Focus Press, 1994.

————. *Street Wise Parents, Foolproof Kids*. Colorado Springs, Colo.: NavPress, 1992.

Kotlowitz, Alex. *There Are No Children Here*. New York: Anchor Books, 1992.

Kramer, Rita. *At a Tender Age: Violent Youth and Juvenile Justice*. New York: Henry Holt, 1988.

Kunkle, Fredrick. *Pray for Us Sinners*. New York: Warner Books, 1996. The tragic story of a New Jersey teenager's murder case.

Larson, Bart, and Wendell Amstutz. *Gangs in America*. Rochester, Minn.: National Counseling Resource Center, 1993.

Leman, Kevin. *Keeping Your Family Together When the World Is Falling Apart*. Colorado Springs, Colo.: Focus on the Family, 1992.

Lucado, Max. *In the Grip of Grace*. Dallas: Word, 1996. A powerful view on changing people, given from a moral and spiritual perspective.

MacArthur, John F. Jr. *The Vanishing Conscience*. Dallas: Word, 1995.

Magid, Ken, and Carole A. McKelvey. *High Risk: Children Without a Conscience*. New York: Bantam, 1987.

Manfredi, Christopher P. *The Supreme Court and Juvenile Justice*. Lawrence, Kans.: University Press of Kansas, 1997.

McDowell, Josh, and Bob Hostetler: *Right from Wrong: What You Need to Know to Help Youth Make Right Choices*. Dallas: Word, 1994.

————. *Josh McDowell's Handbook on Counseling Youth*. Dallas: Word, 1996.

McLean, Gordon, with Dave Jackson and Neta Jackson. *Cities of Lonesome Fear: God Among the Gangs*. Chicago: Moody, 1992.

Mitchell, William, and Charles Paul Conn. *The Power of Positive Parenting*. Old Tappan, N.J.: Revell, 1989.

Mones, Paul. *When a Child Kills*. New York: Pocket Books, 1991.

Moore, Joan W. *Going Down to the Barrio: Homeboys and Homegirls in Change*. Philadelphia: Temple University Press, 1991.

Mosley, Shawn. *The Breaking Point*. South Holland, Ill.: Creative Ways Multimedia, 1996. A street-gang veteran tells his own gripping conversion story.

Murchison, William. *Reclaiming Morality in America*. Nashville: Nelson/Word, 1994.

Officer X. *10-8: A Cop's Honest Look at Life on the Streets*. Northbrook, Ill.: Calibre Press, 1994.

Popenoe, David. *Life Without Father*. New York: Free Press, Simon & Schuster, 1996. A professor of sociology at Rutgers University reports on the importance of the father in a child's life and describes critical changes in our society as fewer children have a dad at home.

Prejean, Sister Helen. *Dead Man Walking*. New York: Vintage Books, 1993. Documents a nun's ministry to a death-row inmate. Also made into a powerful motion picture and video release.

Previte, Mary Taylor. *Hungry Ghosts*. Grand Rapids, Mich.: Zondervan, 1994. Missionary statesman Hudson Taylor's kin— who was for more than 20 years superintendent of the Camden, New Jersey, juvenile detention center—relates her experiences and concerns.

Prothrow-Stith, Deborah, with Michaele Weissman. *Deadly Consequences*. New York: Harper-Collins, 1991.

Reaves, John, and James B. Austin. *How to Find Help for a Troubled Kid*. New York: Henry Holt, 1990. A parent's guide to secular programs and services for adolescents.

Rodriquez, Luis J. *Always Running, la Vida Loca: Gang Days in L.A.* New York: Touchstone Books, Simon & Schuster, 1993.

Rogers, Adrian. *Ten Secrets for a Successful Family*. Wheaton, Ill.: Cornerstone Books, 1996.

Romanowski, William D. *Pop Culture Wars*. Downers Grove, Ill.: InterVarsity Press, 1996.

Rothwax, Judge Harold J. *Guilty: The Collapse of Criminal Justice*. New York: Random House, 1996. A decidedly pro-prosecution view of the justice system from a former public defender who went on to a distinguished career as a New York judge.

Sachs, Steve. *Street Gang Awareness.* Minneapolis: Fairview Press, 1997. A veteran juvenile probation officer provides important details on youth-gang culture, attitudes, appearance, and symbols.

Samenow, Stanton E. *Before It's Too Late.* New York: Times Books, 1989. An important practical help for parents about the need to take a firm stand with a wayward child.

————. *Inside the Criminal Mind.* New York: Times Books, 1984. This is possibly the best volume ever written to understand and deal with the criminal mentality.

Sanders, William B. *Gangbangs and Drivebys: Grounded Culture and Juvenile Gang Violence.* New York: Aldline de Gruyer, 1994.

Sheindlin, Judge, with Josh Getlin. *Don't Pee on My Leg and Tell Me It's Raining.* New York: Harper-Collins, 1996. Billed as "America's Toughest Family-Court Judge," Sheindlin speaks out bluntly, if not always agreeably, on juvenile justice.

Silberman, Charles E. *Criminal Violence, Criminal Justice.* New York: Vintage Books, 1980.

Sinart, David, and Edward Barnes. *The Corner: A Year in the Life of an Inner City Neighborhood.* New York: Broadway Books, 1997.

Sizemore, Finley. *When Caring Parents Have Problem Kids.* Old Tappan, N.J.: Revell, 1989.

Smarto, Don. *Keeping Ex-Offenders Free.* Grand Rapids, Mich.: Baker Book House, 1994. Smarto is the vice president of Good News Jail and Prison Ministry. Earlier he was the founding director of the Institute for Prison Ministry at Wheaton College in Wheaton, Illinois.

Spence, Gerry. *With Justice for None.* New York: Times Books, 1989. A distinguished criminal defense attorney provides a disturbing look at the workings of our justice system.

Stott, John, and Nicholas Miller, eds. *Crime and the Responsible Community.* Grand Rapids, Mich.: Eerdmans, 1980.

Strack, Jay. *Good Kids Who Do Bad Things.* Dallas: Word, 1993.

Taylor, Carl S. *Dangerous Society.* East Lansing, Mich.: Michigan State University Press, 1990.

Trent, John. *Go the Distance: The Making of a Promise Keeper.* Colorado Springs, Colo.: Focus on the Family, 1996.

Tuite, Patrick, with Grace Arons and Norman Mark. *Ignorance of the Law Is No Excuse.* Chicago: Kendall-Hunt Publishing, 1996. An excellent look at the law and possible consequences for young people, prepared by an outstanding criminal defense attorney.

Van Ness, Daniel W. *Crime and Its Victims.* Westmont, Ill.: InterVarsity Press, 1986.

Van Ness, Daniel W., with Karen Heetderks Strong. *Restoring Justice.* Cincinnati: Anderson Publishing, 1997.

Williams, Willie J. *Taking Back Our Streets.* New York: Scribner's, 1996.

Wilson, James Q., and Richard J. Herrnstein. *Crime and Human Nature.* New York: Simon & Schuster, 1985. A comprehensive overview of crime and its origins.

Wright, Bruce. *Black Robes, White Justice.* New York: Lyle Stuart Publishers, 1994.

Appendix D

Organizations with Helpful Resources

American Correctional Association, 4380 Forbes Blvd., Lanham, MD 20706-4322. Ph.: 800-222-5646. Maintains and constantly updates publications and videos for sale on all aspects of crime and corrections.

Amer-I-Can, 1851 Sunset Plaza Dr., Los Angeles, CA 90069. Ph.: 310-657-4838. Founded by football legend and movie star James Brown, this organization teaches gang members, convicts, and troubled youth to take personal responsibility for their actions. Principal operations are in California, Ohio, and New Jersey.

The Bureau for at-Risk Youth, P.O. Box 760, Plainview, NY 11803-0760. Ph.: 800-99-YOUTH. Distributes videos on gangs and violence prevention.

Chicago Crime Commission, 79 West Monroe St., Chicago, IL 60603. Ph.: 312-372-0101. Provides training guides for communities and a special report on youth gangs.

Community Nonviolence Resources Center, 3630 Fairmead, Pasadena, CA 91107. Ph.: 818-351-8398. Offers training and consultation.

Compassionate Friends, P.O. Box 3696, Oak Brook, IL 60521. Ph.: 630-990-0010. Gives support to parents whose children have died.

Cross in the City, P.O. Box 590571, Houston, TX 77259-0571. Ph.: 281-488-3651. James Leslie is the executive director of this ministry to kids in the criminal justice system, especially young gang members.

Focus on the Family, Colorado Springs, CO 80995. Ph.: 719-531-3400. Designed to help parents raise their children in a God-

279

honoring way. Also offers resources for families such as: radio and television programs, books, videos, and magazines— including *Plugged In*, which provides reviews and commentaries on the latest music, movies, and TV aimed at youth.

God's Posse, 62 Catawba St., Roxbury, MA 02119. Ph.: 617-427-2702. Gives counseling to at-risk youth, ministry to incarcerated youth, and gang intervention.

Good News Jail and Prison Ministry, 2230 E. Parham Ave., #200, Richmond, VA 23228-2226. Ph.: 804-553-4090. Provides chaplaincy ministry to correctional institutions and local jails around the country.

International Juvenile Officers Association, 59 Seventh St., Garden City, NY 11040. Ph.: 516-747-2948. This professional organization of law-enforcement youth officers offers conferences and training resources.

Kids Across America, 1429 Lakeshore Drive, Branson, MO 65616. Ph.: 417-335-8400. A uniquely effective camping program designed for inner-city kids. Joe White, president.

MAD DADS (Men Against Destruction—Defending Against Drugs and Social Disorder), 3030 Sprague St., Omaha, NE 68111. Ph.: 402-451-3500. Organizes men to act as mentors and friends for at-risk youth across the country.

Murder Victims' Families for Reconciliation, P.O. Box 208, Atlantic, VA 23303.

The National Counseling Resource Center, P.O. Box 87, Rochester, MN 55903. Ph.: 507-281-8800. Provides educational materials on youth gangs and violence, as well as the occult.

The National Gang Crime Research Center, Box 990, Peotone, IL 60468-0990. Ph.: 773-995-2494. Professors George W. Knox and Thomas F. McCurrie and their staff produce the scholarly *Journal of Gang Research* each quarter, as well as books. The Center also hosts an annual training conference for law-enforcement and community leaders.

Neighbors Who Care, P.O. Box 16079, Washington, DC 20041. Ph.: 703-904-7311. Implements church-based victim-assistance programs in cities.

Nicky Cruz Outreach, 6925 Lehman St., Suite 101, Colorado Springs, CO 80918. Ph.: 719-598-2600. Provides seminars and literature on gangs.

Prison Fellowship, P.O. Box 17500, Washington, DC 20041-0500. Ph.: 703-478-0100. Founded by Charles Colson, this organization is the largest volunteer prison ministry in the world.

Project Intercept, 9888 Carroll Center Rd., Suite 235, San Diego, CA 92126. Ph.: 619-271-0700. Offers mentoring programs for at-risk youth.

Rainbows, 1111 Tower Rd., Schaumburg, IL 60173. Ph.: 800-266-3206. A support group for children of divorced parents in many communities in the U.S. and abroad.

Search Institute, 700 S. 3rd St., Minneapolis, MN 55415. Ph.: 612-376-8955. Dr. Peter Benson and his staff provide excellent material on the needs of young people and how they can be met, including his book *What Kids Need to Succeed,* published by Free Spirit in Minneapolis.

STARS (Students Taking a Right Stand), P.O. Box 8936, Chattanooga, TN 37414. Ph.: 800-477-8277. Provides training, consultation, books, and videos.

Straight Ahead Ministries, 9 Charles St., Westboro, MA 01581. Ph.: 508-366-9797. Conducts Bible studies in juvenile detention facilities in New England and Georgia, as well as providing aftercare halfway homes.

Youth for Christ (Juvenile Justice and Youth Guidance ministry programs and resources), USA: P.O. Box 228822, Denver, CO 80222-8822. Ph.: 303-843-9000. Canada: 1212 31st Ave. N.E., #540, Calgary, Alberta, Canada T2E 7S8. Ph.: 403-291-1195. United Kingdom: P.O. Box 5254, Halesowen, West Highlands B63 3DG.

If you're interested in helping at-risk youth or incarcerated men and women, start by volunteering with established ministries such as the ones listed above. They provide good training and preparation, an effective programming structure to make the most of a variety of talents and skills, and invaluable ongoing support and encouragement. Involvement with correctional inmates should always be done as part of an established program. Any personal mail to inmates should be channeled through a sponsoring agency to avoid con games and pleas for funds from inmates who sometimes try to take advantage of those eager to help.

More Inspiring Resources From Focus on the Family®

A Man Called Norman

For many, loving the person next door is as easy as lending a lawnmower, fetching a stray newspaper, walking a pet or watering a few plants. Discover what Jesus truly meant in this heartwarming story about one man's willingness to reach out and touch the life of his neglected, elderly neighbor. Paperback.

Molder of Dreams

Encouragement is a powerful force, and one that lasts. In this compelling account, 1986 Teacher of the Year, Guy Doud, shares a moving message on the profound difference affirmation and love will have in the lives of others. . . *when* we're willing to invest the time. Paperback.

Surprised by God

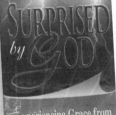

If you've ever wanted a new start, allow Stephen Arterburn to introduce the Giver of second chances. Recounting many of the wrong turns he's taken in life, this honest and poignant book reveals the conclusion we all ultimately must reach: Only God offers the fulfillment for our hearts' desires, and only His grace will see us through. Hardcover.

Gianna

Hers is an amazing testimony of God's grace—and the horrors of abortion. Mere weeks before Gianna would have been born, her mother had a saline abortion. But it didn't work, and this book shares the touching story of one woman's choice, God's plan and how He's worked in the life of a teen girl. Paperback.

• • •

Look for these books in your favorite Christian bookstore. You can also request a copy by calling 1-800-A-FAMILY or by writing Focus on the Family, Colorado Springs, CO 80995. Friends in Canada may call 1-800-661-9800 or write Focus on the Family, P.O. Box 9800, Stn. Terminal, Vancouver, B.C. V6B 4G3. Visit our Web site— www.family.org—to learn more about the ministry or to find out if there is a Focus on the Family office in your country.

8BPXMP

FOCUS ON THE FAMILY®

ⲱelcome to the ᴣamily!

Whether you received this book as a gift, borrowed it from a friend, or purchased it yourself, we're glad you read it! It's just one of the many helpful, insightful and encouraging resources produced by Focus on the Family.

In fact, that's what Focus on the Family is all about— providing inspiration, information and biblically based advice to people in all stages of life.

It began in 1977 with the vision of one man, Dr. James Dobson, a licensed psychologist and author of 16 best-selling books on marriage, parenting, and family. Now an international organization, Focus on the Family is dedicated to preserving Judeo-Christian values and strengthening the family through more than 70 different ministries, including eight separate radio broadcasts; television public service announcements; 11 publications; and a steady series of award-winning books, films and videos for people of all ages and interests. And it's all done for one purpose: to encourage and strengthen individuals and families through the life-changing message of Jesus Christ.

●   ●   ●

For more information about the ministry, or if we can be of help to your family, simply write to Focus on the Family, Colorado Springs, CO 80995 or call 1-800-A-FAMILY (1-800-232-6459). Friends in Canada may write Focus on the Family, P.O. Box 9800, Stn. Terminal, Vancouver, B.C. V6B 4G3 or call 1-800-661-9800. You may also visit our Web site—www.family.org—to learn more about the ministry or to find out if there is a Focus on the Family office in your country.

The Rev. Gordon McLean directs the Juvenile Justice Ministry of Youth for Christ in the Chicago area. The program serves with chaplains in youth correctional centers and offers ongoing contacts and support when a youth is released back to the community. The ministry contacts are:

Juvenile Justice Ministry
Metro Chicago Youth for Christ, Inc.
324 E. Roosevelt Road
Wheaton, Illinois 60187

Phone: 630-588-0700
Chicago phone: 312-443-1932

261.8331
M1634

99562

LINCOLN CHRISTIAN COLLEGE AND SEMINARY

3 4711 00153 3522